Also by Cindy M. Meston

Women's Sexual Function and Dysfunction
(Ed., with Irwin Goldstein, Susan R. Davis, and Abdulmaged M. Traish)

Also by David M. Buss

Evolutionary Psychology:
The New Science of the Mind

Personality Psychology:
Domains of Knowledge About Human Nature
(with Randy Larsen)

The Murderer Next Door:
Why the Mind Is Designed to Kill

Handbook of Evolutionary Psychology (Ed.)

The Evolution of Desire:
Strategies of Human Mating

The Dangerous Passion:
Why Jealousy Is as Necessary as Love and Sex

Sex, Power, Conflict:
Evolutionary and Feminist Perspectives
(Ed., with Neil Malamuth)

Why Women Have Sex

Why Women Have Sex

*Understanding Sexual Motivations—
from Adventure to Revenge
(and Everything in Between)*

⚬

CINDY M. MESTON, PH.D.
AND DAVID M. BUSS, PH.D.

TIMES BOOKS

Henry Holt and Company   ·   New York

Times Books
Henry Holt and Company, LLC
Publishers since 1866
175 Fifth Avenue
New York, New York 10010
www.henryholt.com

Library of Congress Cataloging-in-Publication Data

Meston, Cindy M.
    Why women have sex : understanding sexual motivations—from adventure to
revenge (and everything in between) / Cindy M. Meston and David M. Buss.
        p. cm.
    ISBN-13: 978-0-8050-8834-2
    1. Women—Sexual behavior.   2. Women—Psychology.   3. Sex (Psychology)
I. Buss, David M.   II. Title.
    HQ29.M472 2009
    306.7082—dc22   2009008389

First Edition 2009
Designed by Victoria Hartman

Printed in the United States of America
1   3   5   7   9   10   8   6   4   2

To all of the women in our study
who bravely shared
their sexual experiences with us

CONTENTS

INTRODUCTION
Inside the Sexual Mind

Why women have sex is an extraordinarily important but surprisingly little-studied topic. One reason for its neglect is that scientists and everyone else have assumed that the answers are already obvious—to experience pleasure, to express love, or—at the very heart of the biological drive to have sex—to reproduce. So, more than five years ago, we decided to undertake an intensive research project, involving more than three thousand individuals, to uncover the mysteries of women's sexuality.

When our scientific article "Why Humans Have Sex" was published in the August 2007 issue of *Archives of Sexual Behavior*, it generated an avalanche of interest. What that media coverage revealed, however, was just the tip of the iceberg. In that original study, we identified 237 distinct sexual motivations that covered an astonishing variety of psychological nuance. These motives ranged from the mundane ("I was bored") to the spiritual ("I wanted to get closer to God"), from altruistic ("I wanted my man to feel good about himself") to vengeful ("I wanted to punish my husband for cheating on me"). Some women have sex to feel powerful, others to debase themselves. Some want to impress their friends; others want to harm their enemies ("I wanted to break up a rival's relationship by having sex with her boyfriend"). Some express romantic love ("I wanted to become one with another person"); others express disturbing hate ("I wanted to give someone else a sexually transmitted disease"). But none of these reasons conveyed the "why" that hid behind each motive.

Through statistical procedures, we clustered the motivations into natural groupings. We then set out to explore women's sex lives in richer detail in a new study designed specifically for this book. And we integrated our research with all the latest scientific findings—from our labs and from the labs of other scientists throughout the world—to present what we believe is one of the richest and deepest understandings of women's sexuality yet achieved.

Why Women Have Sex brings these insights to life with detailed descriptions of women's actual sexual encounters; the motives that impel women to have sex; and the theory behind why each of those motives exists in women's sexual psychology. Although human sexuality has been the primary focus of our scientific research for many years, this project proved to be more illuminating about women's sexuality than we ever expected.

How did we end up collaborating on this extraordinary project? As it happens, we have offices right next door to each other in the psychology department at the University of Texas at Austin, where we are both professors. Given our shared professional interests, we've had many conversations about human sexuality. The topic of conversation turned one day to sexual motivation, and we started discussing a simple question: Why do people have sex?

As coauthors, we combine uniquely complementary domains of expertise. One of us, Cindy M. Meston, is a clinical psychologist and one of the world's leading experts on the psychophysiology of women's sexuality. The other, David M. Buss, is an evolutionary psychologist and one of the world's scientific experts on strategies of human mating. Our collaboration allowed us to develop a deeper understanding of women's sexuality than either of us could have achieved working alone.

Viewed from both clinical and evolutionary perspectives, women's sexuality poses interesting questions. Why do women desire some qualities in a mate, yet are repulsed by others? What tactics do women use to attract their preferred sex partners? Why do some women fuse love and sex psychologically? Why are erotic romance novels so much more appealing to women than to men? Why do some women have sex to keep a mate, whereas other women use sex to get rid of an unwanted mate?

The scientific study of sex, or "sexology," is a multifaceted field spanning the disciplines of psychology, sociology, anthropology, evolutionary biology, and medicine. For the past several decades, sexology has focused on three core issues: defining and understanding what sexual behaviors, attitudes, and relationships are normal or healthy; ascertaining how biological factors, life events, and personal preferences or circumstances shape our sexual identities and desires; and discovering how human sexuality affects, and is affected by, social relationships. Clinical psychologists are especially interested in the extent to which a person's sexual choices and responses can be modified or improved. Evolutionary psychologists study adaptive functions of the components of human sexual psychology, as well as why sexual motivations sometimes malfunction in the modern environment.

Since the late nineteenth century, sex researchers have primarily used three scientific methodologies for investigating human sexual behavior: case studies, questionnaires and surveys, and behavioral observation and assessment. The case-study method involves careful, in-depth description of individuals with sexual problems or anomalies. For example, early sexologist Richard von Krafft-Ebing (1840–1902) observed a high prevalence of masturbation among his patients, which led him to conclude (erroneously) that masturbation was the source of all sexual variation. Based on case studies, psychologist Sigmund Freud (1856–1939) theorized that childhood erotic drives shaped adult sexual behavior.

The forerunner of survey research was Havelock Ellis (1859–1939), who emphasized the vast individual diversity in sexual behavior—and wrote a memoir detailing his "open marriage" to a self-identified lesbian. In the 1940s and '50s, Alfred C. Kinsey (1894–1956) and his collaborators Wardell B. Pomeroy, Paul H. Gebhard, and Clyde E. Martin redefined the way Americans viewed their sex lives with the publication of two reports describing the sexual activities of men and women. Kinsey and his team fashioned a standardized interview that they used to gather the detailed sex histories of approximately 18,000 men and women across the United States—the largest survey ever of human sexual practices. Kinsey personally recorded 7,985 of the histories.

Robert Latou Dickinson (1861–1950), a practicing gynecologist in New York, pioneered the laboratory observation of women's sexuality with his development of a glass observation tube to view and document women's internal sexual anatomy. Kinsey also used direct observational techniques to study sexual response, but the current era of laboratory sex research began with the work of William H. Masters (1915–2001) and Virginia E. Johnson (b. 1925), who were married from 1971 until 1992. In contrast to the limited observations made by their predecessors, Masters and Johnson recruited nearly seven hundred men and women to participate in studies at their lab, where they documented the physiological changes that occur with sexual arousal and orgasm. They uncovered the role of vaginal lubrication in sexual arousal, the physiology of multiple orgasms, and the similarity between vaginal and clitoral orgasms in women.

Since the publication in 1966 of Masters and Johnson's landmark book *The Human Sexual Response*, a relatively distinct branch of lab research has emerged: *sexual psychophysiology*. Studies in sexual psychophysiology investigate the complex interplay between the psychological (feelings, emotions and thought processes) and the physiological (hormones, brain chemicals, genital engorgement, and lubrication) in human sexual behavior.

Psychological sexual arousal is typically measured using questionnaires that ask how "turned on" or "turned off" a person feels in a certain context and whether his or her mood is positive, negative, relaxed, or anxious. In the early days of sexual psychophysiology, researchers interested in measuring human physiological arousal with adapted devices used in other species. For instance, penile erection monitors for men can be traced to machines used by horse breeders in the late nineteenth century to prevent masturbation in stud horses! In the early 1970s, two doctors developed a probe that could be used to measure thermal conductance in sheep vaginas. They claimed the device "caused no discomfort for the waking sheep" during the experiments, which lasted up to four hours. Although the device proved too cumbersome and invasive for use in women, its design is not terribly different from modern vaginal probes.

Today, researchers measure physiological sexual responses, particularly genital blood flow, using a number of techniques. In women, studies involve vaginal photoplethysmography (a light-sensing device), pulsed wave Doppler ultrasonography, pelvic magnetic resonance imaging, sensors that measure changes in the temperature of the vagina or labia, and thermal imaging of thighs and genitals. In addition, sexual psychophysiologists often record changes in heart rate, respiration rate, body temperature, blood pressure, and sweat gland activity. While these nongenital measures can provide information about a person's physiological state during sexual arousal, they do not specifically indicate sexual response, since emotions such as anger, fear, anxiety, and even laughter can also trigger these changes. More recently, researchers have turned to functional magnetic resonance imaging (fMRI) to identify the areas of the brain involved in human sexual response and behavior.

All of these contemporary techniques allow researchers at the Meston Sexual Psychophysiology Lab and similar labs around the world to study the full spectrum of sexual response. Over the past eleven years, the Meston Lab has investigated questions such as: What is the relation between levels of genital arousal and feeling psychologically aroused? How do early traumatic sexual experiences impact a woman's ability to become aroused physically and mentally in adulthood? How does a woman's body image impact her overall sexual function and satisfaction? What is the impact of cigarette smoking and other drugs on men's and women's ability to become sexually aroused? How do antidepressants impair women's ability to become aroused and have an orgasm and how can we overcome these sexual side effects? Does the act of having sexual intercourse alter sex hormones in a way that can impact a woman's overall sex drive? And why does anxiety sometimes increase and sometimes decrease women's sexual functioning?

Psychological and physiological methods are also used to test evolution-based hypotheses about women's sexual psychology. To some, it may seem odd to consider these questions through the lens of evolved sexual desires, evolved mate preferences, and an evolved psychology of sexual competition. Indeed, in the field of biology proper, until the 1950s it was viewed as unrespectable to speak of evolutionary processes having sculpted "behavior" at all, with proper biologists sticking closely to anatomy and physiology. The science of evolutionary biology has changed radically since then. The sexual organs, after all, are designed for sexual behavior! Anatomy, physiology, and psychology cannot be divorced from the behavior they were designed to produce.

Many people, when they think about evolution, draw up images such as "nature red in tooth and claw" and "survival of the fittest." Although competition for survival is certainly part of evolutionary theory, in fact it is not the most important part. Indeed, Darwin himself was deeply troubled by phenomena that could not be explained by this so-called "survival selection." Marvels such as the brilliant plumage of peacocks, for example, simply defied explanation by survival selection. How could this dazzling plumage possibly have evolved, since it is energetically costly and an open advertisement to predators, qualities clearly detrimental to survival? Darwin wrote in his private correspondence that the sight of a peacock gave him nightmares, since it defied the logic of his theory of natural selection.

Darwin's nightmares subsided when he arrived at a second evolutionary theory that turns out to be central to the understanding of women's sexual psychology: the theory of sexual selection. Sexual selection deals with the evolution of characteristics not because of the survival advantage they afford organisms, but rather because of mating advantage. Sexual selection operates through two distinct processes—same-sex or intrasexual competition and preferential mate choice (also called intersexual selection). In intrasexual competition, members of one sex compete with one another, and the victors gain sexual access to the mates of their choice. Two stags locking horns in combat is the stereotypical image of intrasexual competition. Although Darwin stressed male-male competition, when it comes to humans, female-female competition is equally intense. Since males of every species differ in qualities such as physical attractiveness, health status, resource acquisition ability, and genetic quality, females who succeed in outcompeting other females for sexual access to males with beneficial qualities have a reproductive advantage over other females. And the evolutionary process is ultimately not about differential survival success, but differential reproductive success.

In intrasexual competition the qualities that lead to access to more desirable mates get passed on in greater numbers because the victors mate more successfully and produce more or higher quality offspring. The characteristics that commonly lead to loss in these competitions bite the evolutionary dust, since they are passed on in fewer offspring. Although this process is sometimes easier to see in males, for whom competition is often ostentatious, the same logic applies to females, for whom competition is generally more subtle. Among humans, for example, social reputation is a key component of same-sex competition. Social reputation is often gained or lost through subtle verbal signals, gossip, alliance formation, and other tactics that sometimes fly under the radar. Evolution—which simply means change over time—occurs as a consequence of same-sex competition because the victors have greater access to desirable sex partners.

Preferential mate choice, on the other hand, involves desiring qualities in a mate that ultimately lead to greater reproductive success for the chooser. Women who choose to have sex with healthy men, for example, gain reproductive advantages over women who choose to have sex with disease-ridden men. Women remain healthier themselves, since they do not pick up the man's communicable diseases. Their children remain healthier, since they too avoid picking up the man's diseases through close contact. And if the qualities linked to health are partly heritable, as we now know they are, then the women's children will inherit genes for good health. Women's mating desires and the qualities they find sexually attractive have evolved because they led ancestral mothers to make wise choices, both in sex partners and in long-term mates.

Evolved psychological mechanisms go far beyond reproduction to include women's sexual desires, patterns of sexual attraction, mate preferences, the emergence of the emotion of love, sexual jealousy, and much more. Each major component of women's sexual psychology solves an adaptive problem, providing a specific benefit to women—or more precisely, provided a benefit to ancestral women that modern women have inherited. So when evolutionary psychologists use phrases such as "evolved psychological mechanisms" or "psychological adaptations," they do not mean rigid, robotlike instincts expressed in behavior regardless of circumstances. Rather, human psychological adaptations are extremely flexible, highly sensitive to circumstance, and activated only in some social contexts. An evolved emotion such as sexual jealousy, for example, might motivate a woman to have sex with her partner to keep his mind off other women. But a woman usually experiences sexual jealousy only if there is a sexual threat to her relationship.

Moreover, a woman might deal with a sexual threat in a multitude of other ways, such as increased vigilance or an increased outpouring of love. Even when women's sexual adaptations are activated, it does not mean that they must invariably act on them. A woman's sexual desire, for instance, might be activated by a chance encounter with a tall, dark, and handsome stranger, but she may choose not to act on that evolved desire due to a wish to remain loyal to her regular partner, a concern about damage to her reputation, or moral or religious convictions. Psychological adaptations are not inflexible instincts that ineluctably get expressed in behavior, but rather are flexible mechanisms whose expression is highly contingent on context.

Over the past twenty years, the Buss Evolutionary Psychology Lab has used a variety of research methods to explore human sexual psychology. The methods range from observational studies of women's tactics of sexual attraction in singles bars to physiological recordings to imagining a romantic partner having sexual intercourse with someone else. They include self-reports of sexual mate poaching; experimental studies of women's sexual attraction to aspects of men's physique; and hormonal assays of the effects of ovulation on women's sexual desire. Samples include college undergraduates, dating couples, newlywed couples, older couples, and a culturally diverse sample of more than ten thousand individuals from thirty-three countries worldwide. The Buss Lab has studied the dangerous passion of sexual jealousy, why women have affairs, parental tactics to constrain the sexuality of their daughters, the evolution of love, sexual deception, the effects of ovulation on women's sexuality, whether men and women can be "just friends," personality predictors of sexual satisfaction, cues that foretell a partner's affair, derogation and gossip about sexual competitors, and "sexual intelligence."

The notion that many components of women's sexual psychology have an evolutionary function does not imply that all features are adaptive, or that every woman's sexual behavior serves a benefit. Quite the contrary. As we will see throughout this book, some reasons that propel women into sexual encounters are self-destructive and cause personal problems, the loss of self-esteem, and even life tragedies. Some reach clinical proportions and develop into distressing sexual disorders. We cover the entire range of women's sexual psychology, from the lows of sexual disorders and how they can be treated to the highs of attaining and maintaining a fulfilling sexual life.

Our new and never-before-reported study of why women have sex was conducted online between June 2006 and April 2009. Web links and online classified advertisements requested women's participation in a study designed to understand sexual motivations. The survey itself was hosted by a database using 128-bit encryption technology to protect the information from hackers and to ensure the utmost anonymity to the study's participants. The women who participated first completed an informed consent during which they received full disclosure of the survey's subject matter and were assured that they could discontinue the survey at any time. We have shared the women's exact words, after eliminating any details that might identify them to maintain the confidentiality of their responses. We also let the participants know that if they had any concerns about the study or became distressed after answering the questions or sharing their stories, a clinical psychologist would be available to discuss their concerns with them.

The survey began by asking the women if they had ever had sex for one of the 237 reasons we identified in our original study. If a woman's answer was yes, she would then be prompted to describe a specific experience; if no, she was asked about another reason for having sex. The women's answers confirmed, enhanced, and enriched the quantitative findings of our initial investigation of why humans have sex. Most important, they gave real women an opportunity to explain in their own words their motivations for having sex, providing a depth of insight into sexual psychology beyond what could be captured from statistical analysis.

In the course of the study, 1,006 women from a variety of backgrounds shared their experiences with us. They hailed from forty-six of the fifty states (all except Alaska, Montana, Nebraska, and Delaware); eight of the ten provinces of Canada (all but Saskatchewan and Prince Edward Island) and one of the two territories (Northwest Territory); three European countries (Germany, Belgium, and France); and Australia, New Zealand, Israel, and China. The women ranged in age from eighteen (the youngest we accepted into the study) to eighty-six and identified ethnically as American Indian, Asian, black, white (non-Hispanic), and Latino. About 57 percent considered themselves to be part of a specific religious tradition—Christian (Anglican, Baptist, Catholic, Episcopalian, Lutheran, Methodist, Mormon, Pentecostal, Protestant, and Seventh Day Adventists), Jewish, Muslim, Buddhist, Hindu, Taoist, Unitarian Universalist, and pagan or Wicca—while 26 percent said they were agnostics and 14 percent said they were atheists. Though the survey was conducted through the Internet, the participants came from diverse socioeconomic situations: 17 percent reported a family income of $25,000 or less a year; 31 percent an income between $25,001 and $50,000; 33 percent an income between $50,001 and $100,000; and 19 percent an income of more than $100,000.

Of course, we also asked the women about their relationship status and sexual orientation. Approximately 80 percent reported being in a relationship at the time, whereas 10 percent were currently dating but were not in a long-term relationship. Ninety-three percent of the women said they were predominantly or exclusively heterosexual, with 2 percent identifying as bisexual and 5 percent identifying as predominantly or exclusively homosexual. Eleven percent actually did not choose one of these labels, opting for "other"—including gay, lesbian, asexual, bi-curious, hetero-flexible, omnisexual, pansexual, queer, straight-plus, fluid, open, polyamorous, still questioning, and various combinations such as "mostly heterosexual plus a touch of gay."

One of the surprises in our study was that for each reason that impels a woman to have sex, we discovered both successes and failures. Sex was often incredibly pleasurable, giving women a sense of excitement, love, connection, and self-exploration:

> *I have found . . . two things are important—being able to be really intense sexually with the person, while simultaneously being able to laugh heartily and really enjoy the experience of being with the person in a different way. It's almost like the laughter and the sex satisfy two basic human urges simultaneously.*

—heterosexual woman, age 42

Women enjoy their sexiness and their sexuality.

But goals sought through sex are sometimes not reached. Indeed, sex sometimes leaves women feeling lonely, bitter, and regretful. One woman in our study sought sex in order to relieve her loneliness and feelings of being unattractive, but it didn't work out that way:

> *I had sex in my last relationship so I would not feel so damned lonely and unlovable. It was a stupid thing because it ended up worsening the feelings for me. . . . I regret it now because we didn't really know each other very well and were not really sure where we were going. We split up after another month.*
>
> —heterosexual woman, age 39

For every failure, however, we discovered sexual encounters of great success and true poignancy. Here is how one woman described sex as a way of boosting her self-confidence:

> *I had sex with a couple of guys because I felt sorry for them. These guys were virgins and I felt bad that they had never had sex before so I had sex with them. I felt like I was doing them a big favor that no one else had ever done. I felt power over them, like they were weaklings under me and I was in control. It boosted my confidence to be the teacher in the situation and made me feel more desirable.*
>
> —heterosexual woman, age 25

Another believed sex was a means of experiencing God:

> *I can't really describe this experience . . . but pure joy and connection with another person I feel is becoming closer to the cycles of life and the underlying palpable energy of the world . . . in essence, God.*
>
> —heterosexual woman, age 21

Through the voices of real women, wide-ranging scientific and clinical findings, and our own original research, women's sexuality can be seen in all of its textures, whether a sexual encounter leads to pleasure, remorse, emotional connection, or transcendent love.

We believe the end result will aid more informed sexual decision making—when, how, and, of course, *why* to have sex, in a relationship or outside one. Although this is not designed as a "self-help" book, we believe that readers will glean information that they can use in their own lives and share with their sexual partners. We hope that this book provides readers with a new set of lenses for viewing the many nuanced facets of women's sexual psychology.

Why Women Have Sex

1. What Turns Women On?

*Scent, Body, Face, Voice, Movement,
Personality, and—Yes—Humor*

☙ℬ❧

*Personal beauty is a greater recommendation than any letter
of introduction.*

—Aristotle (384–322 BCE)

Sexual attraction is an elixir of life, from love at first sight to the spark
of romance that enlivens a relationship for years. It imbues the great
love affairs of literature and film, whether the star-crossed lovers of
Shakespeare's *Romeo and Juliet* or James Cameron's *Titanic* or the long-
smoldering attraction between Humphrey Bogart's and Ingrid Bergman's
characters in *Casablanca*. And despite the reigning conventional wisdom, the basic biochemistry of attraction is the number one reason
women give for why they have sex.

Despite its relative neglect in the history of psychology, sexual attraction is not simply a topic of titillation. It permeates our conversations—
from gossip columns highlighting celebrity fashion missteps to Web sites
devoted to ranking who is hot and who is not, advertisers exploit it to
sell everything from cars to iPods. Lack of sexual attraction is often a
deal breaker in romances, killing possible partnerships before they even
get off the ground. And when sexual attraction fades with time, it can
propel a partner into the arms of another. For many, sex provides a deep
sense of exhilaration that makes them feel alive. We often cannot describe
what it is that attracts us to another person. Sometimes we resort to

types—latching on to an easily identifiable trait or pointing to a celebrity who has many of the qualities we, and apparently many other people, find most appealing. Many women in our study mentioned a specific physical or personality characteristic that sexually attracted them, yet as many others chose to describe their sexual motivation in the simplest terms: I was attracted to the person. Women also said the person had a beautiful face; the person had a desirable body; the person had beautiful eyes; the person smelled nice; the person's physical appearance turned me on; the person was a good dancer; or more graphically, the person was too physically attractive for me to resist.

This chapter explores what, exactly, women find sexually attractive—and why. Why do musky aromas and resonant voices stir women's sexual desires? If women really are less sexually stimulated by visual images than men are, why do the faces of, say, Antonio Banderas and George Clooney excite so many women? Is there actually something in the way another person moves that can affect women's sexual drives? How can a dazzling personality sometimes turn an average Joe into a man who exudes an irresistible animal magnetism? When does physical attraction overpower everything else?

Because the spark of attraction often operates beneath our consciousness, some of our answers to these questions come from an evolutionary perspective. Evolutionary psychologists start with the working premise that at least some of the characteristics that women find attractive are not culturally arbitrary. (The same is true of the characteristics that men find attractive.) Could the qualities that define sex appeal unconsciously provide signals of the benefits a woman might get from a potential mate? Biologists distinguish two broad classes of evolutionary benefits. *Genetic benefits* are the high-quality genes that can endow a woman's children with a better ability to survive and reproduce. *Resource benefits*, including food, shelter from the hostile forces of nature, and physical protection from aggressive men, help a woman and her children to survive and thrive.

As we will see, some of the things that make women want to have sex with men have their roots in humans' evolutionary past, while others have taken on a life of their own because of how we live, work, dress, and socialize today.

Where Attraction Begins

People are constantly coming into contact with one another—we are nestled into adjoining seats in college lecture halls, bump into strangers at coffee shops, move into neighboring houses on suburban cul-de-sacs, or spend long hours in catty-corner cubicles at the office. This proximity is often the first step in becoming attracted to someone.

Historically, you can see this in who people choose as their mates. Back in the 1930s, a study examined five thousand marriages performed in a single year, 1931, to determine where the bride and groom lived before their wedding. One-third lived within five blocks of each other and more than one-half lived within a twenty-block radius. Several studies over the decades have uncovered similar patterns. For example, in classrooms with assigned seating, relationships develop as a function of how far people are seated from each other. Students assigned to a middle seat are more likely to make acquaintances than those who are seated at the end of a row. With alphabetical seating, friendships form between those whose names start with nearby letters.

Although being near someone does not guarantee that a sexual spark will be struck, repeated contact (up to a point) with someone increases the odds. One study found that a series of brief—that is, no more than thirty-five-second—face-to-face contacts *without even talking to the person* increased positive responses. That is, we tend to like the people we see often more than those we see less frequently. In another study, four women research assistants with comparable physical attractiveness attended a college class. One research assistant attended the class fifteen times during the semester, one assistant attended ten times, another five times, and one not at all. None of the women had any verbal contact with the students in the class. At the end of the semester, the students, both men and women, rated how much they liked each of the research assistants. Attraction increased as the number of exposures increased, even though all of the research assistants were fundamentally strangers to the people in the class.

As it turns out, some amount of familiarity creates liking whether you're talking about a person, a drawing, a word in an unknown foreign language, a song, a new product being advertised, a political candidate, or even a nonsense syllable. The more frequent a person's exposure during the crucial early period of introduction, the more positive the response. Why? We often respond to anyone or anything strange or novel with at least mild discomfort, if not a certain degree of anxiety. With repeated exposure, our feelings of anxiety decrease; the more familiar we are with someone, the better we are able to predict his or her behavior and thus to feel more comfortable around the person.

Once people are in close proximity, eye contact becomes important. The effect of mutual eye gaze is especially strong for women and men who are "romantics" by nature—those who believe in love at first sight, love for "the one and only," and love as the key to relationships. In one study, forty-eight women and men came to a lab and were asked to stare into each other's eyes while talking. The effect of mutual gaze proved powerful. Many reported that deep eye contact with an opposite-sex stranger created feelings of intense love. As one woman in our study put it:

> I find it very arousing when someone is mysterious and doesn't give too much of themselves away upon cursory review. I once had sex with a man because he was looking at me longingly but wouldn't say much. It was a very passionate experience.
>
> —heterosexual woman, age 33

Another study had strangers first reveal intimate details of their lives to each other for half an hour, and then asked them to stare into each other's eyes for four minutes—without breaking eye contact or making any conversation. Participants again reported deep attraction to their study partners. Two of these total strangers even ended up getting married!

Too much familiarity, however, can backfire. Traits that are initially deemed positive can become a source of annoyance. Men who were once described as "funny and fun" become "embarrassing in public." An attractive "spontaneity" transforms into an unattractive "irresponsibility," "successful and focused" into "workaholic," and "strong willed" into "stubborn." Indeed, a certain amount of "mystery" can be sexually motivating for women, or for men for that matter. Not only can mystery stoke attraction; too much familiarity can quash it. As one woman said in her sexual memoir, "proximity can kill sex faster than fainting."

Just as overexposure can douse the fire of sexual attraction, its opposite—novelty—can stoke its flames. Psychologist Daryl Bem sums it up with the phrase "the exotic becomes erotic." Indeed, in college classes in which instructors ask women to list the qualities they find sexually attractive, "mysterious" invariably emerges on the list.

Humans come blessed with five known senses—sight, sound, smell, touch, and taste—and the sensory cues that enter into attraction tend to have greater effect with physical closeness. That's particularly true when considering one of the strongest ingredients in sex appeal, one long neglected by the scientific community: women's acute sense of smell.

The Scent of Sexiness

Scents are famously known to carry strong psychological associations— think about how a whiff of a loved one's favored perfume or cologne can bring to mind the person who wore it, along with a cascade of emotions. Partly, this is due to the unusual design of the olfactory nerve, which extends in a network throughout the brain—unlike the nerves carrying information for the other major senses, which are less wide-ranging. This architecture helps the brain to tie memories of emotional events with olfactory information. The emotion-stirring aspect of smell is important; but smell also turns out to be surprisingly important to women when it comes to basic sexual attraction.

Using an instrument called the "Sensory Stimuli and Sexuality Survey," researchers at Brown University found that women rate how someone smells as the most important of the senses in choosing a lover, edging out sight (a close second), sound, and touch. One woman in our study ranked the attractions of a sexual partner:

> *I was attracted to his smell, his eyes, and his demeanor. Also, his French accent.*
>
> —heterosexual woman, age 23

How a woman smells to a man, in contrast, figures less heavily in his sexual attraction. Perhaps it is because men's sense of smell is less acute than women's. Perhaps it is because visual cues loom so much larger in what turns men on. And it's not just that women think smell matters in whether they are attracted to someone, it's that women's sexual arousal is enhanced by good body odors—and killed by bad ones.

One reason why body odors play such an important role in women's sexual attraction has come to scientific light only recently. The first clue came from an unusual discovery: that a woman's olfactory acuity reaches its peak around the time of her ovulation, the narrow twenty-four-hour window during the monthly menstrual cycle in which she can become pregnant. This led scientists to suspect that women's sense of smell might play a role in reproduction. It was not until researchers began to explore the body's defenses against disease, however, that the connection was made.

The genes responsible for immune functioning—fighting off disease-causing bacteria and viruses—are located within the major histocompatibility complex, or MHC, found on chromosome 6. Different people have different versions, or alleles, of these MHC genes; in the jargon of geneticists, the MHC genes are "polymorphic." It turns out that women can benefit in two ways from mating with men who are *dissimilar* to themselves in MHC genes. First, a mate with dissimilar MHC genes likely has more dissimilar genes in general, and so finding an MHC-dissimilar person attractive might help to prevent inbreeding. Reproducing with close genetic relatives can be disastrous for the resulting children, leading to birth defects, lower intelligence, and other problems. But a second benefit of mating with someone with complementary MHC genes is that any resulting children will have better immune functioning, making them better able to fight off many of the parasites that cause disease.

The puzzle is how women could possibly be able to choose mates who have complementary MHC genes in order to give these benefits to their offspring. In a revealing study, Brazilian researchers had twenty-nine men wear patches of cotton on their skin for five days to absorb their sweat—and thus their body odors. A sample of twenty-nine women then smelled each cotton patch and evaluated the odor on a dimension from attractive to unattractive. Scientists identified the specific MHC complex of each man and woman through blood assays. Women found the aromas of men who had an MHC complex complementary to their own smelled the most desirable. The odors of men who had an MHC complex similar to their own made them recoil in disgust. Amazing as it may seem, women can literally smell the scent of a gene complex known to play a key role in immune functioning.

This highly developed sense of smell can have a profound effect on women's sexuality. University of New Mexico evolutionary psychologist Christine Garver-Apgar and her colleagues studied MHC similarity in forty-eight romantically involved couples. They found that as the degree of MHC similarity between each woman and man increased, the woman's sexual responsiveness to her partner decreased. Women whose partners had similar MHC genes reported wanting to have sex less often with them. They reported less motivation to please their partner sexually compared to the women romantically involved with men with complementary MHC genes. Perhaps even more disturbing to their mates (if they knew), women with MHC-similar partners reported more frequent sexual fantasies about other men, particularly at the most fertile phase of their ovulation cycle. And their sexual fantasies about other men did not just remain in their heads. They found themselves in the arms of other men more often, reporting higher rates of actual sexual infidelity—a 50 percent rate of infidelity among couples who had 50 percent of their MHC alleles in common.

So when a woman says that she had sex with a man because he smelled nice, her sexual motivation has hidden roots in an evolutionary adaptation. At an unconscious level, women are drawn to men with whom they are genetically compatible.

Another reason why a man's scent is so important comes from the unusual discovery that body symmetry has sexual allure. Most human bodies are bilaterally symmetrical: The left wrist generally has the same circumference as the right wrist; the left ear is generally as long as the right ear; from the eyes to the toes, the left and right halves of people's bodies roughly mirror each other. Each individual, however, carries small deviations from perfect symmetry. Two forces can cause faces and bodies to become more asymmetrical. One is genetic—the number of mutations an individual has, which geneticists call *mutation load*. Although everyone carries some genetic mutations (estimates are that the average person has a few hundred), some people have a higher mutation load than others, and those with more mutations tend to be more asymmetrical. The second force is environmental. During development, some individuals sustain more illnesses, diseases, parasites, and bodily injuries than others, and these environmental insults create asymmetries in the body and face. Symmetry, in short, is a sign of good health—an indication that a person carries a low mutation load and has experienced few environmental injuries, or at least possesses the capacity to sustain environmental injuries without their leaving much of a mark.

If body symmetry is attractive because of how we evolved, so is the fact that women are able to detect the scent signature for symmetry, a useful skill when you consider that some asymmetries may not be immediately visible.

But could a woman possibly smell body symmetry? In one study, men wore white cotton T-shirts for two nights. The T-shirts were then sealed in plastic bags. In the laboratory, scientists used calipers to measure the various physical components of the men's bodies, including their wrists, ankles, and earlobes, in order to evaluate their degree of symmetry. Then women smelled each T-shirt and provided a rating of how pleasant or unpleasant it smelled. Women judged the T-shirt odors of symmetrical men to be the most attractive and deemed the odors of asymmetrical men to be repulsive. Four independent studies have replicated the finding.

Women find the scent of symmetry particularly attractive when they are in the fertile phase of their ovulation cycle—precisely the time in which they are most likely to conceive. This apparently reflects an evolutionary adaptation in women to reproduce with men possessing honest signals of good health, including high-quality genes. When women have extramarital affairs, they tend to choose symmetrical men as partners—yet another indication of the importance of symmetry in sexual attraction.

The Power of a Man's Musk

A person's scent can influence not only a woman's mate choice, but also when and how frequently she chooses to have sex and possibly the chance she will become pregnant.

Researchers have shown that exposure to male pheromones can increase a woman's fertility. Pheromones are substances secreted from the glands at the anus, underarms, urinary outlet, breasts, and mouth. In nonhuman mammals, a specialized olfactory structure, the vomeronasal organ, acts as the locus for receiving pheromonal signals, which control most animals' and insects' mating rituals. One study found that frequent sexual exposure to men (at least once a week) regularized women's menstrual cycles, increased fertile basal body temperature, and increased estrogen in the phase of the menstrual cycle following ovulation, called the luteal phase. Another study showed that women who slept with a man two or more times during a forty-day period had a significantly higher incidence of ovulation than those who had slept with a man less often.

Once again, sexual attraction plays a role. Dr. Winnifred Cutler, the director of the Athena Institute, found that exposure to male pheromones influences a woman's sexual attraction to a man. In her study, thirty-eight heterosexual men aged twenty-six to forty-two recorded their baseline levels of sexual behavior and dating experiences for a two-week period. Then for a month they wore either their regular aftershave, or the same aftershave but with an added synthetic version of a pheromone naturally secreted by men. The men did not know which aftershave they were wearing. During the test month, the men continued to record their sexual and dating experiences. The results showed that compared to their baseline levels of sexual activity, the men who wore the "pheromone-charged" aftershave engaged in higher rates of sexual petting and intercourse, had more frequent informal dates, and spent more time sleeping next to a partner. Over the same period, they reported no change in their frequency of masturbation—so the increase in the rest of their sexual activity could not simply have resulted from men having a higher sex drive due to their own exposure to the extra pheromone.

Sensitivity to scent does not just provide a means for identifying good hygiene or emotionally resonant perfumes. Scent also gives women cues about a partner's immune system and body symmetry, and pheromones can unconsciously shape how women become sexually attracted and aroused.

Size Matters

We've seen how body symmetry, because it indicates good health, is attractive to women. Body symmetry is also linked with men's muscularity, and studies conducted both in the United States and on the Caribbean island of Dominica have found that symmetrical men have a larger number of sex partners than asymmetrical men. When women identify the specific qualities that attract them to a sexual partner, they frequently mention "the person had a desirable body"—the sixteenth most frequent reason cited for having sex in our original study. But what sorts of bodies do women find sexually desirable?

Perhaps the most obvious characteristic is *height*. Studies consistently find that women consider tall men to be attractive, although only to an extent—taller than average, but not too tall. In analyses of personal ads, 80 percent of women state a desire for a man six feet tall or taller. Men who indicated in their personal ads that they were tall received far more responses from women. Women prefer tall men as marriage partners, and place an even greater emphasis on height in shorter-term sex partners. Women even take height into consideration when selecting sperm donors!

A study of British men found that taller than average men have had a greater number of live-in girlfriends than their shorter peers. Two studies found that taller than average men tend to have more children, and hence are more reproductively successful. Women seem to find tall men better candidates for romance and reproduction.

Could there be a logic underlying women's desires for tall men? In traditional cultures, tall men tend to have higher status. "Big men" in hunter-gatherer societies—high-status men who command respect—are *literally* big men, physically. In Western cultures, tall men tend to have higher socioeconomic status than short men. Another study found that recruiters choose the taller of two applicants for a sales job 72 percent of the time. Each added inch of height adds several thousand dollars to a man's annual salary. One study estimated that men who are six feet tall earn, on average, $166,000 more across a thirty-year career than men seven inches shorter. Taller policemen are assaulted less often than shorter policemen, indicating that their stature either commands more respect from criminals or causes them to think twice before attacking. Height deters aggression from other men. In the jargon of evolutionary biology, height is an "honest signal" of a man's ability to protect. Women report simply feeling safer with tall mates.

Another answer comes from recently discovered correlates of male height. Tall men, on average, tend to be healthier than short men, although men at the extreme high and low end of the distribution have more health problems. So tall men tend to have better job prospects, to have more economic resources, to enjoy elevated social status, to afford physical protection, and to be healthy—a bounty of adaptive benefits.

(We will see how sizes in other arenas matter in chapters 2 and 7.)

Fit for Sex

Height, of course, is not the only aspect of men's bodies that sexually excites women.

Studies of mate preferences reveal that women desire strong, muscular, athletic men for long-term mating as well as for sexual liaisons. Most women show a distinct preference for a particular body morphology—namely, a V-shaped torso that reveals a high *shoulder-to-hip ratio* (broad shoulders relative to hips). They are attracted to a lean stomach combined with a muscular (but not muscle-bound) upper torso.

In fact, both sexes judge men with a high shoulder-to-hip ratio to be more physically and socially dominant—which may give a clue to its appeal, since women generally are not attracted to men who appear as though they could be easily dominated by other men. Men exhibiting a high shoulder-to-hip ratio begin having sexual intercourse at an early age—sixteen or younger. They report having more sex partners than their slim-shouldered peers. They have more sexual affairs with outside partners while in a relationship. And they report more instances of being chosen by already-mated women for sexual affairs on the side. Shoulder-to-hip ratio also arouses the green-eyed monster: Potential rivals with a high shoulder-to-hip ratio trigger jealousy in men.

Men with strong, athletic, V-shaped bodies tend to succeed in competitions with other men compared to their frailer peers. Across cultures, physical contests such as wrestling, racing, and throwing allow women to gauge men's physical abilities, including speed, endurance, and strength.

Scientific research, though, has discovered that men overestimate the degree of muscularity that women actually find attractive, assuming that they need to pump up more, or puff up more, to be attractive. One study compared the muscularity of men's bodies in *Cosmopolitan* (whose readership is 89 percent women) with *Men's Health* (whose readership is 85 percent men). Researchers rated the muscularity of men's bodies depicted in each magazine. The level of muscularity depicted in *Cosmopolitan* (4.26) was nearly identical to the level of muscularity women rate as ideal in a sexual partner (4.49). Men, in contrast, mistakenly believe that women desire a more muscular sex partner (5.04), which corresponds more closely with the muscularity of men shown in *Men's Health* (5.77).

Images of muscle-bound men have almost certainly fostered men's misperception of what women find most sexually attractive—just as photo spreads of impossibly thin women have led women to overestimate the degree of thinness that men find most attractive. After viewing repeated images of V-shaped bodies, men become more dissatisfied with their own bodies, just as women become more unhappy with their bodies after seeing images of size zero models. Fully 90 percent of American men report that they want to be more muscular. The figure among the less media-saturated Ghana is 49 percent. Ukrainian men lie in between, with 69 percent reporting a desire to be more muscular. As one researcher summed it up, the average man "feels like Clark Kent but longs to be like Superman."

The Face of Attraction

He could have been a model. When he acted interested in me, I couldn't believe it. We had sex once. Strangely enough, he kept calling me afterward. I didn't continue with the relationship for several reasons. One, he was just a pretty face, but I think he was really crazy about me. Two, never date a guy prettier than you are. It's terrible for your self-esteem and your sanity.

—heterosexual woman, age 26

Masculine facial features are heavily influenced by the production of testosterone during adolescence, when the bones in the face take their adult form. From an evolutionary perspective, puberty marks the time when men and women enter the arena of mate competition. They begin to allocate time, energy, and effort to the tasks of mate selection and mate attraction. In men, the amount of muscle mass, as we have seen, contributes to success in competition with other men and sexual attractiveness to women. And testosterone turns out to be the magical hormone that promotes men's muscle mass and masculine facial features.

So why don't all men have masculine faces and ripped bodies? The answer strangely hinges on a negative side effect of testosterone. High testosterone production compromises the body's immune functioning, leaving men less able to fight off diseases and parasites. Now here is the paradox: Only men who are above average in healthiness during adolescence can "afford" to produce the high levels of testosterone that masculinize the face. Less healthy adolescents cannot afford to compromise their already precarious immune systems, and so produce lower levels of testosterone at precisely the time when facial bones take their adult form. A masculine-looking face signals a man's health, his ability to succeed in competing with other men, and his ability to protect. And that is the best explanation for why most women find somewhat more masculine faces (but not the most masculine faces) to be the most attractive.

But when we consider a woman's fertility status and whether she is evaluating a man as a casual sex partner or a husband, the dynamics shift. In a series of scientific studies, women were asked to judge the attractiveness of a variety of men's faces at different points during their ovulation cycle—during the most fertile phase (the five days leading up to ovulation) and during the least fertile, post-ovulation luteal phase. The subjects evaluated the faces for sexiness, their attractiveness as a casual sex partner, and their attractiveness as a long-term mate. Women found above-average masculine faces to be the sexiest and the most attractive for a casual sexual encounter. In contrast, women judged somewhat less masculine faces to be more attractive for a long-term relationship. Women's sexual desires for testosterone-fueled facial cues of masculinity were especially strong during the fertile window of their cycle.

The most plausible interpretation of these results is that women are attracted to men who are likely to be "good dads" when choosing long-term mates, but are attracted to the honest signals of health that masculinity provides when they are most likely to become impregnated. This interpretation, however, raises a puzzle: Why wouldn't women be attracted to highly masculine males for all mating relationships, from dangerous liaisons through lifelong love?

The answer lies in the fact that the more masculine men are less sexually faithful. They are more likely to be the risk-taking womanizing "bad boys" among the male population. Consequently, most women face a trade-off: If they choose the less masculine-looking man, they get a better father and a more sexually loyal mate, but they lose out in the currency of genes for good health. If they choose the more masculine man, they can endow their children with good genes for health, but must suffer the costs of a man who channels some of his sexual energy toward other women. So women's preferences reveal a dual mating strategy, an attempt to get the best of both worlds.

They can choose to have a long-term relationship with a slightly less masculine man who will be sexually loyal and invest in her children, while opportunistically having sex with the more masculine men when they are most likely to get pregnant. DNA fingerprinting studies reveal that roughly 12 percent of women get pregnant by men other than their long-term mates, suggesting that some, but certainly not all, women pursue this dual mating strategy.

Cultures differ, however, in how much women are attracted to facial masculinity. Psychologist Ian Penton-Voak and his colleagues found that Jamaican women found masculine-looking men sexier than did British women. They interpret this cultural difference as a product of the higher rates of infectious diseases in Jamaica compared to England. In cultures in which infectious disease is a more pervasive problem, women seem to shift their sexual choices to men who possess honest signals of good health—men whose faces have been shaped by testosterone.

Conventionally Handsome

People are drawn to those who are *collectively* considered attractive—so much so that a number of women in our study reported having sex with attractive people even when they had no desire to pursue a long-term relationship:

> *I became friends with a man who was very handsome, but for whom I felt no desire to pursue a relationship. He asked me to stay the night in his bed, and despite having misgivings . . . I couldn't resist. He was conventionally handsome but very edgy and non-conformist and he like[d] me a lot.*
>
> —predominantly heterosexual woman, age 36

What does it mean for someone to be "conventionally" handsome? Developmental psychologist Judith Langlois studies the meaning of "attractiveness" in human faces by having subjects rate composite faces—made up of sixteen or more images morphed together—against the individual faces used to create the composites. The composite faces were rated more attractive—and, according to Langlois, if "you take a female composite (averaged) face made of thirty-two faces and overlay it on the face of an extremely attractive female model, the two images line up almost perfectly, indicating that the model's facial configuration is very similar to the composites' facial configuration." The same was true of men's composite faces.

Langlois has also found that infants as young as one year old respond to this kind of "averaged" attractiveness in adult faces. Researchers varied their attractiveness levels by putting on attractive and unattractive masks that were carefully and realistically molded to their faces. The men and women then interacted with, and attempted to initiate play with, the one-year-olds. They discovered that the infants expressed more positive moods and were more involved in play when they interacted with the researchers who were wearing the attractive masks. Even when the stimulus is a doll, studies show that infants spend more time playing with attractive versus unattractive dolls.

There is also a large body of research showing that we are drawn to good-looking people because we make assumptions that they possess a whole host of other desirable traits. They are rated as also being interesting, sociable, independent, dominant, exciting, sexy, well adjusted, socially skilled, and successful. There is some support for these stereotypes.

Attractiveness is moderately linked with popularity, good interpersonal skills, and occupational success, and, to some extent, with physical health, mental health, and sexual experience, which may be partly because attractive people are treated more favorably.

A Knee-Knocking Voice

Singers such as Elvis Presley in the 1950s, the Beatles in the '60s, and Jim Morrison of the Doors in the '70s through contemporary rappers such as Kanye West, Jay-Z, and 50 Cent are—and have always been—famously attractive to women. Part of their sex appeal has undoubtedly been a result of the popularity and social status they command. But there is also a *sound* of sexiness, something about male voices that gives women a sexual buzz.

Voice pitch is the most striking feature of human speech. Before puberty, male and female voices are quite similar. At puberty, remarkable changes occur. Boys experience a dramatic increase in the length of their vocal folds, which become 60 percent longer than those of girls. Longer vocal folds and vocal tracts produce a deeper, more resonant voice pitch. Testosterone triggers the change in boys at puberty, and high levels of testosterone predict deeper voices among adult men.

The first scientific evidence of women's preferences for deeper male voices came from a study in which women rated the deep, resonant voices such as that of Luciano Pavarotti more attractive than the higher-pitched voices such as that of Truman Capote. This may not come as much of a surprise. But three more recent investigations show that mating context is critical in how women choose among men's voices. Evolutionary anthropologist David Puts obtained voice recordings of thirty men attempting to persuade a woman to go out on a romantic date. Then 142 heterosexual women listened to the recordings and rated each man's attractiveness in two mating contexts—for a short-term sexual encounter and for a long-term committed relationship. Although women said the deeper voices were more attractive in both mating contexts, they dramatically preferred the deeper voices when considering them as prospects for purely sexual, short-term encounters. Moreover, women in the fertile phase of their ovulation cycle showed the strongest sexual attraction to men with deep voices.

One hint as to why is found in studies of female frogs, which gravitate toward deep, resonant croaks of male bullfrogs, a reliable signal—for frogs—of a mate's size and health. Now, research on people has revealed two similar reasons that help to explain why women find some men's voices more attractive than others.

The first involves bilateral body symmetry—the health-and-good-genes signal that a person can better withstand the stresses of diseases, injuries, and genetic mutations during development. Body symmetry is more likely to produce deep voices. So when a woman finds the resonance of a man's voice even sexier during her fertile, ovulatory phase, she is attracted to the sound of symmetry for her possible offspring. Attractive-sounding voices also indicate a man's body morphology. Psychologist Susan Hughes found that men with sexy voices, in contrast to their strident-sounding peers, have a higher shoulder-to-hip ratio, the attractive V-shaped body. Women judge men with lower-pitched voices to be healthier, more masculine, more physically dominant, somewhat older, more socially dominant, and more well-respected by their peers.

Do women's attractions to sexy voices translate into higher sexual success for lower-pitched men? One study found that American men with lower-pitched voices had experienced a larger number of sex partners than men with higher-pitched voices. A second study, of the Hadza, a population of hunter-gatherers living in Tanzania, found that men with lower-pitched voices had a greater number of children, possibly as a consequence of having greater sexual access to fertile women.

So it's not that carrying a tune makes much difference—a baritone voice like the actor James Earl Jones's might be mesmerizing because of all it signals about good health, good genes, the capacity to protect, and success in social hierarchies. Many of those sexually alluring musicians had another attractive quality to their credit—a body in motion.

Something in the Way He Moves

Physical movement depends on the strength of a person's bones, muscle tone, and motor control. The ability to move in a coordinated manner, especially through repetitive motions such as walking or dancing, reveals information about a person's phenotype: It broadcasts information about age—notice the difference between the dancing prowess of younger versus older dancers. It also conveys information about energy level, health, and biomechanical efficiency, whether we know it or not.

We found that some women had sex with men simply because they were good dancers:

> I was told that if a man could dance he could perform in bed. I did not believe this and wanted to see if it was true. I met someone who danced on the same order of a stripper. He danced for me a couple of times. We ended up having sex and yes he was as good in bed as he was on the dance floor. . . . He literally danced while having sex. It was wonderful.
>
> —heterosexual woman, age 29

> He was hot. The fact that he was a good dancer made him that much more appealing. I really enjoy dancing myself, so when I see that a person has rhythm, it turns me on.
>
> —heterosexual woman, age 26

Research reveals that women find certain body movements to be more attractive than others. One study had women view digitally masked or pixelated images of men dancing. Women were more attracted to men who displayed larger and more sweeping movements. They also rated these men more erotic. Just as men's faces differ from one another in their degree of masculinity, men differ in the masculinity of the way they walk. Men and women have very distinctive walks: Men's upper bodies sway laterally more than women's. Women, in contrast to men, have a hip rotation in opposite phase to their vertical leg movement, creating that classic hip swivel.

In a fascinating experiment, psychologist Meghan Provost and her colleagues videotaped a series of men and women walking. The subjects donned suits with reflecting light markers attached; additional markers were placed on their exposed skin. Then the researchers created a computer program that took the videotaped data and converted it into points of light that "walked" on a continuum from very feminine to very masculine. Fifty-five women not using oral contraceptives viewed these walking lights on a computer screen and chose the precise walking motion they found most attractive. Women preferred male walkers who were above average on the masculinity of their walk. Women in the fertile phase of their ovulation cycle expressed a stronger preference for masculine walkers than did women in the nonfertile phase of their cycle. These findings provide further support for the attraction value of masculinity—features created by higher levels of testosterone during adolescence that provide women with an honest signal of a man's health.

Other patterns of men's movements provide women with valuable mating information. Nonreciprocal same-sex touching—when a man touches another man's back, for example—is a well-documented signal of dominance. Women see "touchers" as having more status, a key component of a man's mate value. Space maximization movements, as when a man stretches his arms or extends his legs, are another dominance signal. Those who display open body positioning—for example, by not having their arms folded across the chest—are judged to be more potent and persuasive.

Evolutionary psychologist Karl Grammer and his colleagues conducted a study in three singles bars in Pennsylvania. They coded men's nonverbal behaviors and then examined which ones were linked with making "successful contact" with a woman in the bar—defined as achieving at least one minute of continuous conversation with her. They found five classes of men's movements linked with successful contact: more frequent short, direct glances at women; more space maximization movements; more location changes; more nonreciprocated touches; and a smaller number of closed-body movements.

Women are drawn to men who signal interest through eye contact and open body posture and social status through space maximization, nonreciprocal intrasexual touch, and a masculine manner of walking.

The Sexy Personality

Sexual attraction isn't simply a matter of physical bodies drawn magnetically together in search of compatibility. For some women, personality is equally, if not more, important in generating a sustained sexual spark:

It is certainly possible to have sex with someone [whom] you find purely physically attractive, or only feel emotionally connected to, but without a combination of both, the sex feels incomplete somehow. . . . In one case, my partner who I had initially been attracted to . . . showed signs of an unstable personality and many insensitive qualities. Though I remained greatly attracted to his physique, the further I became aware of his actions . . . the less I wanted to continue having sex with him. Conversely, I have been in [a] relationship where I was initially drawn to the person on the basis of their incredible personality and not their looks.

—heterosexual woman, age 21

Our study discovered two key personality characteristics that motivate women to have sex—a *good sense of humor* and *self-confidence*. Here is how two women described what made a sexual partner attractive to them:

I had sex with someone who had a great sense of humor because every time I was with him, I had a great time. I have never had so much fun with anyone else as I had with him. All of those good feelings from all the laughter led to me feeling good with him in other aspects. Sex was just an extension of that.

—heterosexual woman, age 27

I had this boyfriend who wasn't terribly attractive, but he was extremely romantic and could make me laugh just by looking at me. He had an incredible sense of humor that turned me on completely. . . . At some point he cheated, broke my heart and his own, and I ended it. . . . Several years later we evenutally did date again, but that magic was no longer there. But that didn't keep me from wanting him sexually. He was still incredibly funny!

—heterosexual woman, age 40

Another woman summed up the importance of humor about as succinctly as possible: "If there is no laughter, the lovemaking, I am sure, will not be good."

One indication of the importance of a good sense of humor is that it is one of the few personality traits that has its own abbreviation in online dating sites: GSOH. Another is that married women who think that their husbands are witty are more satisfied with their marriages than women who do not. Women rate it as a desirable trait in both short-term sexual and long-term romantic relationships. And studies from the Buss Evolutionary Psychology Lab reveal that displaying a good sense of humor is the single most effective tactic men can use to attract women. But not all men believe this, apparently, as the following quote from comedian Jimi McFarland reveals: "One of the things women claim is most important in a man is a sense of humor. In my years as a comedian, I've learned that they're usually referring to the humor of guys like Brad Pitt, Tom Cruise, and Russell Crowe. Apparently, those guys are hilarious."

Why a sense of humor is so important in sexual attraction has been the subject of much scientific debate. One critical distinction is between humor production (making others laugh) and humor appreciation (laughing at others' jokes). There's a sex difference—men define a woman with a good sense of humor as someone who laughs at their jokes! Men especially like women who are receptive to their humor in sexual relationships. Women, in contrast, are attracted to men who produce humor, and that's true for all types of relationships, from one-night stands to lifelong matings.

The most likely explanation for why women and men alike are attracted to those with a sense of humor is because laughing elicits a positive mood. In our study, several women noted how the relaxing effects of a sense of humor enhanced sex for them:

> *A great body is attractive, but especially as I get older, personality becomes more and more important. Someone who's funny can make you feel more comfortable and relaxed, and a clever wit is attractive in itself.*
>
> —heterosexual woman, age 38

> *The people I have been attracted to and had sex with have all had a good sense of humor. It is more fun if you can relax and laugh together in bed—even while you are having sex! It makes it more fun and honest, because you can try different things without fear of*

*them not liking it and not saying anything, and also if something
strange or unexpected happens, you can laugh about it!*

—heterosexual woman, age 51

A person's mood at the time of an initial encounter is an important
factor in determining attraction—positive feelings lead to positive evaluations of others and negative feelings lead to negative evaluations. In
fact, anyone or anything simply present when positive or negative feelings are aroused also tends to be liked or disliked as a consequence.
Hence the saying "Don't shoot the messenger." If other people just
happen to be there when your feelings are good, you tend to like them;
if your feelings are bad, you tend to dislike them.

The tendency to be attracted to those who make us laugh and elicit a
positive mood can partly be explained in terms of conditioning. After
pairing a particular mood with a particular person on multiple occasions,
eventually the person alone will elicit that mood. Indeed, studies have
found that when women view photographs of strangers while enjoyable
music is playing, they are more attracted to them than when they listen to
music they find unappealing. This probably means that women are more
likely to be attracted to their dance instructors and massage therapists
than they are to their tax accountants and the parking meter attendant.

Being able to make others laugh reveals a certain level of empathy or
perspective-taking—being able to put yourself into the minds of others
in order to envision what they will find funny. Witty humor, like that of
Robin Williams, Jon Stewart, or Ellen DeGeneres, may signal intelligence.
Having a good sense of humor usually signals an easygoing, fun-loving,
adaptable personality. Displaying humor takes social verve, poise, and
self-confidence. Telling a joke that bombs can be embarrassing or humiliating, so timid people usually refrain from trying. Research finds that
women view humorous men as socially skilled and confident.

This brings us to self-confidence, a prime personality trait that
women find sexy. One woman interviewed at a singles bar by sociologist Jerald Cloyd expressed it this way: "Some guys just seem to know
what they are doing. They know how to approach you and just make
you feel good. Then you get those nerds . . . who can't get anything
right. They come on strong at first, but can't keep it together . . . they

just hang around until you dump them by going to the rest room or over to a friend to talk."

Often, self-confidence and humor go hand in hand:

> *I had a relationship with someone who was very, very ugly but who made me laugh. He was very self-confident, as funny people tend to be I guess, so that was what attracted me to him.*
>
> —heterosexual woman, age 29

Self-confidence has attraction value by its own virtues. It is a signal of resources: men scoring high on self-confidence earn significantly more money than men with low self-confidence. It is a signal of self-perceived mate value. Another study, for example, discovered that only men high in self-confidence approach physically attractive women for dates, regardless of their own level of attractiveness. Men who suffer low self-esteem, in contrast, avoid approaching attractive women because they think they will strike out.

The Allure of Sexy Sons

> *I have specifically gone out with PhDs, MDs, JDs, [and] CEOs because I have always thought they were out of my league. Thinking they are so much smarter than I am because of a degree. I really wanted to know what makes them tick and what makes them better than I am. I have slept with all of them. I learned they are no different than a mechanic or factory worker; they just have more money.*
>
> —heterosexual woman, age 42

Henry Kissinger famously noted, "Power is an aphrodisiac." A less-known quote by Kissinger is "Now when I bore people at parties, they think it's their fault." And there's no question that he is right—at least about the sexual attraction of fame. Here is how one woman in our study described it:

> *The people were all kind of B-grade famous. Rock stars mostly. I don't need a paragraph to tell you why. There is an exclusiveness to*

having sex with a celebrity. . . . I think I can speak for most girls when I say I wanted my own song . . . infamy. Maggie May, Julia, Suzy Q, Amy, etc.

—heterosexual woman, age 28

One reason why women find fame sexy is that it generally comes packaged with social status and resources—the subject of chapter 8. In a long-term relationship, vital resources are shared; sometimes these resources flow even if the relationship does not last. But the flow of status and resources cannot explain why women find power and status sexually alluring for sexual encounters that they know will be transient. We need a different explanation for why women want to have sex with movie stars or famous athletes, even though they know it will last for just a few hours or a single night.

One possible explanation is what biologists call "mate copying." In many species, ranging from fish to mammals, females use the mate choices of other females as a basis for their own mate choice. They prefer males who have been "pre-approved" by other females. The higher the quality of the females who have chosen a given male, the stronger the mate copying. The Buss Lab found a similar effect among humans.

The research team showed women pictures of men in three conditions—standing alone, surrounded by other men, and surrounded by women. We also showed men pictures of women standing alone, surrounded by other women, or surrounded by men. Women viewing these photos found the same man more attractive when he was surrounded by women than when he was standing alone or with other men. And the more attractive the women that surrounded a man in the photo, the sexier women found the man to be. This desirability-enhancement effect proved especially strong when evaluating the man's sexual attractiveness. Interestingly, men showed the opposite reaction, a desirability-diminution effect. They found women surrounded by other men to be less desirable.

In fish and other species that lack male parental investment, the primary benefit females gain from mating with males desired by other females is access to his genes. The quality of male genes in these species comes in two basic flavors. The first is genes for healthiness and increased survival that can enhance their offspring's health and survival. The second is known as "sexy son genes." Females benefit by mating with males who are highly desired by other females simply because they will bear sons who will, in turn, be attractive to females. Females who "mate copy" increase their reproductive success through their sexy sons.

The sexy-son hypothesis provides a plausible explanation for mate copying in humans. Women who mate with men who radiate sex appeal in the eyes of other women will have a chance of bearing sons who are similarly sexy to women in the next generation. Obviously, women do not consciously think about these adaptive benefits; they just find men desired by other women sexy. Unlike other species, however, women experience an additional benefit by having sex with these men: access to high-status social circles, beyond their usual peers.

So, Do Opposites Attract?

No doubt we are sometimes attracted to people who are different from ourselves. However, when it comes to actually choosing a long-term sexual partner, it is more the rule than the exception that "similars" attract. Several studies have shown substantial similarity between husbands and wives in their attitudes about faith, war, and politics, as well as similarities in their physical health, family background, age, ethnicity, religion, and level of education. Dating and married couples are similar in physical attractiveness, and young married couples even tend to be matched in weight. The "matching hypothesis"—as named by social psychologists—is so strong that observers react negatively when they perceive couples who are mismatched on levels of attractiveness. There is one notable exception—a beautiful woman and a less-attractive man. In this scenario, consistent with evolutionary logic, people judging the mismatched pairs ascribe wealth, intelligence, or success to the man.

Why do similars attract? In terms of physical attractiveness, one motive for seeking a close physical match to oneself is a fear of rejection. People prefer those similar to themselves in overall "mate value," or desirability on the mating market. Going for someone substantially more desirable is often a losing proposition, for both women and men. And, if a person manages to lure a more desirable mate, there are costs involved—such as needing to be ever vigilant of mate poachers.

Finding someone who shares similar attitudes and beliefs is attractive because it provides a sort of consensual validation or verification of what we already believe. That is, a partner who shares our opinions provides us with evidence that we must be correct. Similar attitudes among mates arouse positive feelings, while dissimilar attitudes elicit negative moods. "Balance," according to social psychologists, is a pleasant emotional state, a harmonious feeling that occurs when two people like each other and agree about some topic. When people like each other yet disagree, balance is lost. To correct the imbalance, one or both parties strive to restore it by either changing his or her own attitude or attempting to change the partner's attitude. Clearly, it is much easier to maintain a pleasant balance if you start out agreeing on most topics.

Finally, similarity augurs well for long-term relationship success. It leads to emotional bonding, cooperation, communication, mating happiness, and lowered risk of breaking up. So although opposites *sometimes* attract, when it comes to mating, "birds of a feather flock well together."

He's My Type

Science can explain why women in general are attracted to certain body and personality types, but can it explain the subtle differences in what individual women find sexually attractive? Some women like curly blond hair, others prefer short dark hair, still others no hair at all. Some like clean-shaven men, others prefer the unshaven, tousled, just-woke-up look. It is not uncommon to hear women say, "He's not my type."

Sexologist John Money believed that we all have a unique template of what we find attractive, a "love map" as he called it. Our "love map" is what guides us to find our ideal mate or, as some like to believe, our "soul mate." According to Money, love maps are formed starting in childhood and are based on our experiences and people we knew early in our developmental past. The nice blond grocery store clerk who always gave you candy—check in the blond hair column. The way your beloved father was always the one holding the floor and telling stories—check in the extraversion column. That miserable old bearded doctor who never smiled and always poked you with a needle—forget facial hair and maybe even doctors. In a sense, these childhood experiences condition us to find certain features attractive or unattractive.

Jim Pfaus, a biopsychologist from Concordia University in Montreal, Canada, has shown that you can even condition sexual preferences in rats—who do not tend to pair-bond—by associating a certain partner feature with a satisfying sexual experience. Perhaps to the envy of some human women, female rats display complex behaviors that allow them to control virtually all aspects of sexual interaction with male rats. They have a particular preference for controlling the pace of copulation, which releases opiates in the brain—a reward mechanism. By pairing paced copulation with an almond scent, Pfaus and his research team were able to condition in the female rats a preference for almond-scented sexual partners. After a period of time, even when the female rats were free to copulate with any male rat, they sought out almond-scented mates.

Some researchers believe that all information gathered while growing up is imprinted in the brain's circuitry by the time of adolescence. While it would be impossible to find a perfect match on all counts, when a sufficient number of "hits" line up with your love map, then attraction blooms. In addition to explaining the wide and subtle variability among women in what they find attractive in mates, love maps can also explain why women tend to date the same "type" of partner over and over again.

The underlying motivations for what women find sexually attractive remain partly subterranean, out of conscious awareness. Women are drawn to the scents and sounds of sexiness. But they do not always know why some men excite their senses while others turn them cold. Women know they find the faces and bodies of some men hot and others not, but remain largely unaware of the hidden adaptive logic behind their desires. Their attraction toward more masculine men at ovulation and less masculine men when not ovulating reveals a secret rhythm of mating wisdom, even though most women remain unaware of these monthly adaptive shifts.

2. The Pleasure of It

Sexual Gratification and Orgasm

☙ ❧

Electric flesh-arrows . . . traversing the body. A rainbow of color strikes the eyelids. A foam of music falls over the ears. It is the gong of the orgasm.

—Anaïs Nin (1903–1977)

Men have sex for pleasure and women have sex for love. That message has been circulating for decades, if not centuries. But is it fact or is it folklore? Can it explain why drugs like Viagra are so popular and effective for men and not for women? Is it because a drug can cause an erection but it can't buy love?

Without a doubt, Viagra-like drugs create sexual arousal more easily in men than in women. But, as we shall see, it has nothing to do with women needing love to get pleasure out of sex. Many women in our study described situations where they had sex simply because it feels good:

I have in the past had sexual relationships with men who were strictly friends just for the pleasure of having sex. In terms of emotions, there really weren't any except the fear that the guy might end up wanting more.

—heterosexual woman, age 27

And sometimes pleasure is their top priority:

Sex for pleasure is the main motivation for most of my experiences. I cannot imagine going into a sexual situation without expecting a pleasurable experience, it wouldn't make sense to me.
—predominantly heterosexual woman, age 36

In fact, of all the possible reasons women gave for having sex, "I wanted to experience the physical pleasure" and "It feels good" were two of their top three. These were also two of the top three reasons for having sex endorsed by men.

So, is it true that men are more pleasure-driven to have sex than are women? Not according to the women quoted in this chapter. Women of all ages described deriving sexual pleasure from genital and psychological changes that occur during sexual arousal and orgasm, and from receiving sensual touch. In this chapter we explore in depth what happens to a woman's mind and body that makes having sex feel good.

The Magic Touch

I was in a nonsexual relationship for thirteen years. After that ended, I needed human touch to be reminded that I could still feel. Sex and physical pleasure helped me feel human again.
—heterosexual woman, age 42

The skin is a woman's largest sexual organ. It comprises an intricate system of nerves sensitive to changes in temperature, touch, and texture. The areas of the skin that are highly responsive to stimulation are often referred to as the "erogenous zones" because they lead to sexual arousal and pleasure. The most commonly cited erogenous zones are the neck, earlobes, mouth, lips, breasts and nipples, genitalia, buttocks, inner thighs, anus, backs of the knees, fingers, and toes. For some women, however, virtually any part of the body can be an erogenous zone. Regardless of which area of the body is involved, sexual pleasure can be intensified by the sensation of having one's skin touched, whether from the slightest tickle and tease of a feather being brushed across a cheek, from the warmth and tenderness of sensing bare skin next to bare skin, or from the giving or getting of a massage:

Sex encompasses a lot of physical pleasure. Just the touching of one body to another is pleasurable, similar to getting a massage or receiving a hug. Kissing brings feelings of warmth and arousal, and genital contact and/or vaginal penetration brings upon orgasm. The combination of all of these factors makes sex more desirable to me than masturbation.

—heterosexual woman, age 28

A woman's nipples and areola, the colored area surrounding the nipple, are supplied with numerous nerve endings that make them especially sensitive to touch. When a woman's breasts are stimulated through touch or massage, blood flows into the breast tissue and tiny muscle fibers enable the nipples to become erect. This can cause the nipples and areola to become even more sensitive, and can add to a woman's overall experience of sexual arousal:

Bumping into him again was perfect timing. . . . I was between regulars, so was he. . . . All I could imagine was the feel of his hands on my body, in my body . . . the stretch, the filling sensation as his cock entered me. . . . I asked him if he'd like to come over for a couple of hours . . . I could feel the moisture seeping into my panties . . . the clenching deep in my groin . . . the sensation of my nipples rubbing against my shirt. . . . Sex is for pleasure, he was a sure thing. It was as simple and as complex as "I want you."

—heterosexual woman, age 41

The sensitivity of breasts varies greatly between women. In a study conducted in the Meston Sexual Psychophysiology Lab, 82 percent of the college women surveyed said that nipple or breast stimulation either caused or increased their sexual arousal. In comparison, only a little over 50 percent of men find nipple stimulation sexually arousing. For 7 percent of the women (and the men), however, stimulation had the opposite effect—it decreased their sexual pleasure. Some women have nipples that become so sensitive during sexual arousal that even the slightest amount of touch can be unpleasant or painful. One factor is breast size: Smaller breasts are often more sensitive than larger ones. Breast sensitivity can also change over time in a woman as a result of hormonal changes during the menstrual cycle, pregnancy, and menopause. As a woman ages, her breast sensitivity tends to decline. That women more than men find nipple stimulation a sexual turn-on is likely related to the fact that starting at puberty, the sensitivity of all areas of a woman's breast becomes significantly greater than that of a man's.

Does it matter who the nipple stimulator is? Not really. Although some women find breast stimulation sexually pleasurable only if it is done by their partners, most women who enjoy the sensations find stimulating their own breasts, or even having their breasts or nipples sprayed by water in the shower or brushed by clothing, to be highly pleasurable.

Genital Arousal

Of course, while the skin may be the largest sexual organ, it isn't generally viewed as the focal one. And with feelings of sexual arousal, changes occur in the genitals that can create all sorts of pleasurable sensations for women.

When a woman is sexually aroused, blood travels to the pelvic areas of the vagina, labia, and clitoris, and to other regions such as the urethra, uterus, and possibly even the fallopian tubes and ovaries. This pooling of blood in genital tissue is referred to as "genital vasocongestion." In a nonsexually aroused state, a woman's vagina is the approximate size and shape of a cooked cannelloni noodle—without the filling. It is four inches long, with ridged, horizontally wrinkled walls. As vasocongestion occurs, the inner two-thirds of the vagina expands considerably in length and width, allowing for the accommodation of a penis or another stimulating object. The upper part of the vagina balloons out, the uterus elevates, and the lower portion of the vagina swells. These changes decrease the vaginal opening and ease the vagina's ability to hang on to any object that enters it. The inner labia, or lips, double or triple in thickness as they fill with blood, which in turn pushes apart the outer labia to make the vaginal entry more accessible. As sexual arousal increases, the clitoris increases in length and diameter and hides under its hood to protect itself from too much stimulation.

Vasocongestion also leads to vaginal lubrication. Most people think that vaginal lubrication comes from a gland inside the vagina, but it does not. When a woman is physically sexually aroused, the pressure of blood engorgement in her vaginal tissue actually squeezes lubrication into the vagina. Even when a woman is not sexually aroused, tiny droplets of lubrication slowly seep through her vaginal walls to keep the sides of the "noodle" from sticking together. Consequently, vaginal engorgement and lubrication are closely related, and both are signs of genital sexual arousal in women. Some researchers have measured genital arousal by having women insert a tampon when they are not sexually aroused, and then removing and weighing the tampon after they experience sexual arousal. How much more the tampon weighs after arousal demonstrates how much vaginal fluid has been absorbed by the tampon. This is a clever but not terribly accurate way of measuring vaginal lubrication. More often, genital arousal in women is measured in the laboratory with a device called a *vaginal photoplethysmograph*. The device, which looks like a clear plastic tampon, contains a photosensitive cell that measures, from within the vagina, the amount of light reflected from vaginal walls, which indicates the amount of vasocongestion.

Women often describe genital vasocongestion as feelings of pelvic "fullness," "tingling," or "pulsing and throbbing." These sensations make some women feel warm and good. They also make some women want to have sex as a way to "resolve" the buildup—like an itch that needs scratching. For some women, genital sensations have an added advantage: Not only do they feel good, they also provide a woman with feedback that her body is turned on. Recognizing this can add to a woman's experience of sexual arousal. For some women, though, feeling turned on and sexually gratified has little, if anything, to do with how their genitals are responding—physiological arousal does not necessarily lead to psychological arousal.

The fact that a woman's genital response does not automatically lead to her psychological pleasure is probably why Viagra and similar drugs have not been nearly as helpful for women with sexual arousal problems as they have been for men with erection problems—despite the fact that the genital tissues of men and women are very similar. Both men's and women's genital tissues consist of a network of tiny blood vessels surrounded by intricate muscles. For a man to attain an erect penis and for a woman to experience clitoral and other genital swelling, blood must flow into these tissues. And in order for blood to enter the genital tissues, the muscles surrounding the blood vessels need to relax. Drugs such as Viagra, Levitra, and Cialis work by causing the muscles in genital tissue to relax for a longer period of time, thus providing more time for blood to enter the vessels. Several studies have shown that the amount of blood that flows into genital tissue during a sexual situation is enhanced in women if they have taken Viagra beforehand. Certain herbal formulas such as ephedrine, yohimbine plus L-arginine glutamate, and ginkgo biloba extract can also have the same effect of increasing blood flow to women's genitals.

Why is it that experiencing genital vasocongestion is more likely to cause pleasurable sexual thoughts, feelings, and sexual desire in men than in women? One explanation is that men are more "in touch with" or have a closer relationship with their genitals than women do. Whether considered from the perspective of anatomy or socialization, this explanation makes sense. A penis is significantly larger than a clitoris and, unlike a vagina, it is on display and ready to be noticed—especially when erect. Men also use their penises to urinate and so, from the time they are toilet-trained, they are taught to touch and hold their penises. Women, on the other hand, are often taught the message "don't touch down there," as if their genitals were a biohazard zone. As a consequence, many women have spent their lives not even knowing how many orifices they have down there. Some researchers have speculated that these gender differences in anatomy might explain why men learn to masturbate at an earlier age than women, and why many more men than women engage in masturbation, and with higher frequency. These gender gaps in masturbation have not changed substantially over the past fifty years. For example, a study conducted in the late 1980s found that 93 percent of men and only 48 percent of women had masturbated by the age of twenty-five—percentages almost identical to those reported by Alfred C. Kinsey and his colleagues twenty years earlier. Among college students, the Meston Lab found that 85 percent of Caucasian men and 74 percent of Asian men said they engaged in masturbation compared with only 59 percent of Caucasian women and 39 percent of Asian women. Gender differences in anatomy might also explain why there are many more penises than vaginas and clitorises with names.

Penetration and the Elusive G-spot

Like most things having to do with sexual pleasure in women, there is great variability in how much women enjoy (or are willing to tolerate) having objects penetrate their vaginas—be they penises, fingers, tongues, speculums, vibrators, dildos, or any other objects, animate or inanimate. All of the nerve endings in the vagina lie in the outer portion of the vagina, near the opening. This means that women are sensitive to light touch or stimulation of their vaginas only when it is applied to this outer region. Further inside the vagina there are sensory receptors that respond to more intense pressure. Vaginas probably evolved this way because having highly sensitive nerve endings threaded throughout the vagina would have made the extended penetration of sex painful.

Because of the way the vagina is designed, some women find stimulation of the vaginal opening the most pleasurable aspect of penetration. And because the nerve endings become less sensitive after repeated stimulation, some women say that penetration feels most enjoyable at first entry. Taking short breaks during sexual activity to focus on other erogenous zones allows the nerve endings in the vagina time to regain their sensitivity. Breaks allow women to reexperience the initial entry pleasure.

Inside the vagina there are two areas that bring sexual pleasure to many women when pressure is applied. One area is the cervix—the small round structure at the far end of the vagina that serves as the opening to the uterus. Although the cervix does not have any nerve endings, it is highly sensitive to pressure and movement. Some women find it unpleasant or even painful to have pressure repeatedly thrust against their cervix. For other women, repeated rhythmic pressure on the cervix is extremely enjoyable. And for some it is even essential for orgasm to occur.

Some women who have undergone a hysterectomy that includes removal of the cervix and uterus report decreased arousal, orgasm, and pleasure during sexual intercourse. Other women who have had the surgery report no changes in their sexual function or pleasure whatsoever.

The differences between these two sets of women may have something to do with the role that cervical stimulation or uterine contractions play in their overall sexual experience. For similar reasons, it is not uncommon to hear that "size doesn't matter"—but this is not always true. If a woman falls into the "cervix-stimulating" pleasure camp, size really does matter. Unfortunately, contorting one's body in order to achieve a better cervical aim can only help so much.

The other area of the vagina that brings pleasure to certain women when stimulated is the G-spot, or Grafenberg spot:

> *I have been with lots of men in my life—probably close to one hundred—and of all those men, only one ever learned how to hit my G-spot. I'm now married and love my husband but I keep thinking about sex with the man with the magic fingers! I swear, when he put pressure on that special spot it drove me crazy—I didn't want foreplay or anything—just more and more penetration.*
>
> —heterosexual woman, age 50

The German physician Ernst Grafenberg, who purportedly first described the region, is the lucky man who has a part of women's anatomy named after him. There has been much debate as to what exactly the G-spot is and whether it really exists in all women. Recently, researchers at the University of L'Aquila in Italy announced that they believe they have finally identified the elusive G-spot. Using ultrasound technology, the scientists measured the size and shape of the tissue located in the front wall of the vagina. Of the twenty women they examined, nine were able to achieve orgasm through vaginal stimulation alone and the other eleven were not. The findings from the ultrasound exams revealed that the tissue between the vagina and the urethra—the area speculated to be the location of the G-spot—was much thicker in women who were able to achieve vaginal orgasms than in the women who were not. This means that some women may have a region of their vaginas that is densely packed with nerve fibers that make it more sensitive and thus easier to have an orgasm through vaginal penetration alone.

The easiest way for a woman to determine whether this area exists in her vagina is to explore with her fingers—two or three fingers are best. To find the area, the woman or her partner should try applying firm rhythmic pressure inside the vagina, upward toward the belly button in the space almost directly below the urinary opening. Some women say that the first sensation they experience when the G-spot is hit is a need to urinate. But with continued pressure this feeling is soon replaced by an intensely pleasurable sensation. Continued G-spot stimulation can lead to deep orgasms that may be more pleasurable than orgasms achieved through clitoral stimulation alone. For most women, however, G-spot orgasms are much more difficult to attain than clitoral orgasms. This is especially true during vaginal-penile penetration, when it is harder to hit just the right area. Rear-entry or woman-on-top intercourse positions give the best shot at the G-spot.

A small proportion of women claim that having an orgasm through stimulation of the G-spot causes them to ejaculate. Researchers have analyzed this ejaculate fluid and have found that, although it comes out of the urethra, it is not simply urine being expelled during orgasm. There has not been much solid scientific research on female ejaculation, but some sex researchers believe the fluid comes from the Skene's gland, an internal gland located near the same area as the G-spot.

What Is an Orgasm?

For men, the answer is straightforward. Although orgasm and ejaculation are controlled by different physiological mechanisms, it is quite rare for orgasm not to be accompanied by ejaculation. So, if one moment a man's penis is erect and ejaculate is expelled through his urethra, and the next moment his penis is soft, then an orgasm has more than likely taken place. Such an overt signal makes it nearly impossible for a man to fake orgasm. In women, the sign that orgasm has occurred is not as obvious, and that makes it harder to define. It also makes it more difficult to know exactly when or if an orgasm has occurred. In fact, sex therapists often see women for treatment who do not know whether they have ever experienced an orgasm.

In the 1950s, Kinsey and his team of sex researchers proposed that "the abrupt cessation of the oft times strenuous movements and extreme tensions of the previous sexual activity and the peace of the resulting state" was a sure indicator that orgasm had occurred in women. In the 1960s, William Masters and Virginia Johnson described orgasm in women as a "sensation of suspension or stoppage." By 2001, there were no fewer than twenty-six distinct definitions of women's orgasm in the research literature. In 2003, the Women's Orgasm Committee for the World Health Organization met in Paris, France, and was given the job of reviewing the extensive research on women's orgasm and creating a definitive description. The group adopted the following:

> An orgasm in the human female is a variable, transient peak sensation of intense pleasure, creating an altered state of consciousness, usually accompanied by involuntary, rhythmic contractions of the pelvic striated circumvaginal musculature, often with concomitant uterine and anal contractions and myotonia that resolves the sexually-induced vasocongestion (sometimes only partially), usually with an induction of well-being and contentment.

Sometimes it even amazes us how researchers can manage to take an extraordinary experience and make it sound like a complicated medical affliction. (Full disclosure: Meston headed the committee.) Here, instead, is how one woman in our study described her orgasms:

> *You get caught up in the moment. You start aching, and sweating. You can feel every inch of your partner beside you. You feel the warmth from their body and start letting your imagination run.*
> —heterosexual woman, age 21

The Physical Experience of Orgasm

One thing that both researchers and women at large agree about is that orgasm is an event that involves the mind and body.

A few seconds after orgasm begins, the vagina, uterus, and anal sphincter undergo a series of involuntary contractions. Vaginal contractions are most often described as being the defining characteristic of a woman's orgasm. These contractions occur at about one-second intervals and vary greatly among women in their number and strength. They also depend on the duration of the orgasm and the strength of the woman's pelvic muscles. Masters and Johnson claimed that the stronger the orgasm, the greater the number of contractions and thus the longer the duration of orgasm. They labeled "mild orgasms" as having an average of three to five vaginal contractions with each lasting 2.4 to 4.0 seconds, "normal orgasms" as involving four to eight vaginal contractions each with a duration of 4.0 to 6.4 seconds, and "intense orgasms" as having eight to twelve vaginal contractions each lasting 4.0 to 9.6 seconds—for a grand total of over two minutes of orgasmic delight.

> *Aching of the vaginal regions and trembling in the thighs. Every muscle in the body tightens and then a huge amount of energy is released. It feels like it comes from between my legs and ascends up my spine, absolutely zapping my brain. Oftentimes I hold my breath, my eyes shut tight, and colors appear behind my eyelids. Immediately afterward I'm very photosensitive, giddily happy, tingly, relieved, and energized.*
>
> —heterosexual woman, age 24

Other researchers, however, have failed to find a link between vaginal contractions and the perceived intensity or duration of orgasms. While many women say they have orgasms without experiencing vaginal contractions, for those women the contractions may just be so weak that they are not detectable.

The function of vaginal contractions is not clear. Some women say that the contractions greatly intensify the pleasure experienced during orgasm. Yet, interestingly, contracting these muscles voluntarily is not especially enjoyable. If you are a woman, you can try this experiment yourself. To learn what muscles are involved, the next time you are urinating, practice starting and stopping the flow. The muscles that you use to do this are the same ones that contract during orgasm. Some theorists have postulated that the contractions evolved to serve as a way to excite the male sexual partner to ejaculate during intercourse, allowing her to capture his sperm. The problem with this explanation, however, is that much to the dismay of many women, men frequently ejaculate before women have their orgasms.

For the small percentage of women who ejaculate during orgasm through G-spot stimulation, vaginal contractions likely help release the fluid from the urethra. It is also likely that vaginal contractions during orgasm help dissipate the genital vasocongestion that occurs during sexual arousal. As described earlier, there is an intense accumulation of blood in the vagina, labia, and clitoris during sexual arousal. Orgasm helps the blood to flow out of the genital tissue quickly. If orgasm does not occur, it takes a substantial amount of time—up to an hour—for the blood to flow back from this tissue. This unresolved vasocongestion sometimes frustrates women as it gives them an uncomfortable feeling, analogous to what men refer to as "blue balls." Blood also rapidly flows out of the nipples and areolae following orgasm. In fact, at orgasm the amount of blood loss from the areolae is so rapid that they become corrugated before they return to their unaroused flat state. The corrugation provides a fairly reliable sign that orgasm has occurred.

Prolactin levels double immediately after orgasm and remain elevated for about an hour afterward. Prolactin is thought to be responsible for the refractory period in men—the period of time post-ejaculation when a man is unable to attain another erection. The refractory period varies greatly between men of all ages, but increases with age; more recovery time is required between erections in older men. In women, however, prolactin does not seem to have the same inhibitory effect. As a result, women are able to have multiple, serial orgasms, with the latter ones being just as good as, and sometimes even better than, the first. Unlike men, women can also attain what Masters and Johnson referred to as "status orgasmus," orgasms that last for several minutes. Another difference between male and female orgasms is that once a man becomes highly sexually aroused he reaches a "point of no return," in that orgasm becomes automatic even if stimulation is stopped. In women, however, if stimulation is stopped, during either clitoral- or vaginal-induced orgasms, the orgasm is abruptly halted. Partners please note.

The Psychological Experience of Orgasm

Women describe a variety of intense mental and emotional experiences that occur during or immediately after orgasm. Women use many adjectives to describe the psychological experience of orgasm: incredible, powerful, fulfilling, satisfying, intense, exciting, euphoric, pleasurable, elated, rapturous, loving, tender, close, passionate, unifying, relaxing, soothing, peaceful, ecstatic, and wild. One woman in our study was particularly eloquent:

> *I feel like experiencing the joy of physical release as well as the emotional high, post-orgasm. I enjoy the process, the end result is not the goal, rather the entire experience is arousing, enjoyable, and productive. Sometimes I want to feel the sexual pleasure so I can re-peat a technique or fantasy. Most of the time my sexual experiences encompass a great deal of oral sex, and depending on my mood I prefer to give or receive or participate in both at the same time! My favorite way to climax is to have my husband perform oral sex while I fantasize about... something (this varies with time and mood—it is sometimes homosexual, sometimes heterosexual, and sometimes I just focus on the moment). I enjoy the feeling of sex.*
> —heterosexual woman, age 28

Is the psychological experience of orgasm the same in men as it is in women? To answer that question, scientists asked men and women to write paragraphs describing their mental experience of orgasm. Later, oth-ers read the paragraphs and guessed whether the orgasm descriptions were written by men or women. In most cases, the raters were unable to accu-rately identify whether the writers were men or women. This suggests that men and women psychologically experience orgasms very similarly.

A number of hormones are released during orgasm—with prolactin, discussed above, and oxytocin being the most prominent. Oxytocin re-lease has been associated with emotional bonding and might explain why some women experience an intense feeling of connectedness with their partners following orgasm. While orgasm can lead to feelings of attachment or bonding in women, emotional attachment is certainly not necessary for women to experience sexual pleasure or orgasm:

> *There have been times when I wasn't emotionally connected to the person I had sex with but I did it because I wanted to feel the phys-*

*ical pleasure of sex and orgasm. . . . One instance was a friend of
mine for a few years. I hadn't had sex in awhile and needed a release. We had dinner at my house, and later that evening wound up
in bed. I felt comfortable with him because he was a friend, and the
sex was really enjoyable.*

—predominantly heterosexual woman, age 28

How to Have an Orgasm

If pleasure can be such a powerful sexual motivation, what exactly triggers a woman's orgasm? In the 1960s, it was proposed that a woman's
orgasm was some sort of spinal reflex caused by nerves firing in the
pelvic muscles as a response to genital engorgement. In the 1970s, the
clitoris became the popular candidate for activating these sensory
impulses—which still were thought to build up to a supposed spinal reflex. In the 1980s, scientists suggested that once sexual arousal inten-
sifies to a certain level, a hypothetical "orgasm center" in the brain is
activated. Today, scientists cannot say exactly what triggers orgasms in
women, or whether there is a special "orgasmatron" in the brain that is
responsible. (Researchers are just beginning to use brain imaging techniques to identify exactly which regions of the brain are involved in orgasm and whether they differ between men and women.)

We do know, however, that orgasms in women can be induced many
different ways. Stimulation of the clitoris and vagina are the most common means. Women usually achieve orgasms through clitoral stimulation much more easily than through sexual intercourse. In fact, most
surveys show that only about 60 percent of orgasmic women are able to
have an orgasm through intercourse alone. It is simply the case that
many women need more stimulation of the clitoris to achieve an orgasm
than is provided by intercourse. Some women worry or think they are
missing out on something big if they are unable to have an orgasm
through intercourse alone. Rest assured, if this describes you, that vaginally induced orgasms are no more meaningful, intense, or pleasurable
than clitorally induced orgasms (although some women who are able to
have orgasms both ways do have their preferences).

The belief that vaginal orgasms are somehow better than clitoral

orgasms can be traced to Sigmund Freud's assertion in the 1920s that clitoral orgasms were "infantile" and that the vagina was the center of a
"mature" woman's sexual response. Freud had a hard time imagining
that the penis was not central to every woman's sexual pleasure, and as a
result, millions of perfectly functional women have doubted their sexual
abilities. In the 1960s, Masters and Johnson reported that all orgasms in
women are physiologically identical, regardless of the type of stimulation that triggered them—putting Freud's theory to bed. There is now
some limited laboratory research showing that a different pattern of uterine and pelvic muscle activity occurs with vaginally induced versus clitorally induced orgasms. However, even if different uterine and pelvic
muscle activity occurs during vaginal compared to clitoral orgasms, it is
a small factor in the overall orgasm experience.

Some women are able to have orgasms from clitoral, G-spot, or cervical stimulation, and some reach orgasm from pressure applied to the *mons
pubis*, the fatty mound of flesh covered by pubic hair that lies directly over
the pubic bone. But women have also reported reaching orgasm through
breast or nipple stimulation, from mental imagery or fantasy, or even from
hypnosis or during their sleep. Thus, orgasms can occur in women without any genital involvement whatsoever. The fact that orgasms can occur
while a woman is sleeping suggests that even consciousness may not be
an essential requirement. Occasionally, "spontaneous orgasms" have been
described in the psychiatric literature where a woman has an orgasm when
there is no apparent sexual stimulus involved.

With or Without a Partner

Assuming that it is acceptable to her, it is much easier for most women
to attain orgasm during masturbation than with a partner:

> *I have never had an orgasm except by myself, so my definition of
> "heterosexual pleasure" is sensuous rather than sexual.*
>
> —heterosexual woman, age 54

In a survey of over 1,600 American women ages eighteen to fifty-
nine, only 29 percent of the women overall said they were able to

have an orgasm with a partner. Sixty-one percent—more than twice as many—said they were able to have an orgasm when they masturbated.

The reason why women are able to attain orgasm more easily during masturbation than with a partner is simple: Most women who masturbate spend time touching and exploring their erogenous zones. They learn through experimentation how much and where to stimulate in order to achieve the most pleasurable sexual experience. Because every woman is unique in where, when, and how much touching is needed to achieve orgasm, even the most sexually skilled partner needs a road map the first few times. What sent Lisa screaming with delight could very well send Linda screaming out of the bedroom. Consider how one woman in our study described it:

> *I enjoy having sex with my husband because he knows how to bring me physical pleasure with very little instruction at this point (we have been together for six years)... I do not have to "work" for the pleasure, I can just relax and enjoy myself.*
>
> —heterosexual woman, age 28

If a woman wants to attain sexual pleasure and orgasm with her partner, communication helps. That means explaining verbally, or with subtle (or not so subtle) hand signals, or by redirecting limbs and fingers to new locations to teach her partner the "no zones" and the "go zones." This is often difficult for women to do. Many say that they are afraid of offending their partners. Indeed, partners who think they are already masterful lovers may not react graciously when told what to do. In addition, many women have been taught by their parents, grandparents, teachers, or religious leaders that when it comes to sex, there are distinct gender roles to be followed: Men are the initiators of sex and "proper" women let them lead. It is not uncommon for women who rely on their partner to figure out what pleases them to remain sexually unfulfilled for years:

> *Sex..., when you are young, is fantastic.... Wait until you are over fifty-five... married or not, sex is really not important... but*

it should be. Men place so much importance on it but know nothing about foreplay [or] its importance, however small it may seem.

—heterosexual woman, age 54

And taking control of one's sexuality, despite how difficult or embarrassing sexual communication can be, often leads to long-term improvements in sexual pleasure:

I began to wonder if my sexual experience is completely in my hands or if my partner can be a big factor in how much I enjoyed it. I have had many partners and have only recently begun to really enjoy sex in a way that is fulfilling and satisfying. For a long time, I suspected it had something to do with my partners, and I'm sure it did, though I think now that mostly it has to do with me. Maybe I know myself and my body better, or perhaps I choose better partners, but I know it's up to me to open up to feeling pleasure.

—predominantly heterosexual woman, age 27

Whereas "good" partner sex generally involves a degree of reciprocity, some women focus on their partner's pleasure to the exclusion of their own:

When I was single, I had sex for my own personal pleasure. Now that I am married, I have sex to please my husband. My own pleasure doesn't seem as important as his. I believe he feels the same way.

—heterosexual woman, age 26

When a partner is involved, women can sometimes lose focus on their own pleasurable sensations during sex and become preoccupied with, for example, how to position their bodies to make them appear most attractive. As we'll see, these sorts of thoughts make it hard for a woman to attain a level of arousal high enough for orgasm to occur.

Orgasm Problems

Women who are unable to have an orgasm, or who have orgasms only very infrequently, often wonder if there is something physically wrong with them. It is true that a number of medical conditions, such as diabetic neuropathy, certain pelvic surgeries, and disorders that impair blood flow to the genitals, such as coronary heart disease and high blood pressure, can lead to orgasm problems in women, as can a number of prescription medications. The good news is that in physically healthy women, scientists have never found anything physical that distinguishes women who are able from those who are not able to have orgasms.

Clinical psychologists and psychiatrists agree that the two most common reasons why women experience orgasm problems are that they are not receiving enough pleasurable stimulation for an orgasm to occur or that something is distracting them from focusing on the pleasurable stimulation. In addition to trying to please a partner or worrying about how they look, potential distractors include worrying about whether the kids (or the parents) next door are listening, contemplating the next day's work and errands, reevaluating a partner's mate value, and—probably the number one "orgasm killer"—guilt. If a woman is raised to believe, for religious or other reasons, that sex is meant only for procreation and within marital constraints, then she is more likely to experience a big dose of guilt rather than a big orgasm when she has sex outside that context.

Cultural expectations can also influence a woman's orgasm ability. Anthropologists who have studied sexuality in women across the globe find that in societies where women are expected to enjoy sex as much as men do, the women have orgasms. Lots of them. For example, Mangaian women are taught to have not just one orgasm but preferably two or three to each one of their male partner's. Mangaian men who fail to give their partners multiple orgasms are not held in high esteem. (Air Rarotonga currently offers four flights per week to Mangaia—the most southerly of the Cook Islands.) By contrast, in cultures where people believe women's orgasms are either unimportant or do not exist, women have more difficulty attaining orgasm. The best explanation for this finding is that if a woman is expected to have an orgasm, she is more likely to be willing to learn or to be taught how. Unlike men, most women do actually have to *learn* how to have an orgasm.

If a woman is unable to have an orgasm because she is distracted from enjoying sexual sensations, the best way to resolve this difficulty is to explore, perhaps with the help of a therapist, what the various distractions are and how to get rid of them. Here is how one woman described her sexual pleasure after liberating herself from sexual guilt:

> *After years of feeling conflicted about the idea of having sex with someone simply because of attraction and the thought that the experience may be fun and satisfying, I have completely owned that desire. I regularly enjoy the thrill of seduction and guiltless, enjoyable sex. I think sex is fantastic. It may even qualify as my favorite hobby. I feel as though I have a strong sex drive and don't see any reason to limit the action on my desire. I enjoy feeling the sense of attraction, flirting, assessing the interest of the other person, and, when the other person is attracted, I look forward to exploring uninhibited sexual experiences.*
>
> —predominantly heterosexual woman, age 33

On the other hand, if a woman is unable to have an orgasm because she is not receiving sufficient pleasurable stimulation, then the best treatment for her is something called "directed masturbation." Directed masturbation involves a series of self-exploration exercises that a woman performs by herself. The purpose is to learn to locate sensitive areas that produce feelings of sexual arousal, and then to manually stimulate those areas to increase the pleasure intensity until "something happens." Many studies of the technique have noted a phenomenal success rate for treating women who have never had an orgasm. One study found that two months after treatment 100 percent of the nonorgasmic women were able to attain an orgasm during masturbation and 47 percent were able to attain an orgasm during intercourse. These women had met for ten sessions with a therapist who taught them how to conduct the directed masturbation exercises at home. But the same study also showed high success rates among women who simply read about the exercises as opposed to having a therapist teach them. Forty-seven percent of these women who had never before had an orgasm became orgasmic during masturbation and 13 percent became orgasmic during intercourse. The book *Becoming Orgasmic: A Sexual and Personal Growth Program for Women*, by Julia Heiman and Joseph LoPiccolo, provides women with an excellent step-by-step guide for conducting directed masturbation exercises.

The Rewards of Orgasm

Just as there has been much scientific discussion about what exactly an orgasm is, there has been a great deal of debate as to whether the female orgasm serves an adaptive function or whether it is merely an incidental byproduct, much as male nipples are by-products of evolutionary development with no apparent function. Because the various physiological changes during a woman's orgasm could increase her chance of becoming pregnant, women's orgasms could serve a reproductive purpose. From an evolutionary perspective, orgasms could possibly even provide information on the quality of a man's genes and the likelihood he would make a good father, thus contributing to long-term fitness.

Early theorists hypothesized that when women had an intercourse-induced orgasm, the orgasm activated ovulation and that allowed conception to occur. Although intercourse-induced ovulation does occur in some species, this idea was discarded when it was shown that women ovulate in the middle of their menstrual cycle, regardless of whether either intercourse or orgasm occurs. Later theorists proposed that the contractions that occur during orgasm in women cause a sort of uterine suction that moves ejaculated sperm through the cervix, uterus, and fallopian tubes much more efficiently. However, studies have now shown that the quickest way to transport sperm into a woman's uterus is when she is in a sexually unaroused state.

As described earlier, during sexual arousal the vagina expands and the uterus and cervix elevate. These changes provide a temporary barrier that reduces the chances of ejaculated sperm rapidly entering into the uterus. This gives the sperm time to undergo a sort of natural selection process whereby the healthy sperm have a better chance of being transported through the fallopian tubes and the incompetent sperm are left behind. Orgasm comes into play by dissipating arousal. At that moment, the passageway is opened for the better sperm to make their journey into the fallopian tubes. One study found that women have more frequent orgasms when their partner is physically symmetrical rather than asymmetrical. As we saw in chapter 1, this finding suggests that women's orgasms may help to secure healthier genes, which might be passed on to a woman's children.

One interesting and rather controversial theory of the purpose for women's orgasms is that women are able to use orgasm as a means for manipulating ejaculate into their vagina. When a man ejaculates into a woman's vagina, only a small portion of the semen and fluid make their way through the cervix. The remainder, referred to as "flowback," seeps out of the woman's vagina. According to this argument, the amount of flowback containing sperm varies with the timing of the woman's orgasm in relation to the time the sperm was deposited into her vagina. In other words, precisely *when* a woman has an orgasm determines how much sperm gets through. Low sperm retention is believed to be associated with women's orgasms that occur less than one minute before ejaculation, and maximum sperm retention occurs when orgasm takes place shortly after sperm is deposited. If a woman has an orgasm more than one minute before the man ejaculates, then sperm retention is, according to one study, the same as if orgasm did not occur. Orgasms, by producing a sense of calm and relaxation, lead some women to lie back and relax after sex. Remaining horizontal reduces the amount of sperm flowback and could also facilitate the chances of conception.

Another way that women's orgasms could play a role in the reproductive process is that, for women who are with men who are slow to ejaculate, the vaginal contractions that occur during orgasm can facilitate ejaculation. And when the hormone prolactin is released during orgasm, it may enter into the vaginal, cervical, or uterine fluids, where it can influence calcium entry into sperm. This in turn helps to facilitate sperm entry into the woman's genital tract.

Orgasm could conceivably increase a woman's reproductive success by improving her chances of getting pregnant through these various physiological means. But they could also do so via a more psychological avenue. To the extent that orgasms can be an immensely enjoyable experience, they could serve as a "lure" or "reward" for women to have intercourse with a particular partner. According to this view, women in our evolutionary past who experienced the sexual rewards of orgasm were more motivated to have sex than women who did not have orgasms. High motivation would lead to a higher frequency of sex and hence a greater chance of pregnancy and reproduction.

In evolutionary terms, reproductive success means not only being able to reproduce, but also having the resources and abilities to care for the child long enough to ensure its survival. To this end, being able to have an orgasm with a certain man could serve as a mate selection device. From the partner's perspective, if a woman is able to have an orgasm with him, it sends him a signal that she is sexually satisfied and therefore less likely to seek sexual gratification elsewhere. When men are assured of their paternity they are more likely to remain committed to a woman and invest in her children.

Caring about a woman's sexual pleasure enough to take the time to learn what turns her on and gives her an orgasm is also a good marker of "sexual selflessness." To the extent that this sexual selflessness might extend to other arenas, it may be a sign that the man would make a better long-term partner and father than a sexually selfish one would. So, by choosing to stay with someone with whom she is orgasmic, a woman might be selecting a mate who will stick around and generously invest in her and her children. Which brings us to love.

3. The Thing Called Love

An Emotional and Spiritual Connection

When two people are first together, their hearts are on fire and their passion is very great. After a while, the fire cools and that's how it stays. They continue to love each other, but it's in a different way—warm and dependable.

—Nisa, !Kung woman from Botswana

"Love is a many-splendored thing." That is probably why stories of romantic love—as opposed to the love we might feel for parents, children, siblings, pets, or platonic friends—abound. In Greek mythology there are the orphaned Daphnis and Chloe, whose passion grows as they mature from children to lovers, and Odysseus and Penelope, who suffer continuous trials during their years of separation. The Hindu goddess Sati so loved her husband, Shiva, that she killed herself in an act of contrite shame—giving her name to the ritual by which a Hindu woman immolates herself on her husband's funeral pyre in a final act of devotion. In Maori legend, Hinemoa swam two miles across the rough ocean to be reunited with her lover Tutanekai. The Han Chinese emperor Ai preferred to cut the sleeve off his robe rather than wake his lover Dong Xian. In the United States, Abraham Lincoln's first love, Ann Rutledge, who died in her youth, was said to have been the cause of his lifelong struggles with melancholy, while the tender companionship of John and Abigail Adams helped sustain them through the Revolution, even when they could only write letters to each other. "Romantic love" is the topic of more than a thousand movies carried by Netflix, and the word "love" appears in the title of more than two thousand songs sold on iTunes. (Trying to count the number of *occurrences* in song lyrics would be a fool's errand.) Romantic love is something so powerful that politicians and religious authorities throughout history and across cultures have tried to control it out of fear that it could disrupt social, political, and religious order.

Psychologists have shown that feeling loved by and emotionally connected to another person are important predictors of a person's overall happiness and satisfaction with life. The denial of such emotions sent more than one of Shakespeare's protagonists to tragic ends: In addition to the usual suspects of Romeo and Juliet, Cleopatra poisoned herself with a snake and Ophelia went mad and drowned.

In our study, the pursuit of love and emotional attachment led many women to the bedchamber. In fact, of the more than two hundred reasons given for having sex, love and emotional closeness were ranked in the top twelve for women. What are these emotions that are so powerful they can evoke fear and despair, happiness and contentment, and can lead to behaviors with euphoric, sad, or tragic endings? Why have scientists studying the brain concluded that love is like a mental disorder or a drug addiction? Can we change a person's ability or desire to bond to someone by changing his or her brain chemicals in the same way we are able to in animals? Can having sex with someone we are only mildly attracted to make our brains release chemicals that keep us attached? In this chapter we explore the powerful emotions of love and bonding and how and why they are integrally linked to women's sexuality.

What Is Love?

According to the well-known psychologist Robert Sternberg's "triangular theory of love," love consists of the distinct components of intimacy, passion, and commitment. *Intimacy* is the experience of warmth toward another person that arises from feelings of closeness and connectedness. It involves the desire to give and receive emotional support and to share one's innermost thoughts and experiences. Here is how one woman in our study experienced this dimension of love:

> *I feel that sex can be one of many physical expressions of love, though sex is not always an expression of love. When I make love with my husband, it is an intimacy, trust, and exposure of myself that I share only with him . . . because I love him. Sex can be a way of fulfilling my husband's needs (physical, emotional, psychological) that can't be achieved any other way and [it] lets him know that I love him and vice versa. Though I have been physically intimate (kissing, petting, etc.) with other people whom I did not love, I have had sex only with people I loved.*
>
> —heterosexual woman, age 29

Passion, the second component, refers to intense romantic feelings and sexual desire for another person. Elaine Hatfield, a distinguished psychologist at the University of Hawaii, has spent decades studying passionate love and how it is expressed. She defines passionate love as a "hot intense emotion" characterized by an intense longing for union with another. It is the "lovesick" part of love that Hatfield believes exists in all cultures. In fact, some cultures even have specific diagnostic criteria for the "symptoms" people get when they fall passionately in love. For example, Hatfield reports that in South Indian Tamil families, love-struck persons are said to be suffering from *mayakkam,* a syndrome characterized by dizziness, confusion, intoxication, and delusion.

When reciprocated, feelings of passion are often associated with feelings of fulfillment and ecstasy:

> *Honestly speaking, sex has never been just a satisfied action for me. It has always expressed something more. . . . I feel so happy having the most wonderful man. . . . Probably it happened because while living far away, for quite a long period of time, we had a great opportunity to realize what we mean for each other, and what true love is, and when I look into his eyes while making love, it is always something which is so difficult to express by*

words . . . but it's like the fullest flowering of the blossom of our love.

—heterosexual woman, age 38

For one woman in our study, feelings of romance and passion served an added bonus—they helped her ignore her boyfriend's less than desirable housekeeping habits:

> *For [my] twentieth birthday, my boyfriend took me out to an amazing seafood restaurant and we had a really incredible time. He treated me like a princess. I felt so loved, and I was so in love, and all the feelings [from] the romantic atmosphere of the restaurant carried over to his grungy apartment and we made love on his bed. That may have been the best sex we've ever had.*
>
> —heterosexual woman, age 20

Commitment, the third component of love, requires decision making. A short-term decision involves whether or not one actually loves the other person, while the long-term decision involves a willingness to maintain the relationship through thick and thin. Many women in our study talked about how commitment was an essential component of love for them. In fact, some said that they used having sex as a way to try to ensure commitment from a partner they felt they loved:

> *My first sexual experience with a [man] was because I wanted the relationship to be committed. We were both sixteen-year-old virgins and had been dating for three months. I pushed for us to have sex because I wanted to show him that I loved him. I wanted to give him something that no one else could have.*
>
> —heterosexual woman, age 25

> *The reason I had sex with my ex-husband? I was young, I was sixteen years old, and I wanted him to stay with me. I thought by having sex it would ensure a committed relationship. It didn't, but at the time you could not have made me see that. I equated sex*

[with] love. And the more that we made love, I thought, the more
he must love me. I was a fool.

—heterosexual woman, age 41

Some researchers believe that the "amount" of love a person experiences depends on the absolute strength of the three components, and that couples are best matched if they possess similar levels of intimacy, passion, and commitment.

Sternberg has identified seven different "love styles" based on the possible combinations of intimacy, passion, and commitment in a relationship. For example, he calls love where there is commitment but no intimacy or passion "empty love." These are the people you see eating together silently in restaurants, who love each other largely out of a sense of duty or lack of options. Love where there is passion and commitment but no intimacy is "foolish love." These are the whirlwind courtships that burn brightly at first and then fizzle out when one or both partners come to the sad realization that they do not have anything—other than sex, perhaps—in common. "Liking love" is intimacy without passion or commitment and, as the name implies, it typifies a close friendship. Its opposite, love with passion and intimacy but no commitment, is what Sternberg deems "romantic love." "Infatuation love" has passion but no intimacy or commitment, while "companionate love" involves intimacy and commitment but is short on passion. Companionate love is quite typical of long-term unions, in which sexual desire can fade with time and familiarity.

Of course the seventh and final love style described by Sternberg is the ultimate, "consummate love," which is the perfect blend of intimacy, passion, and commitment. Few couples who have been together for a long time consistently experience "consummate love." In most relationships, levels of intimacy, passion, and commitment wax and wane with time and circumstance. Thus, it is not uncommon for a couple to experience several forms of these love styles throughout the course of their relationship.

The Drug of Love

Much to the dismay of people who believe that defining love should be left in the hands of poets and songwriters, or, better yet, on the lips of lovers who experience it, scientists are exploring whether love—from infatuation to the consummate style—can be explained by a person's biology. Neuroscientist Niels Birbaumer and his colleagues were the first current-day scientists to examine this possibility. The researchers placed electrodes on the scalps of men and women and measured their brains' electrical activity using an electroencephalograph, or EEG, machine as the participants envisioned a joyful scene with a loved one, a jealous scene, and a control scene—an empty living room. Half of the men and women were passionately in love at the time; the other half were not emotionally involved with anyone. When the researchers compared the brain waves of the people who were and were not passionately in love, they found huge differences in brain activity during imagery of a scene with a loved one. Those who were passionately in love showed much more complex brain-wave patterns and much more widespread activity throughout the brain. As noted by the authors, "Subjects in love carry their emotional 'burden' like a snail's house into the laboratory of a physiologist." And on the basis of their findings, the research team concluded that passionate love is like "mental chaos."

In 2003, a decade after Niels Birbaumer's discovery, Andreas Bartels and Semir Zeki, two neuroscientists in London, began scanning the brains of young lovers to see what it means to "fall in love." They selected seventeen men and women who met the criteria for being "truly, deeply, and madly in love" and observed their brains using a functional magnetic resonance imagery, or fMRI, scanner, which is able to record changes in blood flow to various parts of the brain. When nerve cells in the brain are active, they consume oxygen. Oxygen is carried to the brain by hemoglobin in red blood cells from nearby capillaries. Hence, blood flow to the brain and amount of brain activity are closely related.

As the participants' brains were being scanned, the researchers showed them pictures of either their beloved or nonromantic friends. Only when they were gazing at the photographs of their loved ones did the participants' brains show intense activity in areas associated with euphoria and reward—and *diminished* activity in brain regions associated with sadness, fear, and anxiety. In fact, the pattern of brain activity that occurred when the participants viewed their lovers was not unlike the pattern of brain activity seen when a person is under the influence of euphoria-inducing drugs such as cocaine. The brains excited with love also showed decreased activity in regions associated with critical thought, which might explain why people who are acutely in love often appear to be "spaced out." Or maybe, as the study's authors suggest, when a person decides he or she is in love, critical thought to assess the loved one's character is no longer considered to be necessary.

The "love is a drug" connection has also been noted by psychiatrist Michael Liebowitz of the New York State Psychiatric Institute, who compares passionate love to an amphetamine high. Both can create a mood-enhancing giddiness, and withdrawal of either can cause anxiety, fear, and even panic attacks. Indeed, the body releases a host of chemicals when a person first falls in love—dopamine, norepinephrine, and especially phenylethylamine, or PEA, which is considered a close cousin to amphetamine. The "natural high" caused by these brain chemicals, unfortunately, does not last forever. Liebowitz believes that is why some people, whom he calls "attraction junkies," move from relationship to relationship seeking their next "love high."

Love, the Mental Disorder

In addition to all the wonderful emotions passionate love can cause—euphoria, excitement, contentment—it can also cause intense emotional turmoil. People in love often describe feelings of anxiety, depression, and despair when they are not with their loved ones—even when they are only separated for a relatively short period of time. They tend to spend hours and hours obsessively thinking about their loved ones in much the same way that a person diagnosed with obsessive-compulsive disorder, or OCD, experiences intrusive thoughts.

In the late 1990s, psychiatrist Donatella Marazziti and her colleagues from the University of Pisa in Italy speculated that people who are passionately in love and people who suffer from OCD may have something in common—a decrease in the brain chemical serotonin. Decreased levels of serotonin have long been linked to depression and anxiety disorders such as OCD, and antidepressants such as Prozac work primarily by trying to increase the body's serotonin levels.

To test their hypothesis, the research team selected three separate groups of men and women. One group consisted of people who had fallen in love within the past six months but not yet had sex, and who obsessed about their new love for a minimum of four hours a day. A second group comprised people who were diagnosed with OCD and were not receiving medication. The third, "normal" group was made up of people who neither met the criteria for OCD nor were passionately in love. The researchers took blood samples from each of the participants and tested their serotonin levels. Not surprising, the people who were neither love-struck nor diagnosed with OCD had normal levels of serotonin. The people who were diagnosed with OCD had significantly lower levels of serotonin than did this control group. But most shocking was that, like the OCD group, the love-struck group had levels of serotonin about 40 percent lower than the control population.

A year later, the researchers again tested some of the lovesick participants, and sure enough, once their initial intense phase of passionate love had passed, their serotonin levels returned to normal. Fortunately, the depletion was not permanent.

Helen Fisher, a researcher at Rutgers University who has used fMRI imaging to scan the brains of many people in love, also believes that passionate love—or lust as she refers to it—resembles OCD. Fisher believes that it may be possible to "treat" or inhibit this state if the person "in lust" were to take an antidepressant such as Prozac early on, when the feelings begin, to offset the low levels of serotonin characteristic of OCD. But, she says, once the lust turns into romantic love, it is such a powerful drive that no small Prozac cocktail is likely to stifle it.

Forever Falling in Love

Whether love is a feeling of intimacy and connection, a passionate emotion, or a complex scrambling of brain chemicals, one thing is certain—love is persistent and universal. Proof of love's persistence can even be found in societies that have attempted to undermine it by allowing a man to take more than one wife. For example, members of the Oneida Community, a utopian commune founded in New York State in the nineteenth century, held the view that romantic love was merely sexual lust disguised. The Oneida subscribed to "complex marriages," whereby members were not allowed to have exclusive sexual or romantic relationships with each other, but rather were to keep in constant circulation to prevent a "special love" from forming. Early Mormons also viewed romantic love as disruptive and sought to discourage it. In both of these groups, however, romantic love often persisted among individuals, sometimes underground, hidden from the eyes of the groups' elders.

Similarly, in some polygynous societies with traditions of arranged marriages, passionate love isn't banished—it's simply segregated. In many Arab cultures, a man's elders choose his first wife for him; his second wife he can choose for himself. Among the Taita of Kenya, it is preferable to be the second or third wife, not the first. The women believe that after his first marriage, a man will be more likely to marry for love and, as a consequence, will favor his later wives—and share more emotional closeness and intimacy with them. The first marriage is made out of duty, while the subsequent marriages can be matches of love.

A testament to the universality of love comes from studies that simply ask men and women whether they are currently in love. Susan Sprecher and her colleagues interviewed 1,667 women and men from Russia, Japan, and the United States to find out if they were in love, and in almost every case, a majority of those surveyed said they were: 73 percent of Russian women, 61 percent of Russian men, 63 percent of Japanese women, 41 percent of Japanese men, 63 percent of American women, and 53 percent of American men—leaving the curious question about the differential between women's and men's responses unanswered. Studies examining love in other cultures have also revealed that an overwhelming majority of languages have been used to muse on the experience of love, including declarations of love, love songs, and expressions of pain when separated from a loved one or when love is unrequited.

In the most massive study ever conducted of mate preferences—among thirty-seven cultures located on six continents and five islands, and including 10,047 participants—"mutual attraction and love" proved to be at or near the top in every single culture, being seen as indispensable in a long-term mate. In a study on the link between love and marriage, psychologist Robert Levine and his colleagues asked college students from eleven nations if they would be willing to marry someone whom they did not love but who had all the other qualities they were looking for in a mate. In nations such as the United States, Brazil, Australia, Japan, and England, the majority of men and women insisted they would not marry someone they did not love. In less affluent nations—the Philippines, Thailand, Pakistan, and India—a larger percentage of students said they were willing to marry someone they did not love. Clearly, in nations where parental or religious control over marriage is the norm and poverty is widespread, the decision of whom to marry, in some situations, may be more practical than passionate. Psychologists who have studied the concept of love in different cultures find that how men and women define love does not differ greatly between cultures—be it China, Indonesia, Micronesia, Palau, Turkey, Russia, Japan, or the United States. So, men and women define love in similar terms, but do they share similar experiences when falling in or out of love? Despite common images of giggly teenage girls falling in love with boys they barely (or never) met, and stereotypes of women being the ones who are romantically inclined, research shows that men are actually more likely than women to "fall in love at first sight," which may be the result of an evolutionary adaptation. Men generally are more quickly swayed by physical appearance when choosing a partner than are women, who tend to rely on a wider range of signals, including scent and personality, for the initial spark of attraction. Men in cultures from Argentina to Zimbabwe seek women with small waists relative to their hips, an honest if unconscious signal of a woman's health and fertility. The qualities women seek, particularly in a long-term mate, take a longer period of time to evaluate. "Love at first sight" is just more straightforward for men.

Beyond that first rush of emotion, men also appear to *stay* in love longer: A study that assessed 231 college dating couples from 1972 through 1974 refuted the stereotype that women are the lovers and men are the leavers. The study found that women were more likely than men to break up a relationship, and they were also more likely to see the breakup coming well in advance. Consequently, post-breakup, the women were more likely to view the relationship's demise as having been a gradual process, whereas men saw it as having ended abruptly, seemingly "out of the blue." And when women looked back on their former relationships, they tended to list more problems than men did.

There is also some evidence to suggest that breaking up a relationship is more traumatic for men than for women. Obviously it depends on the circumstances of both the relationship and the breakup, but in general, after a breakup, men tend to report more loneliness and depression. The authors explained their findings in terms of gender differences in social and economic power. Although the study on breakups was done in the 1970s, women today are still more likely to be dependent on men for wealth and status than vice versa. In this sense, it is more important for a woman to scrutinize whom she chooses for a partner in relation to the potential alternatives—providing a "brake" on instant infatuation. Men, often being in a more powerful position in terms of earning status and wealth, tend to worry less about the impact of such choices. So they, more than women, can "afford" the luxury of engaging in "love at first sight" and staying in relationships simply for the romance. It may also be related to what University of California, Los Angeles, psychologist Shelley Taylor calls the "tending instinct." Women, either due to biological predisposition or greater cultural acceptance, have a propensity to respond to stress by caring for or turning to other people for support. Thus they have better support networks in place when a breakup occurs than do men.

The Love-Sex Link

So love endures and creates intense emotions—both good and bad—and it can alter, at least temporarily, our brain chemistry. But, to paraphrase Tina Turner, what's sex got to do with it? The answer, according to our study, is a lot. Of the reasons women gave for having sex, they listed "I wanted to express my love for the person" and "I realized I was in love" as two of their top ten reasons. Women wrote many accounts of how they used sex as a way to get love. Sometimes, as hoped, sex brought love and commitment:

I probably lost my virginity out of a need to be loved. I lived in a small town and was pretty neglected by my mother, she had lots of problems of her own. I never really found any boys that I liked all through school and when I met a guy I really liked when I was . . . a freshman in high school, I had sex with him very quickly. I had never even kissed a boy and I went from first kiss to intercourse with him in a month. He made me feel desired, special, he told me he loved me. . . . Luckily it was a good pick; we stayed together for four years.
—predominantly heterosexual woman, age 25

Sometimes having sex did not bring the actual coveted love but, rather, a temporary illusion of feeling loved:

I was extremely naive at the time, and was hopelessly infatuated with my then-boyfriend. Deep down I knew he didn't care for me as much as I did him, but I managed to convince myself he did, because I wanted to believe it. When I had sex with him, I was elated, almost triumphant, because, to my naive mind, sex was the equivalent of love, and having sex with him was "proof" that he loved me. . . . At the time, that is honestly how I rationalized the decision.
—heterosexual woman, age 25

I was working at my first full-time job and worked with an incredibly sexy guy. I was already a mother . . . and didn't think I would ever find someone to love me [but] I really fell in love with [a coworker]. . . . He was much more experienced than me and verbally taught me quite a few things about sex. We acted on those lessons and I thought he would fall in love with me if I did the things he asked. Some of those things were oral sex and performing a strip tease and talking dirty to him on the phone. I was not very experienced at this time and really thought if I did these things, he would eventually fall in love with me. He didn't, and I still have feelings for him to this day.
—heterosexual woman, age 46

But sometimes it brought neither love nor its illusion:

I fell in love with a man and thought he would love me in return if I just gave him what he wanted. I had sex with him even though he made it clear to me that he was no longer interested in dating me and just wanted to be friends. I slept with him at least five more times before he finally refused to have sex with me any more, stating that friends just don't do that. . . . I found the whole experience extremely painful.

—heterosexual woman, age 28

Many women in our study had sex not to get love per se, but as a way of expressing their love for another person:

Sex to express love is about being able to put feelings into actions. With different kinds of love there are different ways to express that love through action. When I physically and/or mentally desire someone I may choose to show that desire through sexual actions.

—heterosexual woman, age 25

And for many others, sex and love were intricately connected:

Um . . . is there any other reason to have sex? Seriously. Love is pretty much it, as far as I'm concerned.

—heterosexual woman, age 35

That love and sex are linked isn't new. In fact, the connection has been implied since humans first invented writing. In the late 1880s, a small tablet was unearthed from a region that is now Iraq. Inscribed on the four-thousand-year-old tablet is what historians believe to be the oldest love poem yet found. In the poem, a priestess professes not just her *love* but also her *lust* for a king:

Bridegroom, dear to my heart,
Goodly is your beauty, honeysweet.
You have captivated me, let me stand trembling before you;
Bridegroom, I would be taken to the bedchamber.

Apparently, the priestess's rather forward manner did not scare off the king, as later she writes:

> Bridegroom, you have taken your pleasure of me.
> Tell my mother, she will give you delicacies;
> My father, he will give you gifts.

Yet, while love and sex go hand in hand for many women, it is certainly not the case for all:

> *When I first started having sex, I thought it equaled love and commitment. I felt that way towards my partner. I have changed my mind recently.*
>
> —heterosexual woman, age 28

Research has even taught us something about which women are less inclined to require love or emotional involvement before sex. Women who are most open to sex without love tend to be extroverted in personality, and more open to new experiences of all sorts, including trying new and exotic foods and enjoying traveling to other cultures.

Although many women do not require or seek out love before having sex, women, more than men, believe that love should accompany sex. In the Meston Sexual Psychophysiology Lab, over seven hundred college students were asked whether they would agree or disagree with the statement "Sex without love is okay." Approximately half of the students were of European ancestry and half were of Southeast Asian ancestry. Among both cultural groups, men were significantly more likely than women to agree that sex without love was acceptable. Psychologist David Schmitt and colleagues noted similar findings in a massive study involving fifty-six nations.

Findings from a study conducted in the Buss Evolutionary Psychology Lab also indicate a gender difference in the love-sex link. One hundred men and one hundred women were asked to think of people they knew who had been, or currently were, in love. With these people in mind, they were asked to write down five acts or behaviors that the lovebirds had performed that reflected or exemplified their love. An interesting gender difference emerged: Whereas only 8 percent of women nominated "having sex" as an act of love, 32 percent of the men nominated sexual love acts. This finding reveals that there is at least one sense in which sex and love are more closely linked for men—sex seems to spring to mind as a more salient feature of love in the minds of men than it does in the minds of women. So although women are more likely to see love as a prerequisite for sex, men appear to be more likely to see sex as a defining feature of love.

The Bonding-Sex Link

Just as many women in our study said they had sex to give or get love, many women also reported having sex to give or get a feeling of emotional connection. They said they "desired the emotional closeness and intimacy" and they wanted to "communicate at a deeper level," "feel connected to the person," "increase the emotional bond by having sex," and "become one with another person." Their responses reflect a common theme—a desire to attain or enhance an emotional bond with a mate through sex. Once again we found that, contrary to gender stereotypes, there were no substantial differences in how frequently college-aged men and women said they had sex to forge a stronger emotional bond.

Some women had sex to try to form an emotional connection in order to salvage a relationship:

> It was a long-distance relationship that I just couldn't admit was not worth the hassle and [was] going to end it. We had sex because it was pretty much all we did on the rare occasion that we saw each other. I hoped it would bring us closer together and make us think we would really make it. [It] didn't work.
>
> —gay/lesbian woman, age 18

Other women in our study described virtually identical experiences. They reported that having sex to feel emotionally bonded in a failing relationship usually did not work. Often it had the opposite effect, making one or both people realize how emotionally (and even physically) unconnected they had become.

If a couple does feel connected, however, then having sex can certainly serve as a way to intensify their bond:

> *Having sex with someone creates a special bond with that person which is unattainable any other way. I would do this to further how involved I am in a relationship, and to show [my] vulnerability.*
>
> —heterosexual woman, age 25

> *I felt like I was starting to fall in love with this girl. I loved to share things with her, whether they be stories of things in my life, or experiences that we had together. We connected so well mentally and emotionally that . . . I wanted to be connected to her in a sexual sense as well.*
>
> —gay/lesbian woman, age 20

Many women who wrote their accounts of having sex for love and emotional bonding did not distinguish between the two:

> *I almost always have sex in order to feel connected with someone on a physical and emotional level. I feel connected with them before having sex and want to be connected to them as much as possible. It creates the fine line difference between having sex and making love. When I am in love with someone, I connect with them [in] multiple ways and having sex is one of them.*
>
> —heterosexual woman, age 24

> *I do not have sex if I am not in love and to me, being in love means desiring to coalesce with the person for whom I feel such strong emotions. The joining together of two does not simply mean physically, but also mentally and emotionally. Sex is a way of fulfilling all of these aspects at once.*
>
> —heterosexual woman, age 23

Indeed, feelings of connectedness trigger a sense of peacefulness and relationship security that is not unlike the emotional experience of love. Feelings of both love and bonding ward off feelings of loneliness and depression, and they can make a person feel that he or she is part of a team, or one of two halves of a perfect whole:

> *Being completely in love with another where you want to become one—one inside each other—spiritually and physically, exploding to become inside out.*
>
> —gay/lesbian woman, age 43

These themes of "oneness," "connectedness," and feeling "whole" expressed by the women in our study are remarkably similar to those that appear in Aristophanes' definition of love from Plato's *Symposium*. According to the dialogue's account, when humans began life, they didn't look as they do today. Instead, each had four arms, four legs, and two faces on a cylindrical neck. With all their appendages they could run quickly and they were mighty in strength and force; so mighty that they plotted to displace Zeus and the other gods. In retaliation, Zeus sliced them all in half and had Apollo turn their faces around and tie up the cut skin in the middle, forming a navel. Thereafter they forever longed to reconnect:

> Now when their nature was divided in two, each half in longing rushed to the other half of itself and they threw their arms around each other and intertwined them, desiring to grow together into one, dying of hunger and inactivity too because they were unwilling to do anything apart from one another. . . . Each of them is but the token of a human being, sliced like a flatfish, two from one; each then ever seeks his matching token.

It seems that people have been looking for their other, if not their better, half for millennia.

There are other ways that emotional bonding and sex can be related for women. For example, some women in our study talked about the experience of make-up sex in terms of emotional bonding. Women sometimes wanted to have sex after a fight because it helped to reestablish connection with their partners:

> *My boyfriend and I were going through a very rough patch in our relationship. He was convinced that I didn't love him anymore.*

Though we spent hours upon hours talking things through, I didn't feel like we were as close as we had been. I felt like I needed to have sex with him to regain some of that closeness that we had shared before.

—heterosexual woman, age 19

Others said that feeling connected during sex intensified their desire and pleasure during sex:

My current relationship is the first time I've had sex with love present, where there was truly an intense emotional connection and where sex is an amazing feeling of connectedness. By feeling emotionally connected to my partner in this relationship, it makes the sex more intense and allows us to connect even more completely. The first night when we realized that we were truly in love, both of us desired to have sex to consummate that feeling, to complete ourselves, so to speak.

—predominantly heterosexual woman, age 22

In a study conducted in the Meston Lab, we identified four main categories of events or cues that lead to feelings of sexual desire in women. Three of these were tied to attraction and arousal. For instance, women's desire was stoked by explicit erotic cues such as reading or watching a sexual story, "talking dirty" with a partner, or sensing that her body was becoming aroused, including by detecting genital lubrication. They responded to status cues, such as seeing or talking with someone powerful or famous. And they responded to "romantic" cues, such as dancing closely, sharing an amorous dinner, and laughing together. The other category of events that increased women's sexual desire, however, was related to emotional bonding. Feelings of connectedness can cause women to desire sex.

Even if they do not seek out sex themselves, or in cases where their bodies do not respond sexually to their partners' approaches and other cues, some women derive pleasure from having sex because of what can follow the sexual act—cuddling, tenderness, and feeling connected. Here is how one woman in our study described it:

Being asexual, I don't normally have the drive to have sex for a physical reason but I do get emotional enjoyment from it when I'm with my partner.

—asexual woman, age 20

Rosemary Basson, a well-known researcher in women's sexuality at the University of British Columbia, calls this having sex for the "spin-offs."

When a Kiss Is Not Just a Kiss

One reason women cited for having sex turned out to be quite simple: *The person was a good kisser.* Why kissing might impel a woman to have sex, though, turns out to be complex. Viewed from a primatological perspective, it's a strange activity. Other than bonobos, humans appear to be the only primate that engages in osculation, as kissing is technically called. Kissing between romantic or sexual partners occurs in over 90 percent of cultures. People kiss with great relish and variety—gently, shyly, affectionately, exuberantly, lasciviously, hungrily. Human lips are densely packed with sensory neurons, more than most regions of the body, but the tongue, nose, and cheeks also come into play. Typically kissing involves information transfer between most of the senses—touch, olfaction, and taste being the most prominent, although sights (luscious lips) and sounds (the English language has no words for this) cannot be ignored.

One study found that kissing caused a drop in cortisol, a stress hormone, indicating a reduction in anxiety. Kissing conveys information about health status, since bad breath can be a sign of disease or ill-health. Women also seem to use kissing as an emotional litmus test, with the outcome revealing whether they should take things to the next level and sexually consummate a relationship. Kissing seems more important for women than for men for this function. Whereas 53 percent of men in one study said that they would have sex without kissing, only 15 percent of women said they would consider sex with someone without first kissing them. Kissing not only provides vital information about a partner, it also can increase sexual excitement, feelings of euphoria, and a sense of emotional closeness.

"Bad" kissing is definitely a sexual turnoff for most women. One study found that 66 percent of women (as compared with 58 percent of men) admitted that sexual attraction evaporated after a bad kiss. As Alex "Hitch" Hitchens, played by actor Will Smith, told his client in the popular 2005 movie *Hitch*, "One dance, one look, one kiss, that's all we get . . . one shot, to make the difference between 'happily ever after' and 'Oh? He's just some guy I went to some thing with once.'" In short, kissing provides information to a woman about whether she wants to take things to the next sexual level, reveals something about whether someone will be a good lover, may provide information about health and genetic compatibility, and provides a barometer of relationship quality.

The Power of Petting

Earlier in this chapter we saw how being in love actually causes changes in brain activity and the release of certain brain chemicals. Can brain chemistry also explain feelings of emotional attachment and bonding? As it turns out, two of the hormones released by the brain during sex—vasopressin and oxytocin—are linked to bonding in animals, and might also play a role in human attachment.

The biggest increases in vasopressin and oxytocin occur after a woman's orgasm. Vasopressin increases the most in men postorgasm, while oxytocin spikes the most in women. There has not been a lot of research on the effects of oxytocin on human emotions, but some researchers found that taking a nasal spray shot of oxytocin increases feelings of trust and generosity. Others have reported that release of these hormones produces feelings of comfort, safety, and attachment. Oxytocin, which has been called the "cuddle hormone" because it is also released when a person is massaged or caressed, is also thought to possess anti-anxiety and antidepressant effects. Regardless of how it is released, most researchers believe that a natural burst of oxytocin elicits a "feel-good" experience.

Two relationship coaches in New York are banking on this—literally. In 2004, Reid Mihalko, the cofounder of Cuddle Party, began hosting parties at which people, mainly singles, pay thirty dollars for the opportunity to cuddle others for an hour or so. Apparently about ten thousand people have snuggled strangers in the past few years in hopes of rediscovering nonsexual touch and getting an oxytocin fix with no strings attached. (The cuddle parties include "cuddle lifeguards.")

In the research world, oxytocin is best known for the role it plays in maternal behaviors. For example, oxytocin stimulates the uterine contractions that facilitate childbirth, hence its name, which means "swift birth" in Greek. A testament to its effectiveness in this regard is the fact that about 75 percent of American women entering delivery rooms are given synthetic forms of oxytocin, such as Pitocin, to induce or speed up childbirth. In China, which has a much lower incidence of birth-related deaths compared to the United States, cool showers are advised when labor needs a boost. Cool showers stimulate the nipples, which, in turn, cause the brain to produce more of its own oxytocin. It has long been known among midwives that applying ice to the nipples can help release oxytocin. This, too, can help with prolonged childbirth.

Oxytocin also allows the breasts to release milk in pregnant and lactating women and plays a major role in maternal bonding and caretaking in many animal species. Researchers have shown that if you block an animal's natural release of oxytocin by giving the animal certain drugs, mothers stop engaging in normal maternal caretaking behaviors and completely reject their own offspring. The opposite can happen as well. If you inject oxytocin into young rats that have never given birth or even copulated, they begin to nuzzle and protect other females' rat pups just as if the pups were their own.

Bonding in the Brain

There has been a lot of research linking oxytocin to maternal bonding in animals—from rats to sheep. But many researchers believe oxytocin is also involved in sexual bonding, and not just among nonhuman animals.

Diane Witt, a researcher at Binghamton University, proposes that the release of oxytocin can be classically conditioned to the sight of certain people. Recall the Nobel Prize–winning Russian scientist Pavlov and his dogs. Dogs salivate when they are exposed to food—it plays an important role in the digestive process. Pavlov began ringing a bell every time he fed his dogs, and after a while the sound of the bell alone caused the dogs to salivate. The dogs had been classically conditioned to salivate at the sound of a bell. Witt believes that, in a similar way, oxytocin can be classically conditioned to be released by the brain with exposure to certain partners.

For example, a woman meets someone and on the first date she decides he doesn't match up to her ideal—Clint Eastwood—but he's still acceptable enough to date a few more times. Eventually she decides to have sex with him—and oxytocin is released, so she experiences that "oohhh so good" feeling. After having repeated sex, and oxytocin releases, with the same man, she forms a conditioned association. Pretty soon, just seeing the guy can cause her brain to release oxytocin—without even having sex! Suddenly, "Mr. Acceptable Enough" becomes "Mr. Can't Live Without." Some researchers believe that prolonged attachment with a given person actually causes chronically high levels of oxytocin and its close hormonal relative vasopressin, which could feasibly help maintain long-term relationship bonds between women and men.

Not long ago, researchers for the first time connected oxytocin with why some animals are naturally monogamous and others are not. Only about 3 percent of nonhuman mammals form monogamous bonds; the majority mate with many different partners. Some species of prairie voles form long-lasting pair-bonds (sometimes for life). They share nests, avoid meeting other potential mates, and rear their offspring together. Closely related to the monogamous prairie voles are the montane voles, which display a very different mating style. They do not form pair-bonds, and the males are uninterested and uninvolved in parental care. Female montane voles are not exactly devoted parents either—they abandon their offspring shortly after birth.

Given that these two species of voles share 99 percent of the same genes, making them very genetically similar, why do they behave so differently? As it turns out, the voles differ greatly in how they produce and process oxytocin and vasopressin. The attachment-prone, faithful prairie voles have a lot more of these bonding hormones and have a denser supply of receptors in the brain that can detect and use them.

Very recently, it has also been discovered that in prairie voles (but not in the unfaithful montane voles), the area of the brain that is loaded with receptors for oxytocin and vasopressin is also rich in receptors for dopamine, a chemical produced in the brain that has long been associated with reward. When animals (including humans) engage in behaviors such as eating, drinking, and sex—behaviors that are necessary for survival and reproduction—their brains release dopamine. This dopamine surge makes them feel good, essentially rewarding them for behavior that increases the chances they will want to eat, drink, and have sex again. The fact that the faithful prairie voles have these "reward" receptors in the same area of the brain as the "bonding" receptors suggests that having sex with a familiar vole mate is more rewarding than having sex with a new vole. The montane voles, which don't have bonding receptors in the same area of the brain as their reward receptors, would not associate familiarity with feeling good.

Working with these two species of voles, researcher Miranda Lim and her colleagues at Emory University in Atlanta made an amazing discovery: They found that they could turn the normally faithful male prairie voles into regular Don Juans by simply blocking the bonding receptors in their brains. They were also able to do the reverse. When they used a harmless virus to transfer the bonding receptor gene from the prairie vole to the montane vole, the montane vole showed an increase in the number of bonding receptors in the reward area of the brain. And guess what? The normally promiscuous montane vole displayed a strong preference for his current partner over novel females and was ready to settle down and raise the offspring.

Sex stimulates the release of oxytocin and vasopressin in humans just as it does in voles, but can hormonal differences explain why some humans are monogamous by nature and others are not? The Meston Lab is working hard to answer this question. Researcher Lisa Dawn Hamilton has tested whether there are differences in the brains of monogamous and nonmonogamous people. People who were considered monogamous not only chose and preferred to have sex with their current pair-bond, they also did not fantasize or "secretly" lust over other people. Nonmonogamous people, on the other hand, had a pattern of dating multiple partners at the same time or having repeated sexual relationships outside of their primary relationship.

To conduct the study, the Meston Lab team scanned the brains of people identified as monogamous and nonmonogamous while they viewed a series of photographs that depicted a variety of scenes. The images showed erotic scenes (e.g., couples making love), romantic/bonding scenes (e.g., couples holding hands or laughing together), and neutral scenes (e.g., a rural landscape). We then looked to see whether there were differences in activation in areas of the brain known to be rich in reward receptors. We predicted that monogamous persons would show more brain activation in the reward areas when they were shown photos depicting romantic or emotional bonding scenes than would nonmonogamous persons. We expected that sexual pictures would be rewarding to both groups of people, and that they would be more rewarding than the neutral scenes. So far, we have completed the study only in men, but the Meston Lab's predictions have been supported. The reward areas in monogamous men's brains lit up like Christmas trees in response to both the sexual photos and the emotional bonding photos. In sharp contrast, the nonmonogamous men's brains lit up only to the sexual stimuli; they showed very little activation in the reward areas of the brain to the emotional bonding photos. The Meston Lab needs to test this finding in a lot more men before we can conclude that there are "prairie" men and "montane" men, but it does seem that emotional bonding is more rewarding at a very basic biological level for some men than for others.

A Transcendental Experience

While the sexual motivations of voles and men seem to have a lot in common, human sexuality is also shaped by culture, from the way people feel about sex to their ideas about emotional connection. That's especially true when it comes to religion.

The role of sexuality varies widely across religious denominations, with some traditions being much more sexually restrictive than others. The Book of Leviticus, which is part of the Jewish Torah and the Christian Old Testament, has been fundamental in shaping how religion and sex are linked in the minds of Americans. According to Leviticus, God gave Moses a list of prohibited sexual behaviors, along with appropriate punishments for transgressions, which often involved death by stoning or burning. The forbidden behaviors included adultery, incest, sex during menstruation, sex between men, and sex with animals. Leviticus did not prohibit marital sex. In fact, numerous passages in the Old Testament attest to the positive moral status of the marriage bond and of sex within that bond. Leviticus also did not prohibit sex between unmarried men and women. Other biblical passages, however, made it clear that women who were not virgins when they married could be executed (Deuteronomy 22:13–29). No equivalent punishment was laid down for men who were not virgins at marriage.

It is well documented in the field of psychology that violating strict religious guidelines can lead to sexual guilt, which can impair a woman's ability to enjoy sex. Thus it was refreshing to hear from women in our study that the association between sex and religion can be an intensely positive experience. For some women, feeling connected to their partners during sex also made them feel connected to God:

> In Jewish law, it is a mitzvah [good deed] to have sex with a partner on Shabbat, and in Jewish mysticism, there is a form of sexual ecstasy that mimics the union of God and man, and recreation of the world. I can't really describe this experience. . . . But pure joy and connection with another person I feel is becoming closer to the cycles of life and the underlying palpable energy of the world . . . in essence, God.
> —predominantly heterosexual woman, age 21

> It was a dream come true, being with this incredible man. I was able to lose myself and see God, where the edges of the dream-world and the real world met.
> —heterosexual woman, age 23

> I had been thinking about how if God is immanent that meant Christ was in me, and in everyone. If Christ was in me, then he would also be in my partner. I suddenly had this moment where I realized that if we joined ourselves it could be Christ seeking Christ and how beautiful that would be.
> —predominantly heterosexual woman, age 20

For other women, sex did not meet their spiritual expectations:

> I grew up in an environment where we didn't talk about God—or sex. For that reason I lumped them into the same category of things

that seemed special because they were beyond me. When I started dating my boyfriend, I made him wait for a very long time. When it finally happened, I expected the experience to have an almost religious quality to it. It didn't.

—heterosexual woman, age 21

Some insight on how sex is able to create a feeling of connection with God might be found in what happens in the brain during deep religious experiences. In their book *Why God Won't Go Away,* radiology professor Andrew Newberg and psychiatrist Eugene D'Aquili observed that in people who are seeking a deep spiritual connection through prayer or meditation—such as Franciscan nuns and Buddhist monks—an area of the brain called the parietal lobe quiets. The parietal lobe is responsible for collating sensory information—helping us to understand how visual information lines up with spatial environment, for instance. A less active parietal lobe decreases the body's ability to orient itself in physical space and, according to Newberg and D'Aquili, to distinguish between self and nonself. Perhaps some people are so bombarded with visual and spatial information during sex that it creates a somewhat similar experience.

On the other hand, artistic depictions of religious experience, such as the Baroque sculpture *The Ecstasy of St. Theresa* by Gianlorenzo Bernini, also hint at a centuries-old association between religious ecstasy and orgasm—even if enjoying sex for its own sake wasn't part of the equation for most religiously observant women of the day.

The Evolution of Love and Bonding

Although in our initial study we did not find substantial differences between men and women in the *frequency* with which they had sex for emotional bonding reasons, a study conducted in the Buss Lab showed a big gender difference in the *importance* placed on emotional connectedness with a sexual partner. In the study, heterosexual men and women from many different countries were asked a provocative question:

Please think of a serious or committed romantic relationship that you have had in the past, that you currently have, or that you would like to have. Imagine that you discover that the person with whom you've been seriously involved became interested in someone else. What would upset or distress you more: a) imagining your partner forming a deep emotional attachment to that person or b) imagining your partner enjoying passionate sexual intercourse with that other person?

Hands down, women were more distressed by thinking about their partners being emotionally attached to someone else than by thinking about their partner having sex with someone else. This makes perfect evolutionary sense. From a woman's viewpoint, a man having sex with another woman may or may not mean that he is emotionally attached to her—it could simply involve physical gratification. But if a man is emotionally attached to another woman, there is a good chance he is (or will soon be) also having sex with her. If a man is both emotionally attached to *and* having sex with another woman, there is a high probability that he will begin to reallocate his commitment and resources to her instead of to his current partner—a clear threat, in evolutionary terms.

It is worth pausing to recall that, despite our earlier example of prairie voles, sex for the vast majority of species on this planet involves no commitment whatsoever. Humans are the rare exceptions, even among primates, in being one of the few species in which males and females form long-term pair-bonds that last years, decades, and sometimes a lifetime. Among chimpanzees, the primates that are genetically closest to humans, sex occurs primarily when a female enters estrus. During this period of ovulation, the female chimpanzee's bright red genital swelling and scents send males into a sexual frenzy, but outside of estrus, male chimps are largely indifferent to females. Thus, sexual relationships among chimpanzees are short-lived.

Among humans, ovulation is concealed or cryptic, at least for the most part. Although there may be subtle physical changes in women—a slight glowing of the skin or an increase in women's sexual desire—there is little scientific evidence that men can reliably detect when women are ovulating. From an evolutionary standpoint, successful ancestral men typically would have needed to stick around to have sex throughout a woman's menstrual cycle. Without cues to ovulation, a single act of sex results in conception only 3 to 4 percent of the time. Stopping by for an afternoon romp rarely paid reproductive dividends. For this reason, some researchers believe that concealed ovulation probably evolved as a way to increase pair-bonding or commitment in human sexual relationships. This in turn increased the chances that resources would be allocated to a single mate and her children.

But that doesn't explain the powerful emotion of love and why it evolved in humans. Evolutionary psychologists believe that it may be a form of "long-term commitment insurance." If your partner were blinded by an uncontrollable emotion that could not be helped or chosen, an emotion that was elicited only by you and no other, and one that was made all the more powerful by its association with a cascade of sex-triggered hormones, then commitment would be less likely to waver in sickness as well as in health and if poorer rather than richer. On the other hand, if a partner chooses you based on mostly "rational" criteria—say, your access to resources or your lack of resource-eating offspring—he or she might leave you on the same basis—in favor of a competitor with slightly more desirable qualities.

4. The Thrill of Conquest

From Capturing a Mate to Poaching One

ᚼ⬥ᚼ

It is not enough to succeed; others must fail.
　　　　　　　　　　　　　　　　—Gore Vidal (b. 1925)

The reality of sexual competition among women is captured, albeit in exaggerated and artificial form, in the popular television show *The Bachelor*. Each week, millions of Americans tune in to watch a real-life bachelor select among twenty-five women, who primp, court, date, flaunt, make out, and sometimes have sex, in the hope of capturing a mate in the bedroom and at the altar. The real-life bachelors chosen for the show, not surprisingly, embody qualities many women want—they are handsome and self-confident, display a charming personality, and are physically toned, athletic, and professionally successful. In the first thirteen seasons, the bachelors included a successful management consultant, the vice president of a chain of family-owned banks, a self-made mortgage company owner, a professional football player, an actor who played a doctor on the show *ER*, a cosmetics entrepreneur, a doctor who happens also to be a triathlete and naval officer, an owner of several successful bars, a global financier, and an account executive.

During the show, the bachelor goes on a series of dates with the women, sometimes singly and sometimes in pairs or groups. At the end of each episode, women are eliminated from contention. At the end of the series, as tensions mount, the bachelor chooses a winner and (sometimes) proposes marriage. Along the way, the sexual competition becomes increasingly vicious. In addition to verbally disparaging rivals to the sought-after bachelor behind their fellow contestants' backs, the women become increasingly sexual in appearance and conduct, though no sex is actually depicted on the show. As one viewer commented, "The women always succeed in making themselves look like low class high school girls by the end of the season." The show has sometimes been reviled as crass, unrealistic, insulting to women, exploitative, superficial, fake, deplorable, and pathetic. Still, it draws roughly 11 million viewers, mostly women according to the Nielsen ratings, who get caught up in the drama of watching sexual competition. (The first season of the spin-off show *The Bachelorette* let one of the "jilted" women from *The Bachelor* select among twenty-five eligible men.)

When we think of competing for mates, many of us conjure images of men battling one another, or the scenes from nature documentaries in which two stags interlock their antlers in a ritualized fight for dominance. Across human cultures, men more than women do compete with each other in violent physical fights. They scuffle for status on the playing field, whether in the ancient Aztec *ulama* court—where the difference between winning and losing was equated with that between fertility and drought—or in the contemporary NBA mega-arena. Historically men also competed with each other in the realm of hunting for calorie-rich meat to outdo their rivals; in modern societies most men display their status and resources in more symbolic ways, such as in prestige possessions. As one of the cofounders of the support group Dating a Banker Anonymous put it, "It's that he's an alpha male, he's aggressive, he's a go-getter, he doesn't take no for an answer, he's confident, people respect him and that creates the whole mystique of who he is."

In fact, male-male competition is so overt and ostentatious that it probably led Charles Darwin and many scientists after him to overlook what we now know is a powerful evolutionary and psychological force: female-female sexual competition. In our study, women described being motivated to have sex in order to beat out rivals:

My boyfriend loves attention, and early in our relationship [he] be-
gan another non-serious relationship with another girl behind my
back. When I first found out about it, I was devastated, but eventu-
ally made it my goal to make him realize that I'm the only one he
wants. While I was happy to have sex with him, I realize now that
I was also doing it in hopes that I could prove myself better than
the other girl.

—heterosexual woman, age 18

Despite this blind spot among generations of researchers, almost everyone would agree that women compete sexually just as much as men do.

From an evolutionary perspective, the reason is straightforward: Men
differ dramatically from each other in their desirability to women, or, as
the cliché goes, a good man is hard to find. So it's not an understatement
to say that each and every woman alive today is an evolutionary success
story—and it's worth pausing to consider why.

In our evolutionary past, women who prevailed over other women
by gaining sexual access to the most desirable men could gain access to
a variety of reproductive benefits—access to better genes, an increased
likelihood of producing successful sons and daughters, access to superior resources, and a boost in social status. All of these benefits would
have translated in ancestral environments into increased reproductive
success—directly in the form of having more children survive and indirectly in the form of having numerous grandchildren because those
children were healthier and more sexually desirable. Each living woman
has descended from a long and literally unbroken line of ancestral mothers who succeeded in sexual competition.

There is healthy debate among psychologists about how much such
evolutionary imperatives shape women's contemporary motivations
and behaviors and the degree to which individuals' own, conscious explanations of their behaviors should take precedence over scientifically
documented processes that may influence individuals' behaviors without their knowledge. Sometimes, there's a happy match between the
two. We found close correspondence in our study between evolutionary
hypotheses about women's sexual competition and women's expressed
motivations for having sex.

In some ways, women's sexual competition appears to have intensified in recent decades, perhaps because there is so much celebrity media coverage of presumed sexual rivalries, from Debbie Reynolds versus Elizabeth Taylor to Jennifer Aniston versus Angelina Jolie. With the amount of attention given to celebrities and the cultural acceptance of sexually tinged popular entertainment, people are now also liable to consider these very high status individuals as sexual competitors—even if a sexual partner would not have a chance to meet a movie star, let alone find one in a real bed. Rather than simply trying to beat out a rival who lives a few doors down, women (and men) can instead find themselves worrying about whether a sexual partner is imagining having sex with a celebrity—and decide to win sexual commitment by using a variety of tactics.

This chapter explores how women's rivalries play out in the competition for desirable short-term sexual partners, committed long-term mates, and sexual domination over rivals themselves. We examine a particular version called mate poaching, which involves going after a sexual partner who is already in a relationship. We begin by looking at two of the major strategies by which women compete for desirable sex partners: through enhancing their sexual attractiveness and influencing the sexual reputations of their rivals.

A Matter of Attraction

It is no secret that men prize appearance in sexual partners, be they casual or committed. But contrary to what social scientists have been saying for decades, this emphasis is not limited to the United States, Western societies, or cultures saturated with modern visual media. The premium men place on appearance, for better or for worse, is a human universal.

The logic of sexual selection dictates that the mate preferences of each sex define in large part the domains of competition in the other sex. Just as men compete in trying to embody what women want sexually, women compete to embody what men want. And just as men stumble over each other to achieve status, secure resources, and display humor, intelligence, and athletic prowess because these are qualities women find sexually attractive, women compete with each other to develop and display the qualities that men find sexually attractive. High among these qualities is physical beauty.

Harvard psychologist Nancy Etcoff notes that Americans spend more money on enhancing their beauty than they do on education or social services. Within the United States, Americans purchase some 2,136,960 tubes of lipstick and 2,959,200 jars of skin care products every day. Roughly three hundred thousand American women undergo breast augmentation surgical procedures each year. The Buss Evolutionary Psychology Lab interviewed women to find out the most common and effective tactics they use to attract mates—and many centered on a woman's physical appearance:

- learning how to apply makeup;
- wearing facial makeup;
- dieting to improve her figure;
- wearing stylish clothing;
- keeping well groomed;
- getting a new and interesting hairstyle;
- spending more than one hour on making her appearance pleasant;
- grooming her hair carefully;
- lying out in the sun to get a tan; and
- wearing earrings, necklaces, or other jewelry to enhance her appearance.

Not surprisingly, women report using makeup to enhance their looks significantly more often than men (some men do wear makeup these days). Women are twice as likely as men to spend more than an hour per day on their appearance, and are 50 percent more likely than men to lie in the sun or sit under a tanning lamp to achieve a healthy-looking, albeit ultimately skin-damaging, glow. Although men are increasingly devoting money and effort to enhancing their sexual attractiveness, a tremendous imbalance remains—women spend nearly ten times as much on appearance-enhancement products as men do.

Consciously or not, women historically have been consumers of fashion and beauty products that signal attractiveness to men. Women wear heels that make them appear taller and slimmer (as did men for centuries), don clothing that accentuates or creates a low (and attractive) waist-to-hip ratio, use hair products that condition a lustrous, healthy mane, and pad their clothing in fertility-mimicking curves. All of these enhancements aim to make women appear young, free of irregularities such as scars and blemishes, and flushed with good health—in other words, sexually desirable.

Researchers who followed women at singles bars found that "many women said that they went home from work before going out to the bars to do a 'whole revamping': often, they would take a bath, wash their hair, put on fresh makeup and go through three changes of outfits before they went out to the bars—'primping for us counts more than for guys—they don't have to worry about their looks as much.'" Appearance enhancement evokes overtures from a wider pool of potential prospects, giving women a greater pool of mates to choose from.

Whether women are seeking a short-term sex partner or a long-term mate matters a great deal. Indeed, the tactic of appearance enhancement proves to be more effective for women in attracting casual sex partners than it does in attracting long-term mates, undoubtedly because in the long run, men also value other attributes, including intelligence, personality, honesty, and fidelity. Women seeking casual sex partners are far more likely to sexualize their appearance, wearing tight outfits, low-cut blouses that reveal cleavage, shirts that expose bare shoulders or backs, and short skirts that show a lot of leg. Sexualizing appearance is a tactic that often works for women seeking sex partners. Sending sexual behavioral signals also hyperactivates men's sexual psychology: arching the back to enhance breasts, leaning over to show a bit more cleavage, holding eye contact for a split second longer than average, exaggerating the hip swivel while walking, and licking lips seductively. All these tactics stir passions in more men, widening the array of possibilities from which women can exercise sexual choice.

The Competitive Rhythms of Ovulation

Interestingly, the degree to which women sexualize their appearance depends on their ovulation cycle—at least among women not taking oral contraceptives. Evolutionary psychologist Kristina Durante and her colleagues had non-pill-taking women come to her lab twice—once during the fertile window of their cycle and once during the infertile phase. She took full-body photographs of the women at each time and had them draw illustrations of clothing that they might wear to a social event that evening. Ovulating women wore more sexy and revealing clothing to the lab, and drew dramatically more revealing clothing that they would wear to the imagined event, compared with the same women when they were not ovulating. Sexually unrestricted women—those who said they tend toward sexually freer conduct and seek sex with a wider variety of partners—showed this ovulation effect more strongly than the other women. Durante and her colleagues argue that this shift toward sexy clothing reflects increased female-female competition at ovulation for the most desirable sex partners.

Studies conducted in Germany discovered a similar effect by using digital photography to capture what women wore to singles bars and interviewing them afterward. Using a computer program that calculated the percentage of skin revealed by women's clothing choices, they discovered that women in the most fertile phase of their ovulation cycles wore more revealing clothing and showed more skin than women in the nonfertile phase. Ovulating women dress for sexual success. Another group of researchers, led by UCLA evolutionary psychologist Martie G. Haselton, found that women in the fertile phase of their cycles wore nicer and more fashionable clothes and showed more upper and lower body skin than the same women in the low-fertility phase of their cycles.

Women's ovulation cycles also influence their patterns of consumer behavior. One study created a simulated online shopping program designed to track women's spending patterns on items such as clothes, shoes, underwear, jewelry, and other fashion accessories. As we have seen, these are all products that women use to enhance their appearance for competition with same-sex rivals. Near ovulation, women tended to shift their spending patterns toward revealing and sexy items. And the shift was most dramatic when women were led to believe that attractive same-sex rivals were present!

Several other scientific studies support the theory that ovulating women sexualize their appearance for success in mate competition. Women report more desire to go to parties and clubs where they can meet men on their high-fertility days. They are more likely to flirt with men other than their primary partners when they are in or near the ovulatory phase of their cycles. They even judge other women to be less attractive when they rate them near the middle of their own ovulation cycles—a finding that evolutionary psychologist Maryanne Fisher interprets as evidence that women are more sexually competitive with other women near ovulation and feel the urge to "put down" their potential rivals. Finally, when evolutionary psychologist Karl Grammer interviewed women at a discotheque, those who rated their attire as "sexy" and "bold" also indicated a specific sexual motivation: a desire to flirt with men or find a sex partner.

From an evolutionary perspective, women are most competitive for the best mating opportunities near ovulation because this is precisely the time when mating decisions are most consequential. It is the phase in which mating mistakes are most costly, the phase in which women are highest in reproductive mate value, and the phase in which beating out rivals for the most desirable mate yields the greatest adaptive benefits.

The Scarlet Reputation

Women who sexualize their appearance, however, run a risk: damage to their sexual reputation. One woman in our study described a trade-off between success in sexual competition and sexual reputation:

> *I broke it off with a guy after I had been tugged around by him for months, right after a very long-term relationship, and was feeling . . . free. This amazing looking guy came to visit a friend and I knew that I wanted to fool around with him. Then I realized that every other girl in my sight was talking about doing the same thing. The "dorm-slut" was the main person who wanted him, and I just figured that she would have him by the end of the night. . . . I somehow wanted to feel what she felt every time she went home with a random*

guy. So I competed against her in her own game . . . and won . . . at a price.

—heterosexual woman, age 20

The effect of success in these short-term sexual rivalries, of course, varies greatly with the culture. Women risk being labeled with one of the dozens of derogatory words, in the English language alone, for a woman who pursues a short-term sexual strategy. Modern terms include slut, whore, skank, tart, and tramp, while more archaic terms include harlot, hussy, strumpet, wench, bawd, mattressback, window girl, fast-fanny, canvasback, hipflipper, breechdropper, trollop, spreadeagle, stump thumper, and scarlet woman. Beyond this labeling, some women disparage their sexual rivals by spreading targeted sexual gossip about them. A study by the Buss Lab revealed that sexual competition included calling a rival promiscuous; telling others that the woman just wanted to get laid; saying that she had too many past boyfriends; saying that she slept around a lot; saying that she would sleep with just about anyone; and calling a woman "loose."

Derogation of a rival's sexual reputation has a very specific function: to render the rival less desirable to other women as a friend and to long-term mates as a sexual partner. In reproductive competition, a rival's loss has benefits. A woman who limits her rival's mating opportunities by impugning her sexual reputation simultaneously increases her own mating opportunities—at least if the putdown is done artfully. The Buss Lab, for example, found that those using derogation tactics often distance themselves from the derogation by using phrases such as "I've heard that she slept with the whole football team," or "Rumor has it that she got herpes."

You might think that in this age of purported sexual equality, a double standard would not exist; that just as men who sleep with many women rarely sustain reputational damage, a woman who has slept with many men would not—or should not—sustain blows to her reputation. Not so. Not only has the double standard not been eradicated, it appears to be enforced more strongly by women than by men. Evolutionary psychologist Anne Campbell conducted several studies of the sexual reputations of girls and observed that "it was the girls themselves who were most vocal in enforcing this code." The girls avoided befriending, and openly rejected, those who were known as "lays" and "whores" to protect their own sexual reputations. They did not want to be "guilty" by association. As one scientist noted: "The most risky confidences center around sexual behavior and feelings. One reason why so few girls even talk to their closest friends about sexual desire or actual sexual behavior is through fear that their friends might betray them in gossip—spread the rumor that they are a slag [the British slang term for "slut"]. There is no parallel for boys to the risk of betrayal which can destroy a girl's whole social standing." Being branded with derogatory labels puts a woman in a terribly difficult situation, since there is no direct way to refute the claims and they pose a threat to her future mating opportunities.

The Winner's High

With sexual reputation so valuable to women themselves, it seems almost counterintuitive that women would have sex out of a sense of competition. But for some women, the feeling of conquest is enough to motivate them to have sex:

> *In high school I remember feeling very proud of my number [of sexual partners]. . . . I would get a thrill just before sex, thinking to myself "another one! I snared another one!" Conquest.*
>
> —heterosexual woman, age 26

> *I view sex as a fun experience and enjoy the thrill of meeting someone and seducing them. The feeling of having a conquest is exhilarating, like a high.*
>
> —predominantly heterosexual woman, age 20

> *Of course we all want to at some point set our minds to something and accomplish it. When I have done that and accomplished my goal of going home with someone I feel like I have made a conquest.*
>
> —heterosexual woman, age 26

Bragging rights can be a motivation as well. In our study, one woman said she bragged about a sexual conquest not as a way of snubbing a specific rival, but as a means of communicating her sexual power:

> *Ah, a silly thing really. . . . I get so annoyed by these obviously gay boys who openly flirt with females and are all like "oh, I like the aesthetics of the female body, but . . ." and leave it ambiguous whether they would ever do anything about it. So one somewhat drunken evening I challenged one of these guys about it—and we ended up sleeping together. I decided this was a good thing to brag about, converting a gay boy . . .*
>
> —predominantly homosexual woman, age 22

We also discovered a number of women who expressed their competition directly—not simply winning the opportunity to have sex, but beating out other women in the course of doing so:

> *I wanted to win. My best friend always had guys interested in her in high school. Although I was never really interested in guys, somehow this bothered me. So I began to pursue the same men she did to prove I was as good, if not better, than her. When she would convey interest in a particular guy I would immediately pursue him and win him with the offer of immediate sex. This included heavy petting under a desk during class and intercourse in a closet or hidden area of my high school.*
>
> —gay/lesbian woman, age 23

Such offers of immediate sex can succeed when they exploit men's desires for low-cost, low-risk sexual encounters—qualities that are alluring when viewed from both evolutionary and clinical perspectives.

Indeed, it is easier to attract a sexual partner with high mate value for casual sex than for committed mating. In these cases, women's sexual competition may serve the function of gaining status among their friends:

I had sex with a person who was very well known and popular, especially in my area. I didn't do it because I was interested in a relationship, but a few of us girls were very interested in him. . . . I knew the other girls wanted to date him, but I wanted to get him first. I wanted to be the one who stole him away from the other girls. As soon as I got a date with him I knew I was going to have sex . . . and I couldn't wait until the next day when the other girls knew I had been with him. It made me feel great. I was the one who got him. My friends envied me for it.

—heterosexual woman, age 23

When I was younger, my girlfriends and I would go to the bars together. It always felt like a competition as to who could get the guy. After drinks and fun at the bar, sometimes I would take the guy home to . . . my shared apartment and have sex with him there so that my friends would know that I got the guy that night.

—heterosexual woman, age 26

Of course, the thrill of winning is not limited to a single night's competition. In a very public display of presumed rivalry, in 2008 singer and actress Jessica Simpson appeared with her boyfriend, Dallas Cowboys quarterback Tony Romo, wearing a shirt with the tagline "Real Girls Eat Meat." Fans interpreted it as a competitive dig at Romo's previous mate, who is a vegetarian.

Competing for the Committed Mate

Women are sexual rivals not just for short-term matches but also for long-term committed relationships. The premise of *The Bachelor* and *The Bachelorette*, of course, is that the competition *is* for a long-term mate, though only one of the couples—picked by a bachelorette and not a bachelor—has gotten married thus far.

In attracting a long-term partner, sexual rivalry can often be explicit:

I was seeing this woman, and she was quite intimidating because of her age and her wealth. And she also was dating other people besides me, all male. The first time she tried to seduce me, I didn't let her, because I wasn't sure of myself. The second time I let it happen, because I thought it could win her over . . .

—gay/lesbian woman, age 20

But while having sex as a strategy for securing a long-term commitment can succeed, several women in our study reported that, for them, the strategy did not work:

When I was in high school, I had a big crush on this boy. He finally started giving me "attention" and I wanted to be his girlfriend so I had sex with him thinking that if I had sex then he would be interested [in me] . . . Nope . . . That's all he wanted me for.

—heterosexual woman, age 35

As a teenager there were a few times when I felt that having sex would get a guy to stay with me, or that if I didn't have sex they would no longer be interested in me. At the time it felt okay, but afterward it was usually a kind of depressing feeling, especially because it didn't usually have the intended result.

—heterosexual woman, age 33

In sexual competitions, for every winner there is at least one loser, and when sex fails to initiate a long-term relationship, many women say they feel used and depressed. As we saw in chapter 3, the release of oxytocin during sex creates a wave of good feeling and emotional bonding, which may explain this shift in mood. According to Swedish physiologist Kerstin Uvnäs Moberg, oxytocin is part of a "calm and connection system [that] is associated with trust and curiosity instead of fear, and with friendliness instead of anger. The heart and circulatory system slow down as the digestion fires up. When peace and calm prevail, we let our defenses down and instead become sensitive, open, and interested in others around us." Although this change is very useful when a person succeeds in forming a pair-bond, it can make a failed attempt in a competitive situation more emotionally painful. In fact, some scientists believe that "oxytocin withdrawal" can occur when relationships end, and the subsequent depression women feel after a breakup may stem partly from this sudden plunge in the hormone.

Tit for Tat

Sometimes sexual competition occurs not merely because a woman seeks the thrill of conquest or a boost in status among her peers, but because she wishes to exact revenge on a sexual rival:

> *Well, my girlfriends and I were on holiday, and there was a group of boys staying at the same holiday resort. There was one guy that I liked, and another one of my friends liked him too. I might not have acted on it, but my friends and I had a big fight. I can't even remember what the fight was about. So I went for it, flirting away with the guy. I was very young (eighteen) at the time, and very sexually inexperienced. But I decided that I wanted to sleep with this man, just to sort of get back at my friend, and to sort of prove that I was the more attractive/better one of us. So I achieved what I set out to do. I felt angry with her, and proud of myself that I won.*
> —heterosexual woman, age 26

For another woman, having sex with a woman's ex simultaneously gave her a sense of vengeance and triumph:

> *In high school there was this girl [who] hated me because I was good friends with her boyfriend at the time. She tried to make my life hell by stalking me and picking fights. So, a couple of years later I slept with an ex of hers (not the same guy) in hopes that it would get back to her somehow and piss her off. It gave me a sense of closure and me winning in the end.*
> —heterosexual woman, age 22

Sexual rivalries also play out in competition for attention from high-status, short-term sexual mates, particularly those of musical and athletic celebrities. The so-called "bass-player effect" exposes some of the competitive hierarchy among groupies: Typically playing in the background and hence lower in status, the bass player often is less sexually attractive than the high-status lead singer and lead guitar player. The term "groupie," though, is not always considered derogatory among many of the most successful companions to rock stars. Cameron Crowe's 2000 movie *Almost Famous* features a character named Penny Lane, played by Kate Hudson, who is modeled after two real-life "supergroupies" Crowe knew, one who actually goes by the name Penny Lane and the other named Bebe Buell. In real life, Lane denies that she's a groupie, stating instead that she is a "band-aid," and Buell prefers the term "muse" to characterize her somewhat longer-term sexual relationships with musicians Elvis Costello and Aerosmith's Steven Tyler. In addition to the celebrity Buell accrued through her sexual encounters with famous rock stars, she also had a daughter, the movie star Liv, with Tyler—possibly an example of the genetic benefits to be gained from having sex with men who are highly desirable to women.

Groupies are so prevalent in the music world that dozens of bands have written songs about them, including the Beatles' "She Came In Through the Bathroom Window" about a groupie who broke into Paul McCartney's house. (Perhaps the ultimate status accolade of being a groupie is having oneself immortalized in song.) Some groupies seem to chase an extra boost of status by writing "kiss-and-tell" books that publicize their sexual conquests. Pamela Des Barres, another rock supergroupie, rose to be the unofficial spokesperson for the wild music scene of 1960s Los Angeles through her four books, including the aptly billed *Let's Spend the Night Together*. She claims to have shared beds with rock legends Jim Morrison of The Doors, Jimmy Page of Led Zeppelin, and Mick Jagger of the Rolling Stones. Carmen Bryan's memoir *It's No Secret: From Nas to Jay-Z, from Seduction to Scandal—a Hip-Hop Helen of Troy Tells All* describes her relationship with rapper Nas, with whom she had a daughter, and his hip-hop rival Jay-Z, as well as with NBA point guard Allen Iverson, whom she calls a "lean and muscled . . . warrior."

Mate Poaching

Whether they are groupies or simply peers in the same social circle, women who win in sexual competitions stand to gain a variety of benefits, and rivalry can grow tense—all the more so because desirable men are rare in the eyes of many women.

In cultures that practice polygyny, in which men are permitted to have more than one wife, the most desirable men often find several wives. Many women prefer to be the second or third wife of a high-status man rather than the sole wife of a low-status man. This can be explained by the "polygyny threshold hypothesis." Stated simply, a woman can sometimes gain more resources by securing a third or a half of the bounty of a wealthy man who already has wives than she can by getting all of the resources of a poor man who has no wives.

In monogamous cultures, women confront a very different problem: The most desirable men may already be mated, and cultural mores and the rules of most religions sometimes put those "good" men off-limits. Some women have developed a solution to this problem, albeit one that is often seen as socially undesirable: a strategy of *mate poaching*, or luring already taken mates away from their existing partners. Men, of course, poach mates as well.

The practice of mate poaching undoubtedly goes back to the emergence of long-term pair-bonds. The earliest written record of mate poaching comes from the Bible, in the account of King David and Bathsheba. One day King David caught a glimpse of the alluring Bathsheba bathing on the roof of a neighboring house. Unfortunately for the king, she happened to be married to another man, named Uriah. David was not deterred. And the fact that he was king certainly didn't hurt. He succeeded in seducing Bathsheba and got her pregnant. He then devised a treacherous plan to eliminate his sexual rival permanently. He ordered Uriah to the battle front and then commanded his troops to retreat. This exposed Uriah to mortal danger. With Uriah safely in his grave, King David married Bathsheba, a union that yielded four children.

Although the practice of mate poaching is ancient, the phrase did not enter the scientific literature on human mating until 1994, and the first scientific study of human mate poaching was not published until 2001. That study, conducted by the Buss Lab, discovered that 60 percent of American men and 53 percent of American women admitted to having attempted to lure someone else's mate into a committed relationship. Although half of these attempts failed, half succeeded.

Sometimes mate poachers just want sex and nothing more. For short-term sexual encounters, the sex differences were larger, and do not show men in a positive light—fully 60 percent of men reported attempting to lure an already mated woman into a sexual encounter. In contrast, 38 percent of women in the study reported comparable behavior—still a substantial number. One woman in our study described her mate poaching in these terms:

> I was younger, and I used to like my friend's boyfriend, and another friend of mine dared me. She said, "I dare you to have sex with [her] boyfriend," and I said, "Please don't tempt me, because I will do it." So one night I went to their house and she was not there (by the way I knew at the time she was not home). I talked to him for a minute, and he started the situation. He kissed me, then touched me, and we had sex, right there in their living room. It made me feel good, superior to my friend for getting her boyfriend.
> —heterosexual woman, age 27

Given the social stigma sometimes attached to mate poachers, the figures cited above probably represent underestimates of the actual incidence—especially since far higher percentages of both sexes report that *others* have attempted to entice them into leaving an existing relationship. Ninety-three percent of men and 82 percent of women say that someone has tried to lure them out of an existing relationship into a long-term commitment. For short-term sexual flings, the figures are 87 percent of men and 94 percent of women.

Evolutionary psychologist David Schmitt found similar patterns in the most massive study of mate poaching ever conducted—16,964 individuals from fifty-three nations. The reported rates of mate poaching, of course, differ somewhat across cultures. They tend to be higher in Middle Eastern countries such as Israel, Turkey, and Lebanon, and lower in East Asian countries such as Japan, Korea, and China. But in all of the cultures surveyed, substantial numbers confessed to trying to poach a mate. In the Middle East, where in many countries women's sexuality is restricted by Arab custom or Islamic religious law, one might expect few women to engage in mate poaching. Yet roughly 64 percent of men and 54 percent of women admit to succumbing to the lures of a mate poacher. Worldwide, 12 percent of men and 8 percent of women report that their current partner was actually romantically involved with someone else when they first met.

Poachers sometimes insinuate themselves into a couple's life as trusted friends, become emotionally close, and then switch into poaching mode when the opportunity presents itself. "Friends" frequently end up becoming mating rivals. The principle of assortative mating—that "similars" attract—explains why. We tend to pick friends because they share interests and values with us, and they often share the same desirable qualities we possess. Because of assortative friendship, people have an above-average probability of being attracted to the mates of their friends.

Mate poachers are often skilled at driving a wedge into a couple's relationship. One common way of doing this is to imply that the person's current mate is cheating or might be straying. Another is to point out flaws in the partner or in their relationship. For example, a woman hoping to poach a mate might tell a man who's already involved with another woman that his partner doesn't treat him well. Others try to boost a target's self-esteem and sense of desirability, saying such things as "You're too good for her" or "You deserve someone better." The mate poacher's goal is to create a discrepancy between one partner's sense of mate value and the other's, thereby lowering the target's commitment to the existing relationship. Some mate poachers wait in the wings and pounce when the couple has a fight.

A particularly insidious form of mate poaching is what has been called the "bait and switch" tactic. This tactic involves a mate poacher presenting herself to the man as "costless sex," a fling with no strings attached. This creates two potential outcomes, both beneficial to the mate poacher. One is that the man's regular partner discovers the infidelity. The Buss Lab encountered a case in which a mate poacher intentionally left her earrings in the folds of the couple's couch after she had sex with the husband. When the wife discovered another woman's earrings in her house, the infidelity was revealed, and the marriage broke up, rendering the man available. The other outcome involves converting a short-term liaison into a long-term relationship—sometimes stealthily, sometimes unintentionally. The mate poacher either consciously takes the opportunity to develop an emotional and physical connection with the target, or does so unwittingly, and one day the targeted mate realizes that attraction has turned into love.

What makes mate poaching as a sexual motivator of women so fascinating is that women often want to hide their sexual competition from their rivals. Otherwise, a woman risks meeting retaliation—for instance, through derogation of her sexual reputation—and failing to secure her targeted mate. In this sense, mate poaching differs from other forms of sexual competition, which usually involve public displays such as wearing revealing clothing or sending observable sexual signals. Despite women's efforts to minimize the risks associated with mate poaching, it is a mating tactic that carries with it imminent dangers.

This point became apparent from an unusual source: the studies conducted by the Buss Lab of homicidal fantasies that everyday people experience. Much to our amazement, we discovered that the vast majority of people have experienced at least one vivid homicidal fantasy in their lives—in fact, out of more than five thousand participants we studied, 91 percent of men and 84 percent of women said that they had at least one. And sexual competition in its many forms was the main reason both sexes had fantasized about murder.

One particular example brings this to life:

> *My boyfriend is always telling me how gorgeous he thinks Kate Moss is. Really, she is just a skinny, drug-addict bitch. What method did I think about using to kill her? I thought about taking a wire coat hanger and putting it through her eye to make her brain dead. Then I would hang her skinny body up in my closet and show my boyfriend that she isn't so gorgeous after all.*
>
> —heterosexual woman, age 20

It is unlikely that Kate Moss is truly a sexual competitor of this woman. But the media bombard men and women with images of celebrities, sometimes with deleterious consequences. Research has documented that men repeatedly exposed to images of attractive women report lower levels of love and commitment to their regular partners, and men who frequently view sexual pornography often become dissatisfied with the physical appearance and sexual performance of their sexual partners. Women repeatedly shown photographs of attractive women suffer in self-esteem. As Mary Schmich captured it in her "Wear Sunscreen" *Chicago Tribune* column, "Do not read beauty magazines, they will only make you feel ugly." So although most women are not in literal sexual rivalry with the cover girls of the world, in a very real sense gorgeous models and movie stars become competitors by lowering women's self-esteem and reducing the love and commitment of partners. In our psychological world, we are surrounded by imaginary as well as actual sexual rivals.

Revenge for Mate Poaching

Using sex to lure a man out of an existing relationship can, of course, fail. Other women become leery of befriending women known to be mate poachers, and the failed poacher may develop a reputation as "the other woman." Even if a woman succeeds in luring the desired mate away from his existing partner, she may suffer anxiety about how faithful her poached mate will actually be to her. After all, if you've succeeded in luring someone away from a committed relationship with sex, you have firsthand evidence that the person is susceptible to external sexual advances!

One retaliatory tactic has an impact on why women have sex: exacting revenge for mate poaching by having sex with the mate poacher's partner. In our study, women mentioned having sex to get revenge on a cheating mate as well as on the mate poacher, who in both cases was the woman's best friend:

> *My husband cheated with my best friend, so I had an affair with her husband for three months. I did not feel guilty at all.*
> —heterosexual woman, age 44
>
> *I had sex with my ex-boyfriend whom I knew still had feelings for me even though I did not feel the same. My ex-boyfriend had begun dating my best friend and I wanted to get even with her as well as with him.*
> —heterosexual woman, age 22

Women also use sex to exact revenge on sexual partners who succumb to the temptations of a mate poacher, focusing the blame entirely on their mates rather than the poachers:

> *My partner cheated on me once so I thought if I cheated back on him that would make us even, so I went out with some friends one night and ran into a high school friend and we ended up having sex. My partner never found out but it made me feel like I got my revenge.*
>
> —heterosexual woman, age 34

And some women took special delight in using sex to get revenge:

> *My ex was an asshole to me, so when we got out of a relationship, I had sex with his friend. It was fun and I enjoyed it because I knew it would piss him off.*
>
> —heterosexual woman, age 22

> *My husband cheated on me a few years ago. I was a lot bigger after having our daughter so I felt incredibly worthless. In only six months I had lost my weight and cheated on him with his best friend just so I could get the same satisfaction that he did when he cheated on me.*
>
> —predominantly heterosexual woman, age 27

The fact that many instances of sex for revenge involve sleeping with a former partner's best friend highlights the delight and relish with which the vengeance is taken—in this case, retribution for allowing a mate poacher to succeed. It exemplifies one of the many facets of sexual competition—rivalry with other women for desirable sex partners, struggles to attract desirable committed mates, antagonism toward imaginary rivals from visual media, and the insidious threat of sexual interlopers. Because problems of sexual competition have occurred repeatedly over human history, evolution has fashioned powerful defenses that help women to combat them. One defense comes in the form of a much maligned emotion—sexual jealousy—a topic to which we now turn.

5. Green-Eyed Desire

From Guarding a Mate to Trading Up

☙❧

Think'st thou I'd make a life of jealousy,
To follow still the changes of the moon
With fresh suspicions? No; to be once in doubt,
Is once to be resolved.

—*Othello*, William Shakespeare

Sexual competition revolves around *rivals*, which in its Latin derivation means using (or trying to use) the same river as another—and in the Roman empire, a river was an essential resource to be guarded at great cost, the most efficient means of transportation, communication, and trade, and a source for irrigation, hygiene, and general sustenance. Likewise, women use sex to achieve a variety of psychological, physical, and evolutionary ends, sometimes engaging rivals in sexual competition over the same desirable partner.

In this chapter, we're going to look at what happens when rivalry turns defensive, and jealousy—and provoking jealousy in a mate—enters a woman's sexual motivations. As one woman in our study put it:

> *I had been sleeping with someone (and not dating them) for more than six months. My partner, his best friend, and I were drinking together one night. My partner fell asleep and his best friend "seduced" me. I decided I would have sex with him to make my partner realize that other people wanted me.*
>
> —heterosexual woman, age 19

The Puzzle of Jealousy

Understanding why sexual jealousy exists has perplexed social scientists for decades. The traditional and long-held view is that jealousy is an immature emotion, a character defect, and a sign of low self-esteem. In the early 1930s, the well-known anthropologist Margaret Mead posited that jealousy is little more than wounded pride: "Jealousy is not a barometer by which depth of love can be read. It merely records the degree of the lover's insecurity . . . it is a negative, miserable state of feeling, having its origin in the sense of insecurity and inferiority." Other researchers have joined her in contending that jealousy is primarily fueled by damaged self-esteem and the fear of loss or violation to one's "property." Those who endorse this view typically believe jealousy is largely a product of culture, and consequently varies greatly from culture to culture.

At the other end of the spectrum, evolutionary psychologists have proposed that sexual jealousy is a highly functional adaptation. Jealousy, according to this view, is an evolved emotion that gets triggered when there is a threat to a valued relationship. In romantic relationships, threats can come from outside the relationship, as when a mate poacher sexually hits on your partner or attempts to lure your partner away from the relationship. Threats can come when a partner signals cues to sexual infidelity or expresses signs of leaving the relationship. And threats can come from the dynamics of the relationship itself, as when an argument creates a rift that breaks down trust, or when one partner's life circumstances change to create a discrepancy in desirability. Jealousy functions, then, to alert a person to a threat; to devote attention to the sources of the threat; and ultimately to motivate action to ward off the threat.

In general, the more insecure a person is, the more dependent he or she is on a partner. The more threatened their relationship is, the more intense the feelings of jealousy. Consistent with this account, several women in our study wrote about having sex out of jealous feelings, mentioning that low self-esteem played a role in their decision:

> I was dating someone and they had just broken up with me. I was very upset and felt rejected and like my self-esteem had been hurt.

Perhaps a week later I went on a blind date and had sex, and told the girl I had been dating about it (we were still friends) hoping to make her jealous. I didn't find the woman I had sex with to make her jealous [to be] attractive and would not have had sex with her if I had not felt I had something to prove.

—gay/lesbian woman, age 21

It's not something I feel comfortable talking about, and definitely not something I'm proud of. But in the past, when I've just gotten out of a relationship and my self-esteem is at a low point, I've had sex thinking about the person I used to be with in the relationship. It's like, "what would they think if they could see me, wouldn't they be jealous, wouldn't they wish we were still together?" It's a pretty pathetic line of thought, and it shows I'm obviously not over the other person.

—heterosexual woman, age 19

What triggers jealousy and how people respond to it show some similarity and some difference across cultures. In one study, researchers interviewed more than two thousand college students from seven countries—the United States, Ireland, Mexico, Hungary, the Netherlands, the former Soviet Union, and the former Yugoslavia—about how they would feel viewing their sexual partner engaging in a variety of acts with another person. They were asked to contemplate relationship transgressions including flirting, kissing, dancing, hugging, having sex, and engaging in sexual fantasies. Some behaviors—flirting, kissing, and having sex—elicited intense jealousy among all cultures, while others—dancing, hugging, and sexual fantasies—generally triggered weaker emotional reactions in all cultures.

There were, however, some interesting cultural differences in what evoked jealousy. For example, while Americans were not terribly bothered by a partner hugging someone else, Hungarians got their feathers seriously ruffled when thinking about it. Slovaks expressed intense jealousy over flirting but were the least of all groups to be upset by a partner's sexual fantasies or kissing someone else. The Dutch apparently take kissing, hugging, and dancing in stride, but a partner who fantasizes sexually about another person sets off alarms. Compared to the other countries surveyed, dancing with another person was most upsetting to people from the Soviet Union.

Cross-cultural studies of jealousy have shown that sexual infidelity is most likely to be viewed as threatening under certain conditions: 1) if the marriage is required for companionship, status, or survival; 2) if sex is hard to attain outside of marriage; 3) if property is privately owned; and 4) if having children is highly valued. The situations of two tribes described by psychologist Elaine Hatfield illustrate how these conditions have played out in the world. Among the Ammassalik Eskimos, everything required to survive—food, clothing, shelter, and tools—had to be produced. They were completely self-sufficient and depended on one another, and especially on a competent mate, to survive. The Ammassalik Eskimos were also known for their extreme jealousy—not surprising, given that a sexual rival could mean a threat to their survival. In stark contrast to the Ammassalik tribe, the Toda tribe of India practiced a clan economy whereby private property did not exist, clan members shared tasks, and sex was abundantly available. The Toda considered marriage a luxury, not a necessity, and the most common form of marriage was something called "fraternal polyandry," meaning that when a woman married, she became the wife of all of her husband's brothers.

A study of twenty-five thousand people from a variety of ethnic groups in the United States found most people responded to pangs of jealousy in similar ways. They were obsessed with painful thoughts of their loved ones being with someone else, and they sought out evidence of their fears—listening in on their loved ones' telephone conversations, following them, and snooping through their personal belongings in search of names or telephone numbers of potential rivals.

Although some of the jealous behaviors seem irrational, evidence suggests that they have an underlying adaptive logic. Consider the following case:

> One Christmas Eve, a man looked across the street and thought that he observed the neighbor's window lights flashing in syn-

chrony with the lights of the Christmas tree in his own house. He concluded with utter certainty that his wife was having an affair. When brought to counseling by his wife, the man was declared to be "delusional" and to suffer from pathological jealousy.

Certainly, there was an irrational component to the man's jealousy: The Christmas tree lights weren't synchronized. But the husband turned out to be correct in his suspicions! His wife was indeed having a torrid love affair, and was even having it with the neighbor he suspected. Some psychologists propose that jealousy reflects *emotional wisdom*, which gets activated when there is a genuine or possible threat to a romantic relationship. Jealousy flares not just by immediate threats, but also by threats lurking on the horizon of a relationship, such as the observation that one's partner just doesn't seem to want to have sex anymore.

Because infidelity and betrayal are often cloaked in great secrecy, their detection often must be based on cues that are only probabilistically related to betrayal. Like a smoke alarm that goes off when there is no fire, people who incline toward jealousy make what psychologist Paul Ekman calls "Othello's error." In his book *Emotions Revealed*, Ekman recalls the story of Othello and Desdemona, as told in Shakespeare's play. When Othello demands that Desdemona confess to her adultery and betrayal, she asks that he have his presumed rival, Cassio, stand as witness to her fidelity. Othello then reveals that he has killed Cassio. This throws Desdemona into a fit of grief—and Othello assumes that she is weeping over her dead lover. According to Ekman, "Othello's mistake was not a failure to recognize how Desdemona felt; he knew she was anguished and afraid. His error was in believing that emotions only have one source, in interpreting her anguish as due to the news of her supposed lover's death, and her fear as that of an unfaithful wife who has been caught in her betrayal. He kills her without considering that her anguish and fear could have different sources: that they were the reactions of an innocent woman who knew her intensely jealous husband was about to kill her, and that there was no way she could prove her innocence."

The most extreme response to jealousy is seriously punishing or murdering the partner—the flip side of the revenge exacted (or pined for) against rivals that we considered in the previous chapter. It is far more common for men to abuse or kill women out of jealousy than vice versa. Statistics from women's shelters indicate that about two-thirds of women who seek shelter do so because their partner's excessive jealousy had led to assault. Indeed, male jealousy is the leading cause of wife battering and homicide worldwide.

Individuals differ in how they cope with their jealous feelings. Some turn a blind eye, some try to figure out what it was about themselves that led their partner astray and try to change those things, and some try to eliminate the rival in less violent ways. In our study, jealousy led a number of women to use sex in an attempt to eliminate a rival:

> [My] ex was talking to this girl who annoyed me and I really disliked. When the opportunity arose to have sex with him, I took it. I knew he'd tell her and the thought made me happy.
>
> —heterosexual woman, age 24

> [My] ex-boyfriend had slept with another girl and I slept with him again and it seems that part of my reason for doing this might have been in hopes of making that other girl jealous.
>
> —predominantly heterosexual woman, age 20

Chastened by Force

Another response to jealousy involves trying to control a loved one's behavior. Historically, it was almost always men who used this tactic. In medieval times, the nobility locked their wives up with chastity belts to ensure their fidelity. Today, many cultures practice what is referred to as female circumcision or female genital mutilation. Experts estimate that between 80 and 120 million women worldwide have been subjected to some form of cutting of their external genitals during childhood or at puberty. The practice is currently prevalent in twenty-nine countries, most in Africa, but it is also practiced in the Middle East, Indonesia, and elsewhere. Female genital mutilation is particularly associated with Islamic cultures, and although it is not prescribed in the Qur'an, it is referred to favorably in later Islamic texts and is often perceived to have religious significance.

There are three main types of female genital mutilation. *Sunnah* (an Arabic word referring to a traditional religious obligation) is the least invasive form and involves having the clitoral hood incised or removed. Clitoridectomy, a second type, involves having the entire clitoral gland and shaft removed, along with the hood and sometimes nearby portions of the inner labia. Infibulation, which is widely practiced in the Sudan, is the most invasive form of female circumcision. The procedure includes having a clitoridectomy performed but also involves removal of the entire inner labia and the interior parts of the outer labia. The cut or abraded edges of the two outer labia are then stitched together, leaving only a small opening for the passage of urine and menstrual blood. The opening has to be enlarged when the woman first has intercourse, and is often subsequently restitched.

Some cultures that subscribe to these practices believe that a woman who retains her clitoris is ritually unclean or dangerous to the health of a man who has sex with her. The likely underlying aim of the practice, however, is to reduce female sexual desire and activity, especially outside of or before marriage. Removing the clitoris decreases the pleasure of sexual acts, while infibulation makes penetration physically impossible and any kind of genital contact uncomfortable. In many cultures that practice female circumcision, a woman who has not undergone the procedure is not marriageable.

The long-term effects of female circumcision are controversial, especially around infibulation, which can cause serious problems with urination, menstruation, intercourse, childbirth, and fertility. The degree to which the less severe forms impact a woman's ability to have an orgasm or receive sexual pleasure are unclear, given that the practice is generally done before a woman has had any sexual experiences with which to compare the impact of circumcision. Some research indicates that the ability to attain orgasm is not necessarily lost with having only the clitoral hood, or possibly even portions of the clitoral gland, removed. But that is not true of infibulation, where there is often nerve damage that impairs a woman's ability to have an orgasm or even experience physical sexual arousal. Recently, scientists have attempted to surgically replace or repair nerves damaged with this surgery and have shown promise in being able to improve women's sexual pleasure. In the United States, female circumcision was made illegal in 1996. Some African governments have recently banned or strictly limited the practice, although these bans have not had much impact to date.

Given these wide-ranging and serious consequences of provoking jealousy, it seems at first blush strange that some women would have sex intentionally to raise the "green-eyed monster." But they do.

Provoking Jealousy

There is a saying that goes, "whatever you won't do, some other sister is dying to." Dating cheaters teaches you what most people think but won't admit. If your partner is sexually satisfied, the likelihood of him cheating is lessened (this is of course unless he is a big fat cheater, in which case he will cheat no matter what).

—heterosexual woman, age 28

All is fair in love and war, and the intentional evocation of jealousy in a partner is a perfect illustration. In fact, women report evoking jealousy in partners more than men do—31 percent versus 17 percent, according to one study—and use several tactics, all involving sexual behavior.

The most common tactic women use to provoke jealousy is casually mentioning how attractive other men find them—dropping into conversation that a man made a pass, brushed up against them, or asked for a phone number. Another tactic involves flirting with another man in the partner's presence. Sometimes a mere smile will do. Here, gender makes a difference, because men often interpret a woman's smiles as signalling sexual interest, an invitation to approach, and men often act on these perceived signals. Some women evoke jealousy by dancing sensuously with another person in her partner's presence. Others talk about past relationships. Men (and women) sometimes suppress their emotions when this happens. People conceal their jealousy so that they don't appear threatened, covering up an emotion that might betray genuine feelings of insecurity about the relationship. But often they seethe with jealousy inside.

Why would women intentionally evoke jealousy, given that it is a dangerous emotion, known to be linked to physical violence and even murder? One clue comes from the circumstances in which women use the tactic. Although many couples are equally committed to each other, a substantial minority—39 percent according to one study—exhibit an involvement imbalance in which one partner is more committed to the relationship than the other. Within this group, when the man is the more committed partner, only 26 percent of women report intentionally evoking jealousy. In sharp contrast, when the woman is more committed to the relationship, 50 percent of the women resort to jealousy evocation.

Women's strategic provocation of a partner's jealousy serves three functions. First, it increases her partner's perception of her desirability. The sexual interest of others is a gauge of a partner's overall mate value. Second, a partner's response to a jealousy-triggering situation provides a litmus test of the level of his or her commitment. For example, if a man is indifferent when his partner sits seductively in another man's lap, it may signal a lack of allegiance, and the level of his jealousy can be a signal of the depth of his emotional dedication to the relationship. Perhaps most important is the third function—to *increase* a partner's commitment. This is especially true among men, who are much more likely to commit to a woman whom they perceive to be highly desired by other men. A jealous man becomes more smitten, comes to believe that he is lucky to be with his partner, and so doubles his dedication.

Desperate Measures

Rather than merely activating a man's sexual interest, some women have sex with a stranger in an attempt to increase their partner's perceptions of their desirability. Several women wrote about situations where they used jealousy evocation tactics. In most cases, it did not achieve what they had hoped:

I was in love with someone of the same sex and it was not reciprocated, so I had sex with someone of the opposite sex to try to make her jealous . . . it did not work.

—bisexual woman, age 27

When I was twenty, my boyfriend of two years and I broke up. He had fooled around with another girl. So I then slept with his fraternity brother—one of his best friends. I told myself that it was to hurt my ex, but in reality, I did it because I wanted him to be jealous and want me back. That backfired, of course. He not only didn't want me back, but all the guys in the fraternity had a very low opinion of me, including the guy I slept with (sort of a double standard there).

—predominantly heterosexual woman, age 28

One woman described how trying to evoke a partner's jealousy ended badly:

My boyfriend and I broke up, and to make him jealous, I slept with one of his friends at a party shortly thereafter. I was intoxicated, deeply hurt, and his friend was obviously attracted to me. Long story short, we slept together, and it was horrible. I felt awful about it, and my ex was devastated. A line was crossed that night, and it's never been the same since between my ex and [me]. We're still involved in each other's lives, but he has absolutely no trust in me whatsoever and I just wish I had never done what I did.

—heterosexual woman, age 22

And sometimes the tactic backfires and ends the relationship altogether:

I was disappointed with a relationship at that time. I decided to make my partner jealous so that I would be treated better, I guess. But the relationship ended instantly. I decided it was not worth playing games anymore.

—predominantly heterosexual woman, age 23

One main reason that the tactic of having sex with others fails to increase commitment is that people usually desire sexual fidelity in a long-term mate. Studies from the Buss Evolutionary Psychology Lab show that women rank "sexual fidelity" as the second-most valued trait in a long-term mate, right after the most valued (but obviously related) trait of "honesty." Men in the past who were indifferent to their partners' having sex with other men are not our evolutionary ancestors. Modern men are descendants of men who prized sexual fidelity, reserved their commitment for women who demonstrated fidelity (or enforced a demonstration of fidelity on them), and cut their losses with women who did not. Many women are fully aware of this dynamic—which may be why there is still more emphasis on maintaining sexual reputation, and sullying the reputations of rivals, among women than among men. Evoking jealousy through sex with external partners can jeopardize the often fragile bond of long-term mating.

Occasionally, however, there are no negative repercussions. Sometimes it can fulfill a desire:

> *I wanted to make the other person jealous so they'd do what I wanted them to do, so I slept with someone else. The guy I slept with was someone I wanted to screw anyway, so it worked out nicely, for me at least.*
>
> —predominantly heterosexual woman, age 25

Jealousy evocation through flirting can be an effective tactic for increasing a partner's perceptions of desirability and consequently increasing commitment. When women have sex to evoke jealousy, however, it usually is an unsuccessful effort to correct a commitment imbalance—and fails more often than not.

Mate Guarding

My mother taught me to please my man or someone else will.

—heterosexual woman, age 37

Many times, in most of my long term relationships, I have had sex because I felt that to go for too long without sex would risk having my partner leave or go somewhere else for sex.

—heterosexual woman, age 33

Mate guarding refers to a range of strategies, from vigilance to violence, designed to retain a partner. Having sex as a means of defending a relationship is one mate-guarding tactic. Women say they have sex because they want to keep their partners from straying and hope to decrease their partners' desire to have sex with someone else. One woman in our study described how worried she was about the threat of mate poachers:

[I] had an ex-boyfriend that thought he was "in love" with another woman online—never even saw a picture of her, but when they talked online he lived a fantasy, so I always tried to do anything sexual to win over this fantasy woman that would tell him anything he wanted to hear, and that said she would fulfill all his fantasies. I was in a competition with someone who never actually materialized. It was all a game to her, but not to him, so I always had the thought about him comparing me to this "fantasy" and tried to outdo it all the time.

—heterosexual woman, age 41

Nor is sexual mate guarding limited to Western cultures. Among the Muria, a group residing in the Bastar region of central India, women are particularly concerned about their husbands' straying early in the marriage: "Wives are never happy about their husbands' visits to the *ghotul* [a sort of mixed-sex lodge for young people in which sex is common] . . . and may insist on having intercourse before their husbands leave the house, hoping to reduce the temptations that the *ghotul* offers."

Having sex works as a mate-guarding strategy among women for two key reasons. First, it may help to keep a romantic partner sexually satisfied and sexually faithful, in both short-term and long-term relationships. As one woman noted:

I recently found out that my husband was looking into an online dating site on our computer. We had just had a new baby and everything was really crazy. We had not had sex in over nine months. (I had a very difficult pregnancy and was not allowed to have sex for some time.) I asked him about it. We fought about it. The best answer he gave me was that he was bored. I felt responsible for this so I had sex with him so he would not try to find it somewhere else.

—heterosexual woman, age 27

Second, it can serve to broadcast a woman's sex life with her partner to others in her social circle, providing a clear signal to would-be mate poachers to stay away.

Mate-guarding strategies have been documented in a variety of species, from insects to mammals. Usually, but not always, males do the mate guarding. For example, in the veliid water strider, males ride on the backs of their mates for hours, even when they're not copulating, to prevent other sneaky water striders from stealing their mates. Unlike most insects and other mammals, humans generally form enduring partnerships that last years, decades, or lifetimes. Consequently, both women and men are faced with the challenge of how to "hang on to" their mates.

As a highly social species, we are constantly threatened by potential mate poachers who try to lure our partners, be it for brief sexual encounters or for a more permanent relationship. We also face the risk that our partners might be tempted to leave the relationship in hopes of "trading up" to a more desirable partner. Among both dating and married couples, the Buss Lab's research has revealed findings similar to those in our study: Women often use sex in many different ways to protect their relationships. They give in to their partners' sexual requests in an attempt to keep them happy, they act "sexy" to take their partners' mind off potential competitors, and they perform sexual favors or succumb to sexual pressures to entice their partners into staying. Sometimes these strategies achieve the desired function:

My husband always seems happier with [me] after we have sex when I initiate it. He spends more time with me, and doesn't seem to gawk at other women as much.

—heterosexual woman, age 30

I guess I wanted to have sex more, before we broke up (I was a virgin at the time and we'd been going out for six months and I tend not to have the same partner for that long). So I thought I should do it actually after we'd broken up . . . so we did . . . and it somehow had the miraculous power of fixing the relationship. That sounds kind of horrible, doesn't it? Like what kind of people are that shallow. . . . But weird, we start having sex and he starts getting way more invested in me, and acting how he should and being more protective and initiating things and so on. So maybe on a subconscious level it was to prevent the breakup from continuing as much as it was to just do it for the sake of not being a virgin anymore. Either way, it worked.

—heterosexual woman, age 24

But sexual mate-guarding tactics can also fail:

I thought at the time that I found the man of my dreams. That if I gave him sex, he would want only me. Little did I know that I wasn't the only one giving him sex. It was not worth the hassle of trying to keep the man.

—heterosexual woman, age 37

I was young and stupid and thought sex would keep my boyfriend around. I was seventeen years old and it didn't work. It pissed me off and taught me a lesson.

—heterosexual woman, age 40

Sometimes, having sex with someone else serves to lure a man back into the relationship, at least for a period of time, as illustrated by the following case:

My husband had an affair and his girlfriend called me to tell me the details so I joined a gym to get back in shape for him. Instead I met

a handsome, "macho" construction worker and began to see him so that my husband would leave his girlfriend. It worked and that is our pattern for the last thirty years. Sad and pathetic, I know.
    —heterosexual woman, age 50

Some women who engage in "threesomes," the most common among two women and one man, are motivated by mate guarding, as exemplified in the experiences of these women in our study:

My boyfriend . . . had always wanted to have a threesome with me and this other girl, and I had always said no. I did not want it to affect our relationship. Well, the other girl was at the same party and we started talking and kissing all over each other, right in front of him. Then me and the other girl went to an empty room and had sex.
    —heterosexual woman, age 22

Right now, the guy I am with is into swinging. I am not comfortable with that lifestyle, but I love him, so I do it for him. We go to a swing club, and we have sex with other people because it turns him on. It makes him happy, so I do it for him. I just pretend he is my master and I am to follow his every command and it makes it easier for me to get through the night that way. I would never do it on my own. He keeps asking me to have a threesome with my best friend and I keep acting like it is okay, but I am dreading it. I just don't want to have to face her in the morning and pretend like it didn't happen.
    —heterosexual woman, age 32

Of course, threesomes undoubtedly can have other motivations, such as adventure seeking or experimentation, which we explore in chapter 7. But for some women, threesomes and related sexual activities such as swinging and polyamory (the open practice of having more than one sexually and emotionally intimate relationship at one time) are attempts to make their partners happy—and to hold on to them.

Women are motivated to have sex to mate guard because the costs of not doing so can be catastrophic. A woman who fails at mate guarding can lose the support provided by her mate, whether it be material or emotional. A woman whose mate cheats may be at risk of contracting a sexually transmitted disease, passed from her partner's lover to her mate and then to her. She can suffer embarrassment, humiliation, and reputational damage if she is "dumped" for another. Having sex, even though it does not always work as planned, is partly designed to prevent infidelity and keep a couple from breaking up.

Trading Up

Many people believe affairs are morally wrong, and sexual infidelity often can be extremely destructive to the individuals as well as to the couple's commitment. An act of infidelity causes much psychological anguish, a mix of emotions including jealousy, sadness, depression, anger, and a profound sense of humiliation. Sexual infidelity is a key cause of spouse abuse. It sometimes triggers homicidal rages. And in a study of eighty-nine cultures conducted by evolutionary anthropologist Laura Betzig, it proved to be the second leading cause of divorce, exceeded only by infertility.

Despite the damage infidelity causes, when a woman has sex with a partner other than her primary partner, her decision is driven, in part, by a collection of underlying benefits. It may seem strange to speak of "benefits" when it comes to infidelity, but bear with us. First, sex with another partner provides a person with valuable information about his or her own desirability on the mating "market"—information critical to a decision whether to stay in a relationship or leave. If the affair partner is highly desirable, that tells the person that he or she is desirable, too.

As one woman in our study said:

> I felt like if he was moving on and sleeping with other people, I had to do the same, just to keep myself from getting hurt. Not only was it to keep up with what he was doing (to keep a level playing field, I guess) but also for reinforcement for me [against] my insecurity. If I felt that he didn't find me attractive, or wanted something else, I needed to have sex with other people to prove to myself that I still was attractive and desirable.
>
> —heterosexual woman, age 19

If the affair partner finds the woman sexually skilled and satisfying, it reveals that she should not evaluate her mate value based on unsatisfying marital sex. The affair partner also can provide a transitional relationship, functioning as a safety net that ensures some measure of protection from the psychological isolation one sometimes feels when adjusting to the often dramatic changes that come from leaving a long-term relationship:

> *My partner had just indicated some incredible insecurity about our relationship, so I seduced someone else just to give myself the confidence that, if I was dumped, I would still be able to find another partner.*
>
> —bisexual woman, age 20

The affair partner might not be around forever, but the sex provides a psychological boost to ease the transition.

Sometimes the affair partner becomes the love of one's life. This is revealed by women in their stated motivations for sexual affairs. One study found that 79 percent of women who had affairs became emotionally involved with, or fell in love with, their affair partners. Although this finding may seem obvious, it is in stark contrast to the experiences of men, of whom only about a third become emotionally enmeshed. According to one study, most men's motivations for sex outside their primary relationship are more a matter of desire for sexual variety. The importance of emotional connection for women is revealed by another key finding: Most women who have affairs are deeply unhappy with their marriages. Again, although this may seem obvious, it is not true of men. Men who have affairs do not differ from men who remain faithful in terms of their level of marital happiness! Whereas only 34 percent of women who have affairs report that their marriages are happy or very happy, a full 56 percent of men who have extramarital sex consider their marriages to be happy or very happy.

The fact is that roughly a third of all married women in Western cultures will have an affair at some point during the course of their marriage. There is a hidden evolutionary logic behind many pursued affairs.

By providing women with valuable information about their sexual desirability, affairs enhance self-esteem, often provide a beneficial transitional relationship, and sometimes allow a woman to forge a new, more meaningful emotional connection, enabling her to trade up to long-lasting love.

Studies from the Buss Lab on the motivations for sexual affairs support this. One woman said that having an affair made it easier to break up with her husband. Another mentioned that her affair made her realize that she could find someone much more compatible with her than her husband. And a third said that she had married young; her affair made it crashingly clear that she did not have to settle for a man who did not meet her standards.

Finally, by enhancing self-esteem, the flush of sexual gratification can provide a woman with the courage to leave a bad relationship. When a couple experiences sexual problems, partners often internalize them and blame themselves. As we'll see in the next chapter, the problem may actually be the product of a mismatch in sexual drives that makes sex an obligation rather than a pleasure.

6. A Sense of Duty

When Responsibility or Guilt Calls

*I am happy now that Charles calls on my bedchamber less
frequently than of old. As it is, I now endure but two calls a
week and when I hear his steps outside my door, I lie down on
my bed, close my eyes, open my legs and think of England.*

—Lady Alice Hillingdon (1857–1940)

In 1950, the humorists James Thurber and E. B. White wrote, "While
the urge to eat is a personal matter which concerns no one but the person hungry . . . the sex urge involves, for its true expression, another individual. It is this 'other individual' that causes all the trouble." We may
not entirely agree on their dining analysis (how often do members of
your family fend for themselves for food?), but they have a point when
it comes to sex. When partners differ in their sexual needs, there is significant potential for conflict.

Of course, such sexual conflicts can be resolved—or at least avoided
temporarily. Most likely, the person who wants sex will manage to talk
or pressure the other person into agreeing to it. Indeed, agreeing to have
sex in order to stop a partner's nagging was a common reason for having
sex given by the women in our study:

> *[My] husband nags about not having enough sex, so I give in and
> have sex. Such is married life.*
>
> —heterosexual woman, age 53

And one benefit of agreeing to sex was that it was often the quickest and easiest way to resolve a conflict in the relationship:

> *Sometimes, it was easier to just give in and do it when he wanted to rather than put up with listening to him whine and complain about how horny he was.*
>
> —heterosexual woman, age 29

> *I once had sex with a guy mostly to shut him up. We had had sex once before. We were going to bed at the end of a party at a friend's house—I think we were both still a bit tipsy. He started making a move on me and I said I didn't want to do anything because I had to wake up early the next morning for work, plus our friends were sleeping in the same room. But he kept bugging me, saying it wasn't too late, I still had time to sleep, no one else would wake up. I finally gave in, mostly because I figured he'd keep bothering me for another hour if I kept saying no and if I just gave in, we'd have sex for ten minutes and then I'd get to sleep.*
>
> —straight-plus woman, age 19

A second scenario for resolving differences in sexual needs is that the person not wanting sex successfully declines the other person's request. They might do so by pretending to ignore the "come-on signals," by convincing the person that it's not a good time, or by simply telling the person "no" or "later." The success of this approach obviously depends on the partner's persistence, and how determined or comfortable the person is at saying no. Overtly declining a persistent partner's request for sex is something many women find hard to do:

> *It was my first time having sex. I felt pressured to have sex because it seemed like the appropriate time in the relationship to start having sex. I didn't particularly want to, I just didn't know how to say "no" without breaking up the relationship.*
>
> —heterosexual woman, age 24

This was my first boyfriend, and it was an older man. We had been dating for a while, and he was expecting me to put out, and I knew I was supposed to but I really didn't want to for some reason. But I didn't know what that reason was, and I couldn't think of a good excuse, so I was unable to say "no." I also had a fear of appearing inexperienced or being perceived as a "goody-goody." . . . It took me eight years of dating him (and bad sex!) for me to figure [it] out.

—heterosexual woman, age 31

The third potential scenario, which is the topic of this chapter, is that the person not wanting to have sex recognizes their partner's desire and willingly complies.

What are the motives for, and consequences of, agreeing to unwanted sex? In this chapter, we address these questions and discuss in detail what causes mismatches in sex drive—the reason that propels many women to willingly agree to unwanted sex.

Mismatched Sex Drives

Sometimes mismatches in the desire to have sex arise because a person fears pregnancy, dislikes the sexual activity being suggested, or believes it is too early in the relationship to have sex. In heterosexual relationships it is more often the man wanting to have sex earlier than the woman. One study found that college women, compared to college men, expected to date about twice as long before engaging in sexual intercourse for the first time.

In long-term relationships, couples most often disagree about whether to have sex when the partners have mismatched levels of sexual desire. It is rare for both to always to agree on when they want to have sex. As one woman explained:

I'm married, and when you're married, you've got two people with different sexual needs and schedules. It's fairly common for one of us to want sex when the other doesn't, and I regularly have sex because I know he wants it but I'm not particularly interested.

—heterosexual woman, age 27

For some women, a lack of interest in having sex was more the norm than the exception:

> *My sex drive has been really pathetic so sometimes I push myself to have sex now and then even though I'm almost never in the mood.*
> —predominantly homosexual woman, age 27

Most clinicians would probably agree that it is wise to select a mate who has sexual needs similar to one's own. If both desire sex only once every few months, then they are well matched in terms of sexual drive and it is unlikely to become a stressor in their relationship. In fact, hypoactive sexual desire disorder—the term for clinically low sex drive—is only diagnosable if it causes distress. If one partner has chronically higher desire than the other, however, then conflicts and concessions are likely to unfold.

Sometimes couples are fooled into thinking they have compatible sexual needs during the "infatuation" stage of their relationship. This is the period when a couple discovers their attraction to each other and can barely eat, sleep, or think of anything but the loved one. The anticipation of sex can become overwhelming, and the novelty of discovering each other's sexuality is thrilling. The result is insatiable sexual appetites that often disguise their "real" levels of desire. After a few weeks or months, some people welcome the start of the calmer "attachment" phase, which involves a deeper sense of connection and commitment. After all, spending months or years walking around like a lovesick puppy is not conducive to solving many problems of life, let alone survival.

What often comes as a shock, though, is the realization that while they were both well-matched "sex-starved maniacs" when the relationship began, they actually have very different sexual needs in the long-term relationship. By then, it is often too late—they are bonded. And along with the bonding comes a mismatch of sexual desires:

> *I have only slept with one person (my current boyfriend of a few years). After a while, the initial spark went away, so sometimes I*

don't feel "in the mood" when he does. I feel sometimes that it's my
duty to make him as happy as I can, so sometimes I have sex when
I don't necessarily want to.

—heterosexual woman, age 20

Some people are, in a sense, addicted to the infatuation stage. They have unrealistic expectations that the feelings of newness and excitement will last forever. When the spark and excitement start to fade, so does their desire for having sex. There begins another mismatch in desire.

Men Versus Women

The popular conception is that in heterosexual relationships, the woman always ends up desiring less sex than the man. Not true. It is not *always* the woman who wants less sex. There are plenty of couples who show up for therapy because the woman has sexual needs that are not being fulfilled or because she desires sex—just not with her current partner. What is true, however, is that men generally report desiring more sex than do women, and more women than men report a lack of interest in sex.

Studies consistently show that men report higher levels of sex drive than women. This holds true for college students, middle-aged people, and even eighty- and ninety-year-olds. Men are also much more likely than women to say they want more sex than they are currently getting, whether measured among married persons or couples in the early stages of dating. In a study of 1,410 American men and 1,749 American women, 32 percent of women between the ages of eighteen and twenty-nine reported a lack of sexual interest in the previous year, compared to 14 percent of men in the same age group. Although these statistics are higher than the number of clinically diagnosed cases of hypoactive sexual desire disorder among women in the United States, they are consistent with the fact that desire problems stand out as the number one sexual complaint reported by women.

There have been several explanations offered for why men report higher sex drives than women. The most common reason given is that men's high levels of androgens and other hormones are responsible. But there are other possibilities as well. Men and women are socialized very differently when it comes to sex. Traditional sex roles dictate that it is the man who initiates sex, not the woman. So there may be situations where women desire sex but are reluctant to seek it out or ask for it. Men are also often cast as being ever-desirous and ready to have sex. This could actually propel some men to act consistently with these expectations. In other words, some men may aggressively seek sex because they believe that is what successful men are supposed to do.

While it is generally accepted, if not encouraged, for men to engage in sexual exploration once they hit puberty, women are warned of the perilous consequences of sexual curiosity. This fits well with an evolutionary explanation for why men might desire sex more than women. One cardinal feature of women's evolved sexual strategy is the exercise of sexual choice, both in partner quality and in the timing of when sex occurs. According to evolutionary anthropologist Donald Symons, a ferociously high sex drive would interfere with women's mate choices, leading them into untimely sex, sex with inappropriate partners, or sexual infidelities that could jeopardize their primary relationship. On the other hand, a high sex drive in men has been favored by evolutionary selection. It propels them into reproductively beneficial sexual encounters, since a man's reproductive success historically has been more closely linked to the number of fertile women he could inseminate.

Anatomical differences between men's and women's genitals also can impact differences in desire. When men become aroused, their erections provide very visible and direct feedback that prompts an urgent desire for sex. This can happen even when they do not initially seek sex. Nightly erections often occur during REM, or rapid-eye-movement, sleep, the period of the sleep cycle when brain waves slow down and people dream. Men also get erections from accidentally brushing their penises with clothing or in the shower—without the need for conscious sexual thought. The feedback they receive from having an erection, though, can easily change a nonsexual event into a sexual one. Women, on the other hand, receive very little feedback from their genitals when they first start to become aroused. Thus, genital arousal cues do not trigger women to want sex as frequently or in the same way as they do for men.

For men, sexual thoughts, images, or fantasies can also cause erections that can make them want to have sex. Sexual fantasies can also make women want to have sex. Many studies find that women report less frequent sexual fantasies than men, although estimates vary from study to study. In men, estimates range from five sexual fantasies per day to one per day. In women, estimates range from three per day to less than once per month. Interestingly, when sexually compulsive men are treated with drugs that decrease testosterone levels, they report lowered levels of sexual thoughts and fantasies. So perhaps higher testosterone levels cause men to fantasize and think about sex more than women. To the extent that sexual thoughts and fantasies create the desire to have sex, women have fewer of these sexual desire triggers than men.

The Killjoys

While some couples start out with different levels of sexual desire, others are compatible in their levels of desire for long periods of time until something happens to diminish one partner's drive. One woman in our study described it matter-of-factly:

> *Having been with my previous boyfriend for three years, our sex life declined due to my disinterest. At times his discontent with the situation was so overwhelming and disruptive to the rest of our lives that I would feign interest and have sex with him just to make him happy, in part because I felt I wasn't holding up my end of the relationship sexually.*
>
> —heterosexual woman, age 21

Many factors can contribute to low sexual desire in a woman. Some are short-term and contextual, such as feeling too tired after work or child care or not having the privacy to feel comfortable having sex. Others are more enduring and can lead to relationship distress. These include biological causes, such as changes in hormones, pregnancy, medications, or health, and relationship factors, such as decreased attraction to a partner, sexual boredom or frustration, and conflict with a partner. Let's first consider the biological causes.

There are three major categories of "sex hormones": progesterone, estrogen (which comes in three different varieties—estriol, estradiol, and estrone), and the androgens (of which testosterone is the most important). Progesterone is primarily known for its role in pregnancy. It is responsible for "building the nest" by preparing the lining of the uterus for implantation of the fertilized egg. Studies have not shown progesterone to play an important role in women's sex drive, although high levels cause the symptoms of PMS, or premenstrual syndrome—a common desire killer.

Estrogen and testosterone, on the other hand, are critical for women's sexual interest. Estrogen, in addition to protecting the bones and heart (and presumably helping women to remember where they put their keys), is responsible for the vaginal lubrication that occurs when a woman feels sexually aroused. It also helps "plump up" and maintain women's genital tissues. Without estrogen, vaginal intercourse and stimulation of sensitive erogenous zones such as the nipples and clitoris would be painful.

Testosterone, generally considered the "male hormone," might actually play the most important hormonal role in women's sex drive. Like estrogen and progesterone, women's testosterone is produced primarily by the ovaries and a smaller portion by the adrenal glands. According to medical laboratories, the "normal" range of free testosterone for women aged eighteen to forty-six is anywhere from 1.3 to 6.8 picograms—that is, 1.3 to 6.8 *trillionths* of a gram—per milliliter. That's obviously very little, and just by comparison, beginning at puberty the male testes produce somewhere between 300 and 1,000 picograms per milliliter daily.

Testosterone levels decline naturally year by year in women starting around age twenty. But the biggest drop in testosterone occurs around the time a woman undergoes menopause, usually when a woman is in her mid-forties to fifties, and her ovaries dramatically decrease hormone production. It is generally believed that a woman's testosterone levels decrease by about 50 percent between the ages of twenty and fifty. If a woman has a total hysterectomy that includes having both ovaries re-moved, regardless of her age, testosterone production is dramatically decreased. As one woman in our study noted, this can negatively im-pact drive:

> *After thirty-two years, it's hard to think of a single instance [of having sex when I wanted to]. I think it just happens in long-term relationships. In my case, a hysterectomy lowered my libido. There were times when I did not feel like having sex, but just did it for my husband. It was frustrating not to want to do it, and depressing when I did it because it was not fulfilling for me. However, I felt guilty for not having sex as often and wanted to please my hus-band, so there you have it.*
>
> —heterosexual woman, age 52

There is no doubt that a certain amount of testosterone is required for women to experience sexual desire. A lack of testosterone negatively affects how frequently a woman masturbates, fantasizes about sex, and desires sexual activity. Women who lack sufficient testosterone may also lack sensation in their nipples and clitoris, and are unable to become sexually aroused even when stimulated by someone or something that used to turn them on.

How much testosterone is enough? Unfortunately, nobody really knows. The link between testosterone levels and women's sex drive is not straightforward. Although labs give ranges of what is "normal," women vary a lot in how much testosterone they need to feel good. For example, two thirty-five-year-old women could have exactly the same levels of testosterone and one could experience a healthy sex drive while the other complains of diminished desire. This may be re-lated to what the women's testosterone levels were in their late teens compared to their current levels. Adding to the confusion, there are many women who complain of a lack of sexual desire and have per-fectly normal testosterone levels, and there are many women who have low testosterone but high sex drives! Sandra Leiblum, a sex re-searcher, therapist, and author of several books on women's sexuality, suggests that if a woman used to experience sexual desire and no longer does, she should have her blood levels of dihydroepiandros-terone (DHEA) and testosterone checked by her gynecologist or an endocrinologist. If the levels fall within the lowest quarter of the "nor-mal" range for her age, she recommends testosterone replacement therapy.

Testosterone is available by prescription in many forms—pills, lozenges, capsules, and, most commonly, creams that are applied to the clitoris and inner labia. There has been some convincing research that taking testosterone helps restore sexual drive in women with ab-normally low levels, and it has been especially effective for restoring drive in postmenopausal women. Testosterone is also available over-the-counter in the form of DHEA, which converts to testosterone once it is in the body. The standard recommended DHEA dose is 50 to 150 mil-ligrams per day, taken each morning. It usually takes a few months of regular use before a woman will be able to feel any changes. However, women who try DHEA as a means for boosting their testosterone lev-els should know that the production of DHEA, like that of many herbal supplements, is not regulated by the U.S. Food and Drug Administra-tion. As a result, although the bottle label may say the capsules contain a certain amount of DHEA, with some brands the actual amounts may be quite different.

It is important to keep in mind that if a woman has low desire but normal levels of testosterone, then increasing testosterone is not going to help increase her sex drive. There are also potential negative conse-quences of taking testosterone when the body already has enough of its own. Too much testosterone in a woman can put her at risk for liver damage and can lead to the development of facial hair, acne, hair loss, and even the deepening of her voice. These are not generally considered sexy changes, so unless the plan is to decrease her partner's desire to have sex with her, caution must be exercised.

Conception to Chaos

Women's sex drive can change dramatically during and following pregnancy. Some of the reasons are tied to the emotions of expecting.

These include a couple's level of excitement about the pregnancy, the severity of morning sickness or trouble with sleeping, how sexy a woman feels about her ever-expanding body, and whether the couple is worried about the baby's eye being poked by the penis (which can't happen, by the way).

A series of hormonal changes also accompany pregnancy. Estrogen and progesterone no longer fluctuate the way they do prior to conception. They are both simultaneously high to get the woman's body ready for milk production and to keep the uterine lining thick to prevent miscarriage. High levels of estrogen may make a woman feel sexually aroused and interested, but high progesterone may make her too tired and cranky to want to do anything about it.

After childbirth, a woman's sex drive is a lot more likely to decrease than increase, at least for a short time:

> *I had given birth to our son a few months prior and still did not have any sexual drive. We had not had sex since before our son was born and I felt guilty about not being interested. So I pretended to be interested and had sex.*
>
> —heterosexual woman, age 35

This is not surprising given the lifestyle and hormonal chaos that often occurs in those first months. Most women have either vaginal soreness from childbirth or pain and tenderness from cesarean surgery. Most are exhausted from the lack of sleep associated with trying to feed and accommodate a new person into the couple's life.

Hormones once again change dramatically, impacting mood, sleep, and sex drive. With breast-feeding, levels of oxytocin increase—but most likely it is facilitating mother-child bonding rather than bonding with a sexual partner. At the same time, estrogen levels decrease. Because estrogen works with brain chemicals to maintain a sense of well-being, a drop in estrogen can dampen mood and may contribute to postpartum depression.

The oxytocin released during breast-feeding also suppresses testosterone levels, so it could negatively impact women's sex drive. From an evolutionary perspective, both the decrease in sex drive following childbirth, and the fact that the hormonal changes during breast-feeding make conception less likely, serve an important birth-spacing function. Ancestral mothers who had children too closely spaced often found their limited resources spread too thin. A temporary decrease in sexual desire helped ensure adequate spacing between children and hence a better chance that the children survived and thrived. Indeed, in traditional cultures, the typical birth spacing is about three and a half years.

How soon it takes for sex drive to return after childbirth depends on a lot of factors, not the least of which is how long it takes for a woman to feel less sleep deprived and more in control of her life:

> *Being in a relationship for any amount of time, mine being almost six years, there are times when I just don't feel like having sex. I have two children, one two years old, the other one year old, and after I had my daughter (the one-year-old) I was just so tired from being up all night feeding her and taking care of both of the kids during the day, I just wanted to go to bed and sleep, not have sex. But just because at that time my sex drive wasn't what it used to be didn't mean my fiancé's had slowed down any. He was definitely in the mood, kissing my neck, rubbing his hands gently up and down my body, caressing me, doing everything he knows I love, and I was just too tired to react the way he wanted me to, but I didn't want to hurt his feelings and I just felt it was my duty to give him sex when he wanted it, so I did.*
>
> —heterosexual woman, age 22

For a small group of mothers, their sex drive never returns to pre-pregnancy levels, often because the couple moves into parenting mode at the expense of their romantic relationship. Some women get so wrapped up in parenthood that being a mother becomes their primary or sole identity. Planning nutritious snacks for school supplants sexy lingerie and naughty whispers in bed at night. Unless these women's partners continuously remind them, years could pass before they would realize their sex lives no longer exist. When they finally do, the relationship may have become so practical that both partners have forgotten how to feel sexual desire for each other. In rare cases there may also be a physiological explanation. Some researchers believe that pregnancy can sometimes permanently impair the production of testosterone, and that, in turn, could permanently affect a women's desire to have sex.

Rx for Sexual Dissatisfaction

Pregnancy is not the only change in health that can negatively affect sex drive. Most obviously, pelvic cancers, surgeries, or traumas and vaginal and urinary tract infections can directly impair a woman's sexual desire by causing her pain during sex. But pretty much any type of illness can have a negative effect on desire by causing weakness, pain, lack of energy, or poor body image.

Many prescription drugs also impair sex drive, either by influencing the hormones or brain chemicals that directly play a role in women's sex drive, or indirectly by impairing a woman's ability to become sexually aroused and have an orgasm—both of which make sex less rewarding to her. For instance, birth control pills can decrease sex drive if they substantially lower testosterone levels. Oral contraceptives that have the active ingredient desogestrel or norgestimate are especially bad in this regard.

Antidepressants, which are used to treat depression as well as certain anxiety disorders, have long been linked to impairments in sexual functioning. An estimated 96 percent of the women who are taking selective serotonin reuptake inhibitors, or SSRIs—the most commonly prescribed class of antidepressants—experience problems with desire, arousal, orgasm, or all three. Up to one-half of women who experience sexual side effects feel that the problem is significant enough to warrant clinical attention. One woman in our study described how she had struggled with this side effect:

> *My partner has a higher sex drive than me; therefore, I sometimes feel like I should have sex to meet his needs. He doesn't make me*

*feel obligated. I feel that way because I know it is a normal part of
healthy relationships. Because I've battled some anxiety and am on
antidepressants, my drive is very low. I could go months, but that
would not be fair.*

—heterosexual woman, age 38

Antidepressants work primarily by increasing the brain chemical
serotonin, which is diminished in many depressed individuals. Animal studies show, however, that certain receptors in the brain that
"read" serotonin are also responsible for sexual behavior. If you give
those receptors too much serotonin, they suppress sexual functioning. In the past decade, great gains have been made in developing antidepressants that do not activate the brain receptors that influence
sexual behavior. As a result, many of the newer generation of antidepressants such as Serzone (nefazodone), Wellbutrin (bupropion), Celexa
(citalopram), and Remeron (mirtazapine) cause fewer deleterious
sexual side effects than those developed a decade or so ago (such as
Prozac and Paxil). Anti-anxiety medications, such as Valium, Xanax,
Ativan, and BuSpar, and antipsychotic medications, such as Haldol,
Thorazine, and Mellaril, can also negatively impact a woman's sex
drive by interfering with brain chemicals that play a role in sexual functioning.

Finally, some antihypertensive medications that are used to treat
high blood pressure, such as reserpine and clonidine, have been found
to inhibit the blood flow to women's genitals. By doing so, they impair
a woman's ability to become sexually aroused and experience orgasm.
Over-the-counter antihistamines that are used to treat allergies, including Benadryl, Atarax, and Periactin, can also negatively impact sex drive
by drying out the mucous membranes in the vagina.

Women differ in how they respond sexually to medications. In most
cases, if a medication is causing a nasty sexual side effect, there will be
other drug options that may not have the same negative effects. Sometimes the side effects go away after a few weeks, and sometimes doctors
will suggest taking a two-to-three-day "drug holiday" which may help
diminish symptoms.

Psychological Turnoffs

Most people have strong preferences for what physical types they find sexually attractive. If a partner's physical appearance changes over the course of a relationship, sexual attractiveness may be diminished in the eyes of the partner. This is just as true for women as for men.

The most common physical change that people experience as they age is weight gain. Sometimes this has no effect on levels of attraction, but for many women a partner's significant weight gain can be a sexual turnoff. The situation can be complicated, however. Because overweight partners may not feel competitive in the mating market, they may be less likely to leave the relationship or have an affair, which naturally makes the other partner feel more secure in the relationship. The partner who is not overweight may even gain some power in the relationship.

Poor hygiene is another sexual turnoff for many women. If a person is constantly sweaty, dirty, smelly, unshaven, rumpled, smells of cigarette smoke, or has bad breath, who would want to get near enough to have sex? In the "Shattered Dreams" chapter of *Eugenics and Sex Harmony*, first published in 1933, the author described the perils that changes in hygiene can have on a woman's sex drive:

> The wife's dreams of romance are shattered by the stern realities of the work-a-day world. She finds that her knight in shining armor is merely a man who has to be reminded to shave every morning. And who may not infrequently neglect to take his daily bath, unless he is forcibly reminded of this function. She may discover certain habits in him which he has carefully concealed during his courting days. She may find that he delights in smoking some particularly terrible-smelling pipe, which makes his breath almost unbearable. It may develop that he chews tobacco, and that his feet and arm pits exude a most offensive odor, which he takes little or no pains to eradicate by the proper use of formaldehyde solution, or other simple measures. In a thousand different ways her rosy dream of love may be broken into fragments.

Similarly, status and wealth are sexual attractants for many women, and if a partner's status and wealth decrease over time, so can a woman's attraction to her partner.

Less commonly, a woman's desire for sex with her partner may decrease because she realizes that she is more sexually attracted to members of a different gender than her male partner. Or perhaps she knew from the beginning that her sexual orientation was incompatible with her partner's, but was too afraid or unwilling to let it be known until well into the relationship:

> When I was married and our sex life was unfulfilling to me I felt obligated to have sex with my husband to keep him happy. I was his wife and he felt rejected and was suspicious of me having an affair because I wasn't interested in sex with him. We got married when I was only nineteen (he was twenty-seven) and I knew I found women sexually appealing and was attracted to them but when I attempted to discuss this with my husband he didn't want to hear about it. I began to resent him over time because I tried to do what was "expected" of me as his wife, but no thought was given to what I was getting out of our sex life and I don't think he even noticed that I wasn't fulfilled or satisfied. That was the beginning of a wedge driven between us and I feel it was the underlying cause of our failed marriage.
>
> —predominantly heterosexual woman, age 35

Frustrated and Bored

Being with a partner who lacks sexual skills and is unable or unwilling to learn over time can obviously become frustrating and lower the desire to have sex. Some people think that if they dive right in and start vigorously rubbing a woman's clitoris they are being the ultimate selfless lover. But for most women foreplay starts long before the actual lovemaking begins. This is humorously—but also honestly—depicted in the book *Porn for Women*. In one of the book's photo spreads, a handsome man sits at the kitchen table cradling his breakfast coffee and says to his mate, "Ooh, look, the NFL playoffs are today. I bet we'll have no trouble parking at the crafts fair." How a woman's partner treats her in general, and not just right before it's time to "do the deed," can dramatically affect her desire to have sex.

One common complaint among women who have been in long-term relationships is that sex becomes routine, predictable, and thus less enjoyable. Here is how one woman in our study experienced the duty of having sex:

> *I love my husband, but when you've been married for awhile, let's face it—sex just isn't that exciting anymore. It's all so predictable. Even when we try to be "spontaneous" it's almost comical because I can predict his every move. I have sex because I feel I "owe" it to him as his wife, and also because I love him and want to keep him happy. The truth is, though, most of the time I just lie there and make lists in my head. I grunt once in awhile so he knows I'm awake, and then I tell him how great it was when it's over. It seems to be working. We're happily married.*
>
> —heterosexual woman, age 48

Because heterosexual women are more likely to marry or enter a long-term relationship with a man older than themselves (compared to the opposite scenario), they often must adapt to the sexual and other health problems of aging mates before they are faced with the same sorts of issues. Changes in a partner's sexual functioning can decrease a woman's desire to have sex in many ways. If, for example, a partner develops premature ejaculation, whereby he ejaculates before or shortly after beginning vaginal penetration, the woman may lose interest in sex because it becomes too frustrating for her. Similarly, if a man develops problems getting or maintaining an erection, a woman's desire to have sex with him may wilt as well.

Psychologist Lorraine Dennerstein of the University of Melbourne in Australia conducted a study among a large group of middle-aged women and found that sex drive decreased with the length of their relationships. The longer the women were in a relationship, the more likely they were to experience low sex drive.

The same study measured women's sex drive before, during, and after they passed through the menopausal transition. For some women, menopause had no effect on their sex drive. For others it tended to lower their sex drive. For a small group of the women, however, sex drive increased with menopause. What caused these women's boost in sex drive? Was it a successful sex therapy they had engaged in? Did their partners change in some positive way? Did they discover new sex tricks? No, the best explanation was that the women who showed an increase in sex drive were most often the ones who had found a new sex partner.

Learning and experimenting with new techniques, watching or reading a sexually arousing story together, having sex spontaneously and at times and locations that are not the usual, or planning a romantic getaway with no demands or distractions are just a few of the techniques that can keep boredom at bay among couples who have been sexually active together for a long time.

Relationship Decay

At times, having a fight with one's partner can increase sexual arousal and help couples reconnect. But repeated fighting and squabbling wears down most couples over time, as portrayed in the country and western song by the Notorious Cherry Bombs, "It's Hard to Kiss the Lips at Night that Chew Your Ass Out All Day Long."

Often, it is hard to figure out cause versus effect—did the constant fighting cause the decreased sexual interest, or did the decreased sexual interest cause the fighting? Often, it goes both ways. Sometimes the fighting revolves not over sex per se, but over differences in the need for nonsexual intimacy. Many women describe needing to feel good about their partners and close to them in order to want to have sex with them. And feeling close may require intimate conversation or quality alone time, not just sexual foreplay.

Among lesbian couples, there is sometimes so much intimacy in the relationship that psychological "fusion" or "merging" takes place. These couples have such an intense desire to relate to each other that all personal boundaries, individuality, and separateness disappear. While this may epitomize the ideal of intimacy to some women, it often has a negative impact on women's sexual desire. Some therapists think avoiding sex becomes a way to achieve some distance that is desperately needed in the relationship. Others think that for some women, having sex is a way to achieve closeness and knock down personal barriers. In couples where there are already no barriers, sex becomes unnecessary.

Often a woman has a hard time pinpointing why she no longer desires to have sex with her partner. The change may have taken place slowly over time, perhaps due to an accumulation of too many misunderstandings, disappointments, and frustrations. One woman in our study told the story of how her lack of sexual attraction to her husband led her to wrongly conclude there was something wrong with her sexually:

> *About seven years into my marriage, I went out for dinner with a male friend of both myself and my husband. My husband stayed at home with the children. . . . This friend and I decided to attend a party [and] we stayed out really late. I was having fun and feeling reckless and free for the first time in years. On the way home, I leaned over and kissed my friend, which surprised both of us. It surprised him because I gave no previous indicator of attraction to him. And it surprised me because I never enjoyed sex with my husband and believed something was wrong with me because of my disinterest in sex. He pulled over to a secluded spot, and we made out. Although we did not have sex that night, it precipitated the sex we had weeks later, beginning an affair and the eventual dissolution of my marriage. In retrospect, I had wanted to leave an unhappy marriage even though I didn't realize it at the time. My life revolved around my children and I assumed I was sexually dysfunctional. Suddenly, that night, something awoke in me and I became a sexual being again. I realized that I did like sex . . . just not with my husband.*
>
> —heterosexual woman, age 47

When You Want to Say No but Say Yes

When a couple is mismatched in their sexual desires, it is usually, but not always, the man who desires more sex. If men have evolved a higher sex drive and are socialized to feel more comfortable initiating sex than women, then women necessarily will be presented with more opportunities to comply with unwanted sex. But do they actually *choose* to comply more frequently than men do?

Research indicates that women agree to unwanted sex more often than men do—but not by as great a margin as one might predict. One study of married couples found that 84 percent of wives and 64 percent of husbands "usually" or "always" complied with having sex when their spouse wanted to and they did not. Researcher Lucia O'Sullivan found that when encounters were measured over a two-week period, women were more likely to agree to unwanted sex than men (50 percent versus 26 percent). When they were measured over a year, however, there were no meaningful differences between men and women. Women may comply with unwanted sex more often then men do, but given enough time, virtually everyone in a sexual relationship will experience unwanted sex at least once.

In our study, three main themes emerged in the reasons women gave for why they willingly agreed to have unwanted sex: to maintain the relationship; because they felt it was their duty; and because they felt it was the "nice" thing to do. For some women, having unwanted sex to maintain the relationship meant using sex to avoid a fight:

> *I was in a long-term relationship with a partner who had a very high sex drive. I have a very low sex drive and this was a source of anger and frustration for my partner. At times, in an attempt to avoid an argument or fulfill what I felt my role in the relationship was, I would have sex when I didn't feel like it.*
>
> —heterosexual woman, age 25

> *Sometimes, as a woman you do not feel like having sex . . . either being too tired or just too busy. But, being in a married relationship*

you must put the other person's needs in front of your own at times.
So I do not know that it would be called nagging . . . but my spouse
does get crabby, frustrated, and distant . . . when he has gone a lit-
tle long without having sex. I have at times just given in to sex . . .
to keep all peace in the household. Mind you, I am always ex-
tremely glad that we did have sex after the act.

—predominantly heterosexual woman, age 32

In every long-term relationship, there are times when partners'
needs differ and sacrifices have to be made in order to maintain the relationship. Sacrifices can be simple, such as agreeing to go to a restaurant
you are not crazy about but that your partner likes, or complex, such as
agreeing to relocate to accommodate a partner's career change. Agreeing to unwanted sex can be seen as a similar form of functional relationship sacrifice.

How much a person is committed to the relationship will generally
determine how willing they are to make sacrifices. If a person views the
relationship as providing more benefits than costs, commitment is increased. If he or she has already invested a lot of time, money, resources,
and effort into the relationship, then it becomes harder to throw it all
away and end the relationship. A person's commitment is also influenced by the perception of viable mating alternatives. A person who is
afraid to be alone and does not envision desirable men or women lining
up for dates will be more committed to their relationship.

Research has not directly addressed the question of whether having unwanted sex successfully helps to maintain relationships. When
people feel their partners have made important sacrifices for them,
they become more committed. Of course, that sometimes requires
that the person *cares* that the partner is making a sacrifice. The effects
of sexual sacrifices likely depend on how discrepant the partners' sexual desires actually are, whether the sacrifices are in some way reciprocated, and whether the sacrifice is viewed as an act of generosity and
nurturing.

On the other hand, some people may not take kindly to learning
that having sex with them is viewed as a "sacrifice."

The Wifely Duty

In addition to agreeing to sex despite mismatches in drive, many women, particularly married women, had unwanted sex because they viewed it as their duty:

> *I have been married for thirty-two years. It seems only natural to me after that long of a time, that once in a while you have sex with your husband only because you feel that it is your duty.*
>
> —heterosexual woman, age 53

The idea that sex is part of the marital contract is alluded to in many religious texts. For example, the Christian Bible states in First Corinthians 7:2–3 that it is both the wife's and husband's duty to have sex with each other: "But since there is so much immorality, each man should have his own wife, and each woman her own husband. The husband should fulfill his marital duty to his wife, and likewise the wife to her husband." In Judaism, the duty is placed more on the husband pleasing his wife sexually than vice versa. The Talmud specifies both the quantity and quality of sex that a man must give his wife while taking into consideration the husband's occupation. The husband is not permitted to take a vow of sexual abstinence for an extended period of time or to take lengthy journeys that would deprive his wife of sexual relations.

While for some women believing that sex is a marital duty may be embedded in their religious beliefs, for others the notion stems from generations of cultural expectations that the man was the breadwinner in a marriage. In return, it was the wife's responsibility to raise the children, run the household, and "please" the man. Pleasing the man included fulfilling his sexual needs, regardless of how different they were from one's own. As described in the book *Sexual Pleasure in Marriage*, published in 1959, "loving" wives were also expected to do so with great enthusiasm:

> Individual differences being what they are, some wives most certainly will experience less frequent desire than their husbands . . .

loving wives always have made this accommodation for their husbands and probably always will. Even if a wife's pleasure is less intense on some occasions, she is happy in giving pleasure to her mate. The wife who is too often merely compliant runs some risk that her husband's urgency, or his expanding erotic taste, may send him occasionally into the arms of another who, for the moment at least, appears to offer more abandoned and spontaneous forms of pleasure. Obviously, unless she is a consummate actress, she cannot pretend to a burning passion she does not feel. But her honest appreciation of her spouse's need for variety, her genuinely welcoming attitude, her avoidance of a patronizing manner will serve her well in the intervals when her own passion is not intense.

Although today in Western cultures it is more the norm than the exception that women as well as men to work outside the home, these messages are still conveyed from older, more traditional generations to many young women. Caretakers—whether mothers, fathers, nannies, or grandparents—are exceptionally powerful sources of influence on how a girl grows up to view herself as a sexual person. It is not known exactly how family messages are accepted by a child, or why some messages are taken in and others are not. It is apparent, however, that whatever creates sexual anxiety for a woman in adulthood is often closely related to what produced anxiety for her primary childhood caretaker.

"Nice" Girls Sympathize

Women are socialized to be nurturers. They are taught from an early age to show empathy and compassion and to be sensitive and aware of other people's feelings. Women, for the most part, are the ones who give soup to the sick, cookies to the elderly, and . . . sex to the forlorn? Several women in our study described using sex as a way to nurture people who were feeling bad about themselves. More than a few women in their late teens and twenties reported having sex with men because they felt sorry for them:

It was an old friend (we grew up together) [who] was very upset that he was a virgin still and also that he had never found someone he trusted/loved/cared about, etc., to have sex with. I think he was kind of hung up on the issue that men are supposed to have sex as soon as they can . . . not be waiting for someone special like women are supposed to. We were attracted to each other and had talked about the possibility of dating, but he lived across the country at the time and nothing came of it. Eventually, he visited home and we ended up kissing and messing around on my couch . . . he was certain that he wanted to have sex and I was feeling sorry for him so I agreed. It wasn't a big deal for me because I had had sex before and I knew and trusted him . . . but it was a bad idea in the long run . . . I had always thought I wanted to only be in a serious relationship before having sex and this experience taught me that this is really what I wanted.

—heterosexual woman, age 25

One woman reported having sex because she felt sorry for a man who was unable to get dates:

I hate letting people down, or hurting them, when I think that I can avoid it. I've even had relationships based on this in the past, when I don't really feel attracted to someone, but I don't want to lose the close friendship I have with them. . . . For a specific instance, I started talking to a guy on Facebook about a movie interest that we had in common. He wanted to meet me in person, so we decided to get lunch together. He showed that he was interested in me right away, and told me all of his horror stories about how he could never find girls that liked him, etc., etc., etc. To make a long story short, I ended up dating him just to make him feel better about himself, and because I felt like I had led him on, so I "owed him."

—heterosexual woman, age 22

Having sex out of a sense of nurturing obligation wasn't limited to young women or casual sexual activity. One woman in our study described having sex with a man because he had just gone through a divorce and she felt bad for him:

The person was interested in me and we hung out. I liked him, but I certainly wasn't attracted to him. He had recently been divorced, so it was a sympathy lay.

—heterosexual woman, age 44

And within established relationships, several women in our study talked about willingly having unwanted sex because they wanted to make their partner feel loved:

In long-term relationships, I feel that sex is an important thing that helps resolve problems and prevents new problems from arising. In some of my relationships, I have felt that there has been unequal interest in sex, so I have "started" the sex stuff because I felt the other person wanted it, and I wanted him to be happy. I have found that I am generally less interested in sex than my partners are, so I sometimes make a conscious effort to initiate sex so that my partner feels wanted, loved, and secure.

—heterosexual woman, age 23

Some women said they wanted to prevent their partners from feeling bad or rejected:

After making up from a fight with my girlfriend, I was exhausted and upset, as was she. She initiated sex; I felt that to decline would be to reject her, which I didn't want to do. I wanted closeness, though not necessarily of the sexual sort, but was willing to compromise with her.

—gay/lesbian woman, age 19

Is Saying Yes to Unwanted Sex Ever a Good Idea?

Women frequently engage in consensual unwanted sex when, for a number of situational, biological, or relationship reasons, they desire sex less often than a partner. Sometimes women agree to unwanted sex because they believe that it is their duty to please their partners, or because it is their temperament to try to please people. At other times, women engage willingly in unwanted sex because they feel it is helpful, if not essential, to maintaining a relationship. If a woman's motivation to have sex is embedded in a desire to feel good about herself as a mate or a person in general, then doing so can result in a pleasurable experience for both partners.

As we will see in chapter 10, when a woman has unwanted sex because she is coerced or forced, with rare exception she experiences intense negative emotional consequences. And if a woman's motivation is based on fear of negative consequences, she often feels guilty, resentful, or remorseful afterward. But this is not necessarily true when women *willingly* consent to unwanted sex.

In fact, one study found that only 29 percent of men and 35 percent of women experienced any type of emotional discomfort as a result of engaging in consensual unwanted sex. As we have seen, women in our study experienced a range of emotional responses as a consequence of agreeing to have sex when they did not desire it. Some said the event made them "extremely glad" or it "boosted [their] confidence." Others described it as a "bad idea" that they later regretted. Some viewed it as a healthy aspect of a relationship:

> When my fiancé needs to feel closer to me or release tension, I feel that I owe it to him to have sex with him. Even if I'm not particularly "in the mood" at the time. He has done the same for me on numerous occasions. I feel that it's part of a healthy, loving, monogamous relationship to be able to see your partner's needs and help them in any way you can. I never feel anything but the satisfaction of knowing that I have given to him all that I can, as he does for me.
>
> —heterosexual woman, age 25

And for some women it was just not an issue at all:

> Tired, but he wanted it. No big deal. I do it to him too.
>
> —heterosexual woman, age 24

What determines whether a woman will feel happy or remorseful after engaging in consensual unwanted sex? Probably the best predictor is whether the behavior occurred because of what psychologists refer to as *approach* versus *avoidance* motives. Approach-motivated behaviors refer to acts done in an effort to achieve a positive or pleasurable experience. In the sexual arena, this would mean, for example, that a woman agrees to have unwanted sex because she wants to make her partner happy and to feel that she is a good mate. That motivation would likely result in her feeling good about her decision. Avoidance-motivated behaviors, on the other hand, refer to behaviors undertaken to avoid negative or painful outcomes. This could mean agreeing to have sex out of fear of losing one's partner or making the partner angry or disappointed. Consenting to sex to avoid negative outcomes more often than not leads to feelings of shame and remorse.

There are also approach-motivated reasons for having sex that are focused on the woman rather than her partner. Sometimes, having sex when a woman is not really in the mood can actually "jump-start" her sex drive. Here is how two women in our study experienced this:

> *I had a headache and just wanted to sleep, but my boyfriend kept kissing me and pressing a bit. We were in a long-distance relationship, seeing each other for the first time in a few weeks, so I relented after not too much pressure. But once I started to respond to his pleas, I found myself getting more and more "into it," I guess you could say.*
> —heterosexual woman, age 24

> *There have been instances where I have told my partner that I did not feel like having sex. On the occasions when I have had sex due to my partner's insistence, it has been because his insistence came in the form of foreplay (romantic kissing, petting, etc.), and I found that I had changed my mind about wanting to have sex.*
> —heterosexual woman, age 24

The notion that having unwanted sex can make a woman desire sex once she gets started can most easily happen if she is in a state of "sexual neutrality." Being sexually neutral means not consciously think-ing about or wanting to have sex, but also not being completely averse to the idea. Whether a woman's neutrality turns into sexual desire depends on a number of things, including how skilled her partner is at foreplay, how easily her body responds to sexual stimulation, and the degree to which bodily changes that occur during arousal feel good to her psy-chologically as well as physiologically. And some of these factors are within a woman's control—particularly for those women who say that they sometimes have sex to gain more sexual experience.

7. A Sense of Adventure

When Curiosity, Variety—
and Mate Evaluation—Beckon

ℭℬℬ

An American Virgin would never dare command;
an American Venus would never dare exist.
> —Henry Brooks Adams (1838–1918)

Historically, being sexually adventurous or experienced, especially prior to marriage, was not considered a positive attribute for women. Women who engaged in sexual intercourse prior to marriage were considered "soiled" and were unlikely to wed—unless, of course, they were clever enough to be able to fake virgin status. Women who remained chaste until marriage, on the other hand, were considered respectable, honorable, trustworthy, and pure. In fact, the word "virgin" is listed in the dictionary as being synonymous with "pure," and things virginal have long been considered pristine, untouched, unsoiled, and white—hence the traditional white wedding dress and the phrase "virgin snow." Even olive oil is better if it is "extra virgin."

Virginity in women has been considered a valuable commodity socially, spiritually, and even politically. Mary of the Christian New Testament may be the most famous virgin of all time. Because of her unique ability to give birth to Jesus, the son of God, without having to engage in the dirty, sinful sex part, the Virgin Mary remains the model of virtue for Christian women. But even among the nonreligious, virginity in wives, sisters, and daughters was highly valued by men. Among the aristocracy, marrying off an undefiled daughter was a way of guaranteeing that bloodlines remained unpolluted. From an evolutionary perspective, controlling a woman's sexual activities and preserving her virginity prior to marriage—through the chastity belts or circumcision that were described in chapter 5—was the surest way for a man to guarantee the lineage of his children. What a woman got in return for protecting her virginity was the eligibility to marry "well" and receive the necessary food, shelter, and social status that came with it. Before women were able fully to join the workforce, this was often their best option.

The importance of remaining a virgin until marriage has changed—at least in the Western world. One study tracked the importance Americans attach to a woman's virginity from the 1930s to the end of the twentieth century. In 1939, a woman's virginity was rated as the tenth most important of eighteen characteristics in a wife. By 1985, the importance of virginity had dropped to near the bottom of the list, and has remained there ever since. Women in our study illustrate this change:

> *I was in college and all my friends had experienced [sex] and I wanted to know what it was like. Thinking about how everyone in the world knew what sex was and that people started wars and killed over it . . . it made me curious and I felt a sort of "pressure" to find out about it.*
>
> —heterosexual woman, age 24

Many women in our study gladly traded in their virginity for the chance to explore their sexuality. And women said they frequently had sex because they wanted the experience—they wanted to try out new sexual techniques or positions, see what sex was like with someone other than their current partners, act out a fantasy, or improve their sex skills. Some women simply "wanted to see what all the fuss is about," and others were just plain curious—either about their own sexual abilities or those of another person. In this chapter we discuss the motivation for, and consequences of, women's sexual adventurism.

Valuing Virginity (or Not)

Despite all the fuss associated with preserving virginity, until the eighteenth century medical doctors actually warned about the perilous effects of long-term virginity. They claimed that remaining a virgin for too long could lead to ill health. The "closed" body of the virginal woman was thought to be prone to such ailments as chlorosis, a condition that caused young women to turn pale green, and "womb suffocation," wherein the womb roamed around the body, causing disturbing "uterine fits." In situations where girls were thought to be dangerously sexually frustrated, yet not ready to be married off, getting a dose of the supposed "health-giving" semen was obviously not an option. So medieval doctors instead suggested that trusted midwives assist the girls with masturbation. Even by today's sexually liberal standards, this type of activity would raise more than a few eyebrows.

The value of women's virginity shifted dramatically with the introduction of the birth control pill in 1961. The resulting freedom to have sex without the fear of pregnancy fueled the sexual revolution of the 1960s and '70s. Indeed, there are substantial differences in the rates of premarital sex reported by women before and after the year 1960. In the landmark 1953 Kinsey report surveying nearly six thousand American women, 40 percent reported being nonvirgins before marriage. In a 1994 survey of more than 1,600 American women, approximately 80 percent of the women who were born between 1953 and 1974 reported having had premarital sex. Several studies recorded a large uptick in premarital sexual activity among women during the 1970s. The average age for a woman to lose her virginity also radically changed during this time period. In 1950, the average age for a woman to first engage in sexual intercourse—or at least admit to it—was twenty. In 2000, the average age was sixteen.

We do not really need statistics to show us how the value of virginity in North America has changed since the 1950s. We can instead look at popular culture. Recall the lyrics to the Everly Brothers' 1957 hit "Wake Up Little Susie," which tell the story of a couple who fell asleep in a movie theater and missed their curfew: "We fell asleep, our goose is cooked, our reputation is shot." The song clearly demonstrates the social ostracism associated with having premarital sex at that time. Now contrast that tale of woe with Rod Stewart's "Tonight's the Night (Gonna Be Alright)," released in 1976. The lyrics implore a virgin to yield to her desire for her lover, to "spread your wings and let me come inside." There's no shame in sex, and no one will stop them.

For many women in our study, virginity was considered neither sacred nor valuable. Several viewed it as something they just wanted to be done with—like taking a dose of bad-tasting cough medicine:

> *I sort of felt like I just wanted to get it [virginity] over with. It was fine and now I have that out of the way.*
> —heterosexual woman, age 25

Other women said it was something they wanted to do to fit in with their peers:

> *I lost my virginity at seventeen because I felt like everyone else I knew was having sex and the idea of going to college a virgin was not what everyone else was doing. I was kind of scared at the time, but in retrospect I honestly don't regret it.*
> —heterosexual woman, age 21

> *When I was in high school, I was the last of my friends to lose her virginity. Most of them had had sex by thirteen and at sixteen I was far behind them. So in order to prove that I was not afraid of sex or intimacy, I had sex—if only to tell them I did.*
> —heterosexual woman, age 27

Perhaps in reaction to this cavalier attitude toward virginity among many American women, virginity—to be or not to be—has today made its way into the political realm. Former president George W. Bush approved a one-billion-dollar abstinence campaign. Although it was targeted at both men and women, many believe it was primarily intended to reinforce the idea that sex outside of marriage is a bad thing for women—regardless of how safe or consensual it might be. Slogans such as "Would you eat a cookie that already had a bite out of it?" were intended to shame people into remaining virgins until marriage. Young people who completed abstinence programs wore silver rings to display publicly their vows of chastity. But was the program successful at changing young people's sexual habits? The results released by the U.S. Department of Health and Human Services in 2007 showed no evidence that the programs actually affected rates of sexual abstinence.

Of course, not every American woman wants to lose her virginity as soon as possible or before she gets married. A woman's attitude toward her own and other women's virginity is undeniably influenced by cultural and religious expectations. Cross-cultural studies of sexuality reveal important differences in both these attitudes and the rates of premarital intercourse, even between ethnic groups living in the same country. To some extent, a woman's feelings depend on how acculturated or enmeshed she has become with the prevailing North American assumption, reflected in mass-media depictions of sexuality and most women's actual behavior, that women have sex before marriage.

A study conducted in the Meston Sexual Psychophysiology Lab of more than four hundred Canadian university women showed that 72 percent of women of European ancestry had engaged in premarital sex compared with a much lower 43 percent of Southeast Asian women, most of whom were ethnic Chinese. The age of first intercourse also differed among Canadian ethnic subgroups. European-ancestry women lost their virginity at age seventeen, on average, and Southeast Asian women at age eighteen. A study just completed in the Meston Lab among more than nine hundred American university women also found differences, although less pronounced, in rates of premarital intercourse based on ethnic group. Seventy-six percent of European-ancestry, 71 percent of Hispanic-ancestry, and 66 percent of Asian-ancestry women reported having had premarital sex.

North America is not the only place where sexual liberalization is taking hold. Among Chinese women living in Shanghai, a recent survey of five hundred single men and women discovered that only 60 percent said virginity was a requirement for a spouse. While this number is still high compared to Western cultures, it is substantially lower than earlier findings. In fact, results from a cross-cultural study published in 1989 indicated that Chinese women and men both viewed virginity as indispensable in a spouse. At the other end of the continuum were Swedes, who thought virginity was irrelevant or unimportant. The cultural differences are probably caused by differences in women's economic independence. In 1989, women in Sweden were much more economically independent than Chinese women and thus, not having to rely on men for resources, they were freer to explore their sexuality. For women, more economic freedom translates into more sexual freedom.

A recent legal case in France demonstrates the extent to which culture and religion can still influence a woman's freedom to engage in premarital sexual activity. The case involved a young Muslim couple whose marriage was annulled in 2008 because the groom discovered that his bride was not a virgin. According to Muslim tradition, the couple is to consummate their marriage during the wedding night party, after which the groom proudly displays a blood-stained sheet as evidence of his new bride's purity. Much to this groom's dismay, he left behind in the bedroom a pure white sheet—one of those few instances in which purity and whiteness do not go hand in hand with virginity. So the groom sued for an annulment. The case created a furor throughout Europe with feminists, women's rights activists, the media, civil rights organizations, and some government officials. Some argued that it was unacceptable for the law to be used to repudiate a bride on religious grounds. Those in support of the court ruling claimed it had nothing to do with religion, but rather that the bride's nonvirgin status qualified as a "breach of contract."

Cultural pressures to remain a virgin prior to marriage may be especially difficult for immigrant women who feel conflicted between the sexual norms of their new culture and those of their culture of origin. In cultures where virginity remains a prerequisite for marriage, single women who are not virgins may face dire consequences, not just from their would-be husbands, but often from their fathers, brothers, and sometimes their entire communities. When the virginity stakes are high, a woman's word just doesn't cut it. Definitive proof is required. This has led, throughout history, to all sorts of cockamamie "virginity tests" such as measuring a woman's skull, timing the duration of her urination, assessing the shape of her breasts or the clarity of her urine, and testing the effect of male earwax on her vulva. In the Middle Ages, if a woman was covered with a piece of cloth and fumigated with the best coal but she didn't smell it, she was declared a virgin. (At least this test gave women a 50 percent chance of giving the right answer.)

For at least the past five hundred years, a broken hymen has been the standard marker for lost virginity. The word "hymen" is Greek for "membrane," and in the past, the term referred to any membrane in the body, but at some point it became uniquely associated with the membrane in a woman's vagina. Some people think the hymen is a tightly stretched piece of skin that covers the entire inside vaginal opening. Not so. Hymens like this do occasionally show up in gynecologists' offices, but they are deemed "imperforate hymens." Such hymens are considered to be birth defects that require minor surgery in order to open the vagina for sex and other health reasons.

The truth about hymens is that they are membranous tissues that cover only part of the opening to the vagina—sort of like a flap of skin. They come in many different shapes and sizes, and they change in dimensions as a woman ages—whether or not she has had intercourse. Some are tough, some are weak; some have blood vessels and bleed when torn, and others do not. Weak hymens can break relatively easily during activities such as bike or horseback riding (tampons may stretch a hymen, but tearing is unlikely), and sometimes they even disintegrate on their own during childhood. The bottom line is that our modern-day "test" of a woman's virginity may not be much more reliable than measuring the size of her skull.

But people are not likely to give up on the "bleeding hymen test" anytime soon. In fact, the latest craze in gynecological surgery is "hymenoplasty"—a thirty-minute operation that repairs a woman's torn hymen. In France, following the case of the Muslim woman who had her marriage annulled, a flurry of Muslim women sought out the surgeries. Medical tourist packages in France offered deals whereby women could go to Tunisia and have the surgery performed for about half the usual 3,500 euros. Having minor surgery is, perhaps, a bit better than inserting blood-filled bags of bird innards into a vagina (an earlier virginity "restoration" technique). But some say that allowing medical doctors to "bring a woman's odometer back to zero," as it is referred to in the Italian movie *Women's Hearts*, is only going to perpetuate the myth that an intact hymen is a reliable test of virginity. Others argue that if a minor surgery means avoiding severe beatings or an acid attack—not uncommon forms of punishment for nonvirgins in societies that place a very high value on a bride's virginity—and allows a woman to be accepted within her community, then it is a good thing.

Just Curious

After I broke up with the first person that I had sex with, I wondered if sex with different people was dramatically different, so I had sex with another boy that I knew and . . . yeah, it was definitely different.

—predominantly heterosexual woman, age 18

Women of all ages in our study reported having sex simply out of curiosity. Some were curious about what a certain person was like in bed or whether the person would live up to their sexual reputation. Some met expectations:

In college, I was friends with a guy who had a reputation for being good in bed. After we had been drinking, I brought up his reputation to him. He asked me if I wanted to find out if it was true (we had always been flirtatious with each other). To his surprise, I said yes. It was one of the best sexual experiences I had!

—heterosexual woman, age 27

Others did not do so:

I met someone while in college and heard [good things] about his sexual behavior. I began to date him, mainly because of what I had heard from a friend. We had sex one time in the first week we were dating. I was disappointed, but glad that I had found out for myself. I ended the "relationship" after that.

—heterosexual woman, age 26

Some women reported being curious about what sex would be like with someone of a gender they had not had sex with before:

> *After my first long-term romantic relationship (two years, ended when I was eighteen), I still had only had one sex partner and a heterosexual one at that. I felt it was time to explore my sexuality and sought out several female partners to do so with. I did that not only to see what it felt like with another person, but another gender as well.*
>
> —predominantly heterosexual woman, age 20

or with a person of different ethnicity:

> *I was about eighteen . . . and the thought that went through my head at the time was "Um, wonder what an Arabic or Italian guy is like in bed?" I guess I wanted to know how each race was in bed. Thinking about it now, I know that was stupid. But at the time I [had] slept with two Puerto Ricans, two white boys, and I wanted to try something new.*
>
> —heterosexual woman, age 22

Does having sex with a member of a different race or nationality make a difference between the sheets? There are certainly many racial stereotypes about who the greatest lovers are, but they are based solely on movies, romance novels, and popular folklore. There has never actually been any scientific investigation into whether people of a certain race make better lovers than those of a different race. There is substantial variability in sexual attitudes and abilities among people of any race, as well as huge variability between women in what they enjoy sexually. That said, people of different races and ethnicities look different, accents make them sound different, and different diets can even make them smell different. Put together, these qualities offer a bounty of novelty for the senses, and when it comes to sex, novelty can be very sexually arousing.

One dimension of novelty is gender, and studies show that gender affects sexual satisfaction. Women who have sex with women are more likely to have orgasms during sex than women who have sex with men. There are several possible explanations for this. First, sex between a man and a woman generally involves intercourse, and intercourse is not the easiest way for a woman to experience an orgasm. Second, in many heterosexual relationships, it is the man who wants sex more often than the woman. As a result, women often go along with sex to please their partners with no aspiration of attaining an orgasm for themselves. This is less likely to be the case among lesbian couples. According to a study by sex researchers William Masters and Virginia Johnson that compared the sexual repertoires of homosexual and heterosexual couples, women may actually be better than men at knowing how to sexually satisfy another woman. Women know women's bodies. If they are sexually experienced, they know what, where, when, and how to touch to make a woman feel good sexually. Masters and Johnson called this "gender empathy."

Hands down, the main thing women in our study were sexually curious about was whether penis size made a difference, and if so, what difference it makes:

> The first person I had sex with was not well endowed. I figured it couldn't get any worse than that. The second guy I had sex with was very well endowed. I wanted to experience the difference.
>
> —heterosexual woman, age 22

> I have a friend [in] whom I have absolutely no romantic interest. We don't even have a whole lot in common, but he's a generally nice person. One night, probably 3 a.m. or so, we were bored and hanging out in my room when he started scratching my head and neck, which is one of my bigger turn-ons. Things sort of escalated, mostly because it was something to do. I'd never had plans to have sex with him, but he was constantly talking about how his very large penis had put a damper on his sex life because girls were afraid of it. I decided to see for myself what it was like. It was a purely curious thing because I'd only had sex with average (or very below average, in one case) sized men. It was, indeed, the largest penis I'd seen outside of pornography, probably nine inches long and three inches in diam-

eter. I can see how some girls might have been intimidated. I fig-ured, what the hell, and went for it. It took some effort to get it in, but once it was there it could barely move around. It was probably one of the least satisfying sexual encounters I've had because it's hard to hit the right spots when it's stuck in one place.

—predominantly heterosexual woman, age 24

A three-inch by nine-inch penis is definitely outside the normal range. According to most surveys, the average penis ranges from five to six inches in length when erect and three to four inches in length when flaccid, or nonerect. Contrary to popular belief, penis length is not closely related to height. In Masters and Johnson's study of over three hundred flaccid penises, the largest was 5.5 inches long (about the size of a bratwurst sausage) and belonged to a five-foot-seven-inch-tall man; the smallest nonerect penis was 2.25 inches long (about the size of a breakfast sausage) and attached to a stocky five-foot-eleven-inch man. If a woman enjoys having her cervix stimulated during sexual intercourse, then size can matter. For most women, it is going to take a good five or six inches in length to reach the cervix when a woman is sexually aroused.

When people talk about penis size, they are usually referring to penis length. But according to one study, penis width may be more important in determining if a potential mate "measures up." Psychologist Russell Eisenman and his fellow researchers at the University of Texas in Edinburg asked fifty sexually active university women whether penis length or penis width was more important for their sexual satisfaction. A surprising forty-five out of fifty women said that width was more important. Only five said length felt better, and none said they were unable to tell the difference. A wider penis could provide greater clitoral stimulation during sexual intercourse as well as more stimulation of the outer, most sensitive portion of the vagina.

Taking a Test Drive

Some women in our study described wanting to have sex with someone as a sort of "relationship screening test." That is, they wanted to see whether the person was "good enough" in the sack to warrant a relationship:

> *I think that this is a normal evolution in a relationship. If I have gone out with a person a few times and it leads up to sex, I am curious to know how the sex is. If it is awful, there are few circumstances that would compel me to stay in the relationship. If it is good, then it becomes [a] reason to stay in the relationship.*
>
> —predominantly heterosexual woman, age 23

> *I've had sex with people I've dated to see if I liked sleeping with them, so I could decide whether I wanted to keep going out with them or not. My experiences with that have been mixed but mostly positive. For example, that is what I did with my current boyfriend and I was happy that I already knew what it would be like to have sex with him before I made any decisions about what kind of a relationship I wanted us to have. My feelings at the time were that things were going well, and that seeing what it was like to have sex with him was the next logical step.*
>
> —bisexual woman, age 24

One woman wanted to make sure sex wasn't better elsewhere before she walked down the aisle:

> *My boyfriend and I had discussed the possibility of marriage. Then, I started to get cold feet. I wondered if the sex that my boyfriend and I were having was good enough. So, I had sex with someone else that I thought would be good in bed.*
>
> —predominantly heterosexual woman, age 20

Using sex as a relationship screening test obviously stands counter to the old tradition of women waiting until they are married to have sex. It also says loud and clear that *good sex* is an important aspect of relationships for many women—important enough that lack of it can be a deal breaker. Women in our study who wrote about testing sexual compatibility before committing to a relationship were mainly younger, in their twenties and thirties. But research shows that sex plays an important role in relationships for women across the life span.

In a study conducted by National Family Opinion Research, Inc., 745 American women aged forty-five years and older answered surveys on the importance of sexuality in their lives. Almost half of the women between the ages of forty-five and fifty-nine felt that having a satisfying sexual relationship was important to their overall quality of life. The National Council on Aging reported similar findings among a group of American women aged sixty years and older. Among the women who were sexually active, two-thirds said that maintaining an active sex life was an important aspect of their relationship with their partner.

Practice Makes Perfect

[To get experience] is pretty much a constant reason [why] I have sex. I definitely think there's always room for improvement, and I feel it is important to be a skilled participant when you are having sex with someone. As a woman, I don't want to be a "dead fish." I want to be involved and actually contribute. It makes it better for both partners.

—heterosexual woman, age 20

Many women in our study, particularly younger women, cited improving their sexual skills as a motive for gaining sexual experience. Some women said they wanted to gain sexual experience to avoid the humiliation of being viewed as sexually inexperienced:

The first time I had sex, a big part of the reason was that I was nineteen and felt like it was time I "learn how" to have sex.... So the first time I had sex, it was with someone much older whom I didn't really care about, and it was mostly just because I wanted to know what I was doing the next time. To clarify: it wasn't that I wanted to lose my "virgin" status; being a virgin didn't bother me, per se. It was just that I felt like someone of that age was expected to know what they were doing sexually, so I did what I thought I needed to in order to learn what I was doing.

—heterosexual woman, age 23

When I was fourteen, I was really concerned about being horrible at performing fellatio. I never had, but I wanted some practice before I began dating someone I cared about—someone whose opinion of my [skill at giving] oral sex I cared about. My friends and I used to hang out late at night in a parking lot and watch some guys BMX and flirt with them. One night, one of them . . . asked me if I would flash one of his friends . . . to cheer him up. I laughed and he offered me [five] dollars. I did it and then tossed off, "That's not all I'll do," and began to walk away. One of the guys caught up with me a block away and asked if I would give him head for [five] dollars. This was exactly what I had wanted. I agreed, but said I would not swallow. He asked, Would I if he gave me [more]? I still said no. So I did it in my friend's backyard and it was pretty awkward. I gagged and almost threw up. I felt really exposed. After he left, I began to feel kinda shitty, like I had just sold my self-respect. I was kind of ashamed, but got over it in a day or so.

—"straight-plus" woman, age 19

One woman said she wanted the experience so that sex would be better on her wedding day:

I had decided that I wanted to have sex before marriage, primarily because you want to know what to do and how to act when you're married. It would almost be embarrassing or awkward if you were lost in what you were doing especially if one partner is a virgin and the other isn't. . . . I think there is a lot of pressure and importance on the consummation of marriage. It's a pretty big deal to a lot of people, so they want it to be "perfect."

—heterosexual woman, age 20

Most of the women who had sex primarily to improve their sexual skill did so because they believed it would contribute to an overall better sexual experience—not just for their partner, but for themselves as well:

> *I have had sex with my boyfriend to make my sexual skills better for the both of us. I see it as each time I have sex I'm also choosing to do it to heighten my skills so we can both have an even better experience than the last.*

—heterosexual woman, age 20

Sexual science has documented that the more sexually experienced a woman is, the more likely she is to have an orgasm. The reason is simple: The more a woman has sex, the more opportunities she has to learn what feels good to her sexually and how to have an orgasm. Sexual experience can also explain why it is often said that women "peak in their thirties"— a saying backed by research as early as the classic survey conducted by Alfred Kinsey in the early 1950s. Kinsey found that women's total orgasm frequency from all sexual "outlets," including intercourse and masturbation, was highest around age thirty. A more recent study on the sexual desire of 1,414 Canadian and American women of different ages also found a sexual peak among women in the thirty-to-thirty-four-year-old age bracket. Women in these age brackets also described themselves as more "lustful," "seductive," and "sexually active" than women in any other age category studied. In North America, most women in their thirties have had numerous sexual experiences and have had sex with a variety of different partners. According to one study, approximately 25 percent of women in their thirties have had sex with five to ten different partners since age eighteen, and just over 10 percent have had sex with more than twenty-one different partners. By contrast, only about 15 percent of women in their late teens and early twenties have had between five and ten sexual partners, and approximately one-third have had sexual intercourse with only one person. Consequently, women in their thirties usually have enough sexual experience to know how to attain sexual pleasure. Compared with women in their teens or twenties, they also tend to be more confident. Along with confidence comes the ability to communicate sexual needs and desires to a partner.

The link between sexual experience and sexual satisfaction in women is not quite so clear-cut. In the short term, the more sexually experienced a woman is, the more likely she is to seek out sexually satisfying experiences. But in long-term committed relationships, being sexually experienced may not always be a good thing. For example, what if a woman finds a partner who is perfect in many ways—the couple share the same interests and life goals and are attracted to each other, and the partner is intelligent, kind, and loyal—but her "near perfect mate" is seriously lacking in the lovemaking department and doesn't seem to have what it takes to be able to learn? Then what? Some would argue being sexually experienced prior to marriage is not a good thing—that not knowing what else is out there is better in the long run. If you have never tasted fine French Champagne, then a sparkling California wine tastes just dandy. However, based on the responses of some of the women in our study, achieving sexual pleasure may not be negotiable in their relationships.

Whether being sexually experienced prior to marriage is good or bad depends on many unique characteristics of each woman. If a woman chooses the "no sex before marriage" option and is content with whatever will unfold, then that is the right choice for her. But if she later spends her nights fantasizing about other men, or is drawn into having an affair simply out of curiosity, then it might have been better if she checked out her options beforehand:

> I lost my virginity to my fiancé when I was fifteen years old and by the time I had been with him for two years and knew I wanted to marry him I realized that I wanted to see what it was like to have sex with other men. I ended up cheating on him, which we have worked past now. I regret it every day but I think I needed that experience in order to move forward with my relationship.
>
> —heterosexual woman, age 18

If a woman chooses the "informed shopper" option, she then runs the risk of having to deal with the fact that her chosen mate may not live up to her sexual memories. That fiery sex with Fabio on the beach while vacationing in Greece may be hard to replicate back home years later when the children are screaming and the dog needs walking and both partners are exhausted from work. If a woman holds on to such memories and compares her current sex life with that of a passionate encounter she had in the past, then undoubtedly she is going to feel that she has made a disappointing compromise in the sex department. But if a woman is able to put such past experiences into their proper context, and to recognize that wildly passionate lovers do not always make the best long-term mates, then there is no reason such memories should negatively impact her current sex life.

Variety Is the Spice of a Sex Life

In the Meston Lab, rarely a month goes by that someone from the media does not call to ask for a scientific explanation as to why people are claiming that some new herb or food or sexual practice causes supersized orgasms. More often than not, the explanation boils down to *novelty*. People get bored when situations get too predictable—like always having sex at the same time, in the same position, or in the same location. Trying something new, such as giving oral sex after eating extra-strength Altoid mints (a craze we were asked about in 2008), creates new sensations, catches your attention, and spices things up.

Women in our study described engaging in sexual encounters because they craved some variety in their sex lives:

> *I don't consider myself to be monogamous. I enjoy being sexual with different people because everything they do is different.*
> —predominantly heterosexual woman, age 28

> *My girlfriend and I are both into S&M, she's more experienced than I am. Often, after hearing or reading about new activities or techniques, we make a point to try them during our sexual encounters in order to give us more experience with them.*
> —predominantly homosexual woman, age 21

For some women, adding variety to their sex lives meant adding another person to the mix, along with their current partner:

> *When I was in a lesbian relationship, my girlfriend and I decided to have sex with a former girlfriend of mine just to spice things up*

a bit. My ex and I were still friends and there was no jealousy be-
tween her and my current girlfriend.

—pansexual woman, age 33

I've been in a relationship for nearly nine years and after a while
the spark tends to fade. [My] husband and I agreed that we would
open the relationship to allow us both to partake of others. We both
felt hopeful that this would lead to more intimacy in our relation-
ship, which it has. We are now polyamorous.

—polyamorous woman, age 30

At times, a woman may seek other partners as a solution to a mismatched sexual drive with her partner:

I am a very sexual woman and enjoy specific ways of lovemaking.
My husband and I do not share the same drive and even when we
do, he finishes quickly and does not pay attention to my needs. I've
chosen many different partners over the years, for many different
reasons. I've had sex with a coworker, several married men, and
also tried a threesome (male, female, female). I have had sex with
a younger man who worked at my child's high school. I have met a
man online whom I had a long-term affair with, strictly sexual.
I've felt some emotional involvement with these people, but [I] cer-
tainly [have] not [been] "in love" with any of them. It's for fun,
great sex, and expressing myself. It is exciting and a bit dangerous.

—heterosexual woman, age 39

Long ago, researchers who studied sexual behavior in rats discovered
that if you drop a male rat into a cage with a willing female rat, he engages in enthusiastic copulation. He will mount her repeatedly until he
is completely tired out and ready for the rhetorical post-ejaculatory
"cigarette and nap." But if you replace his former sexual mate with another willing female, he becomes randy all over again. In fact, every
time you replace the female with a new female, the male rat shows re-
newed vigor and begins copulating afresh. He will keep going and going

with new females until he nearly dies of exhaustion. Scientists believe this happens because the rat's brain releases dopamine when he is presented with a new female. Dopamine excites the brain's reward receptors, which keeps him coming back for more. Amusingly, the name given to this phenomenon is "the Coolidge effect." Story has it that when President Calvin Coolidge and his wife were touring a farm in a small American town, the farmer proudly showed Mrs. Coolidge a rooster that "could copulate with hens all day long, day after day." Mrs. Coolidge suggested that the farmer tell that to Mr. Coolidge, who was elsewhere at the time. When the farmer later related the story, the president asked if it was with the same hen. When the farmer replied that it was not, the president told him to tell that to Mrs. Coolidge.

Does the Coolidge effect exist in humans, causing some people to stray from or even avoid monogamous relationships? As we discussed in chapter 3, dopamine is released during sex in humans, and, as with rats, it serves as a major reward mechanism. Dopamine has been linked to addictive behaviors ranging from alcoholism to gambling, and some scientists believe it plays a role in sexual addiction as well. To test the Coolidge effect in humans, most universities would not allow researchers to run an experiment to see how many times a person can get aroused and have sex with different people; the best they can do to approximate the situation is to test how aroused a person gets in response to repeated presentations of erotic stimuli. This test has been done in both women and men. Researchers present, for example, either a series of ten erotic scenes involving different people or a series of ten different scenes of the same couple engaging in sex. During each presentation, the scientists measure how sexually aroused the viewer gets in response to the erotic image. Then they look to see whether, over time, there is a difference in how aroused the viewer was by scenes of different couples versus scenes of the same couple. When the study was done in women, researchers found that women were similarly aroused—both genitally and mentally—by erotic scenes of the same couple and of different couples—even up to the twenty-first presentation. When the study was done in men, however, a very different pattern of arousal was seen. After a few presentations, men were more aroused when they saw erotic pictures of different people than when they saw the same couple. Scientists call this habituation, and it is defined as a systematic decrease in the strength of a response—including a sexual response—resulting from repeated stimulation.

These studies suggest that habituation to the same sexual partner may be more likely to occur in men than in women. Keep in mind, though, that the studies used only photographs, not real people. Thus, they did not involve any decision making about actually engaging in sexual behavior. Humans have evolved much more sophisticated brains than rats. Consequently, when a human chooses a sexual partner, it is a much more complex process than simply responding to a surge of dopamine.

There is no doubt that women differ considerably from each other in the degree to which they seek sex with a variety of different partners. Many factors determine whether or not women choose to be monogamous. Sexual desire also plays a role in women's mating strategies. Women with high levels of desire who are mated with men who desire sex less often may seek out other partners simply to get their needs met. Opportunity plays a role—women who are frequently presented with sexual offers may, over time, become tempted. Relationship satisfaction plays a role; women who are less satisfied with their relationship are more likely to have an affair. Life goals play a role. A woman who is just beginning to explore her sexuality, or a woman who just ended a twenty-year marriage, may enjoy her newly found sexual freedom and not want to commit to one sexual partner. On the other hand, a woman who has dated many men and had many different sexual partners may be ready for one stable, committed sexual partner.

An Adventurous Personality

A woman's personality can also play a role in determining whether she would enjoy having sex with a variety of partners. In a study of 16,288 people in fifty-two nations (spanning North America, South America, Western Europe, Eastern Europe, Southern Europe, the Middle East, Africa, Oceania, South Asia, Southeast Asia, and East Asia), psychologist David Schmitt found that two personality traits were linked to sexual variety seeking in women—*extraversion* and *impulsiveness*. Extraversion describes individuals who are sociable, gregarious, and thrive on social interaction. Impulsiveness describes those who leap before they look, act on the spur of the moment, and have less inhibition about acting on their urges. The study showed that the more extraverted and impulsive women were, the more likely they were to seek sexual variety.

Similarly, a study of 107 married couples conducted in the Buss Evolutionary Psychology Lab found that impulsivity was linked to infidelity in women. But an even greater predictor was the personality trait of *narcissism*—a personality cluster defined by the attributes of being self-centered, grandiose, and exhibitionistic, feeling a strong sense of entitlement, arrogance, and being interpersonally exploitative. In the Meston Lab, a survey of 121 women aged eighteen to forty-seven found that individual differences in *perfectionism* were also related to relationship fidelity and sexual variety seeking. Those high in the trait of perfectionism set unrealistically high standards for themselves and others: They expect perfection, and this leads them to evaluate themselves and others stringently. The study found that women who scored high in perfectionism had engaged in sex with more partners than women low in perfectionism, and they also were more likely to have been unfaithful in a sexual relationship. Perfectionists appear to hold unrealistic or unattainable demands of sexual performance from their partners, which causes them to be continuously disappointed in the bedroom and consequently to look elsewhere for sexual gratification.

In our original scientific paper on why humans have sex, we found that college-age men were more likely than same-age women to report having sex because "the opportunity presented itself" or because they wanted more sexual variety and experience, and in his cross-cultural study, David Schmitt came to the same conclusion. In each of the fifty-two different regions studied, men and women were asked, "Ideally, how many different sex partners would you like to have over the next . . . ?" He had the participants answer with respect to several different time reference points, ranging from one month to their remaining lifetimes. In every region studied, and at every time point assessed, men said they wanted more sexual partners than did women. For example, using "next month" as a time reference, overall about 25 percent of men wanted more than one sexual partner. The highest percentage was seen in South America, with 35 percent of men wanting more than one sexual partner in the next month, and the lowest was in East Asia, with about 18 percent of men desiring multiple sex partners in that period. The percentage of women who wanted more than one sexual partner in the next month was dramatically different. They ranged from a high of about 7 percent of women in Eastern Europe to a low of about 3 percent of women in East Asia.

The women profiled in this chapter devalued virginity. Sex was neither forced nor prescribed; it was an opportunity for exploration and adventure with new partners or using new techniques. They placed a high premium on sexual pleasure—their *own* pleasure.

In the widely discussed book *Female Chauvinist Pigs,* journalist Ariel Levy argues that women today—who alter their bodies cosmetically, take pole-dancing classes during lunch break, and attend Cake parties where audience members assess the breast sizes of women simulating sex on stage—are not feminists who demonstrate how far women have come in terms of sexual freedom. Rather, she says, women who make sex objects of other women or themselves only prove how far women have left to go. Levy calls for a new wave of feminism in which sex for women is passionate—a primal urge, to be explored freely. The women whose stories are shared in this chapter might typify this new wave of sexual liberation.

8. Barter and Trade

The Value of Sex—Literally and Figuratively

cℰℬɔ

The dress is for sale. I'm not.
—Diana, *Indecent Proposal* (1993)

In September 2008, twenty-two-year-old Natalie Dylan decided that she wanted to pursue a master's degree in family and marriage therapy—but realized that she needed to raise the money for her tuition. She had considered her options, including the one that her older sister had chosen: working as a prostitute (which in three weeks earned her enough money to pay for her education). Dylan decided to auction off her virginity, partly as a fundraiser and partly as a study of women's sexual value—and within five months, a reported ten thousand bids had been placed for it, with the high bid rising to nearly $4 million. When she was interviewed about the tactic, which drew worldwide attention, she said, "I think me and the person I do it with will both profit greatly from the deal."

Stephanie Gershon yearned to explore the Amazonian rain forest before leaving Brazil to complete her college education back in the United States. Her efforts to locate a tour guide who would take her past the edge of the forest, however, came up empty. When a local busboy at her resort started to flirt with her, she questioned him about the rain forest.

Could a tourist such as herself, she wondered, survive alone in the jungle for a couple of weeks? "He laughed and told me I was nuts," said Gershon. But when he revealed that he had deep knowledge of the jungle, having grown up there, Gershon turned on the charm. She was not attracted to the busboy, but sent out flirtatious signals anyway. She wanted him to become her jungle guide. Her sexual magnetism succeeded. The busboy managed to get out of work, and they left for the jungle:

> It was amazing. We built our homes out of palm leaves, I saw animals I'd never seen before, he taught me the medicinal properties of all the plants, we picked fruit off the trees, we swam with and ate piranhas. And, of course, we had sex . . . for almost two weeks. It was a good barter both ways. I got to stay in the jungle, and he got to have sex with a cute young American girl.

Gershon reported that she did not feel at all uncomfortable or sleazy about the arrangement. In exchange for the sex, she gained memories of an Amazonian adventure that will last her lifetime.

Although Natalie Dylan's and Stephanie Gershon's barters are perhaps more exotic than most, a recent study of 475 University of Michigan college students supports the view that some women are motivated to have sex not because they are sexually or romantically attracted to the person, but simply to get things they want. Despite the fact that the University of Michigan is an elite institution of higher learning, with students coming from homes that are typically above average in income, 9 percent of the women reported that they had initiated an attempt to trade sex for some tangible benefit. Of these, 18 percent occurred in the context of an ongoing romantic relationship; the vast majority—82 percent—did not. But while some women barter sex to get the necessities of life to survive, as we will see later in this chapter, dire need was not the motivation of these college women. As the study's author noted, "It's more about getting what you want than getting what you need, unless you think everyone needs a $200 Louis Vuitton bag."

Our own study of why women have sex confirmed that Michigan undergraduates are not alone in their sexual motivations. Among the reasons women listed:

- I wanted to get a raise.
- I wanted to get a job.
- I wanted to get a promotion.
- Someone offered me money to do it.
- I wanted to make money.
- The person offered me drugs for doing it.

Nor is sexual barter limited to Americans. Exchanges of gifts and sex occur in every culture. Anthropologist Donald Symons set out to elucidate this phenomenon from a cross-cultural perspective. Using the Human Relations Area Files, considered to be the most massive database of ethnographic studies, Symons categorized gifts that were received in contexts such as courting, wooing, and extramarital affairs, determining whether men or women or both gave the gifts, whether the gifts occurred between lovers or directly in exchange for sex, and the relative value of the gifts given. The gifts were identified along the following lines: 1) only men give gifts; 2) men and women exchange gifts, but men's gifts are of greater value; 3) men and women exchange gifts and there is no mention of relative value (in no cases were men's and women's gifts specifically stated to be of equal value); 4) men and women exchange gifts, but women's gifts are of greater value; 5) only women give gifts. He specifically excluded from his analysis gifts given in the context of marriage and paid prostitution.

To his surprise, Symons discovered that the fourth and fifth categories proved entirely unnecessary, since not a single society met their criteria. In contrast, 79 percent of societies fell predominantly into the first category, with only men giving gifts; 5 percent fell into the second category, in which both sexes gave gifts, but men's gifts were more valuable; and the remaining 16 percent of societies fell into the third category, in which there was no mention of the gifts' relative value. As a heterosexual woman in our study put it, "Sex equals gifts."

It is especially intriguing to find this sexual asymmetry in cultures high in sexual equality and in which there is tremendous sexual freedom and opportunity for both sexes. Anthropologist Marshall Sahlins's studies of the Trobriand islanders provide an interesting illustration. Trobriand women expect gifts in exchange for sex:

In the course of every love affair the man has constantly to give small presents to the woman. To the natives the need for one-sided payment is self-evident. This custom implies that sexual intercourse, even where there is mutual attachment, is a service rendered by the female to the male. . . . This rule is by no means logical or self-evident. Considering the great freedom of women and their equality with men in all matters, especially that of sex, considering also that the natives fully realize that women are as inclined to intercourse as men, one would expect the sexual relation to be regarded as an exchange of resources itself reciprocal. But custom . . . decrees that it is a service from women to men, and men have to pay.

These observations, along with an avalanche of other findings, strongly support a basic fact about human economics: Women's sexuality is something that women can bestow or withhold, something that men want and value highly, and consequently something that women can use to secure resources that they desire. Women, in short, have the power in many sexual transactions.

In the most traditional hunter-gatherer cultures, the transaction is an exchange of sex for food. Among the Sharanahua of Peru, for example, "Whether men prove their virility by hunting and thus gain wives or offer meat to seduce a woman, the theme is an exchange of meat for sex." Janet Siskind, the anthropologist who studied the Sharanahua expressed bafflement at this since she knows "of no real evidence that women are naturally or universally less interested in sex or more interested in meat than are men." Yet one woman in our study made a strikingly similar point:

> *Being "gifted" for sex, or financially compensated, provides a stimulus of excitement with a wealthy man equivalent to passion with a physically powerful man. Financial protection equals physical protection.*
> —heterosexual woman, age 58

The key issue is not whether women and men differ in their enjoyment of sex, nor whether the sexes differ in their interest in having sex (let alone in consuming meat!). The mystery is why women sometimes seem to hold such a commanding position in the economics of sex.

The Golden Egg

The most plausible evolutionary answer to the mystery of women's greater power in the sexual arena—why women's sexuality is so valuable and seemingly scarce that men worldwide willingly pay for it—lies with the fundamental asymmetries in human reproductive biology, and the sexual psychology that has evolved as a consequence.

We've already seen how women's hefty investment in pregnancy, when viewed from an evolutionary perspective, has favored a sexual psychology that seems to make women less desirous of having multiple sexual partners. But the gender differences in reproductive biology really start with the asymmetries between sperm and egg. Sperm are little more than genes traveling an eighth of an inch per minute via a stripped-down swimming machine. Sperm are dwarfed in size by women's nutrient-filled eggs. The normal human sperm is a mere three microns wide and six microns long, while the normal human ovum, at maturity, is a whopping 120 to 150 microns in diameter. So from the very start of conception, women make a larger contribution than men do. Compounding the asymmetry, women are born with a fixed number of eggs, which cannot be replenished. Men, in contrast, produce roughly 85 million new sperm each day. Today, these differences in relative value play out in how much women get paid for donating their ova versus how much money men get paid for donating sperm. Compensation for egg donation usually starts at five thousand dollars, and can be several times that amount for women who meet certain physical and psychological conditions. Sperm donors, in contrast, typically receive only $35 per donation, although some with highly desirable traits—such as height, a V-shaped torso, an attractive face, high intelligence, and high social status—may get as much as $150.

This difference between the sexes widens as a consequence of the nine-month pregnancy that women endure in order to produce a child. Women's heavier reproductive investment in producing their offspring means they are by far the more valuable reproductive resource. As a general rule, the more valuable the resource, the more people compete for access to it. Men must compete with each other for sexual access to women. Women can afford to be choosy since they are in greater demand when it comes to sex.

Evolutionary psychologists posit a number of explanations for women's disproportionate sexual power. The first derives from men's evolved sexual strategy for what is called short-term, low-investment mating. Because ancestral men could increase their purely *reproductive* success by having casual, no-strings-attached sex with multiple partners, one component of their evolved sexual psychology is a desire for access to mates. The *desire for sexual variety* is reflected in men's sexual fantasies, which are far more likely than women's fantasies to focus on sex with strangers, multiple partners, and partner switching during the course of a single episode. Men are four times as likely as women to report having had sexual fantasies about more than a thousand different partners. Although there may be some reporting bias—perhaps because women are culturally conditioned to be more reticent about disclosing information about their sexuality than are men—the sex differences are profound and verified by many studies. Because of men's desire for sexual variety, women, in men's eyes, are perpetually in short supply.

Men possess another psychological tic, the *sexual overperception bias*, which is the tendency to overinfer women's sexual interest based on ambiguous information. As demonstrated in the evocations of jealousy described in chapter 5, when a woman smiles at a man, men often infer sexual interest, when in many cases the woman is simply being friendly or polite. Other ambiguous cues—a touch on the arm, standing close, or even holding eye contact for a split second longer than usual—trigger men's sexual overperception bias. As a consequence, women can exploit men's overperception bias for economic gain, in what has been called a "bait and switch" tactic, a strategy that involves persuading men to expend resources as part of courtship, but then failing to follow through on an implied "promise" of sex.

Research has also found that most men find most women at least somewhat sexually attractive, whereas most women do not find most men sexually attractive at all. The Buss Evolutionary Psychology Lab discovered that men lower their attraction standards for casual encounters. Empirically, they are willing to have sex with partners who meet just minimal thresholds on traits they themselves rank as desirable, such as intelligence and kindness. In contrast, women typically maintain high standards in whom they choose, whether for casual or pair-bonded sexual encounters.

Several other gender differences in how women and men are sexually aroused and respond to arousal cues give women extra leverage in sexual economics. Men are generally more likely than women to become sexually aroused through visual stimulation. Simply the sight of an attractive woman can lead a heterosexual man to become aroused, and this gives women, who tend to be less keyed to visual attractions, an edge. Men also appear to be less willing to tolerate states of sexual abstinence and to have a greater drive to have sexual intercourse, regardless of circumstances.

It is important to keep in mind that men do not have a conscious motive to "spread their seed." Furthermore, the desire for sexual variety and quantity reflects just one of their mating strategies, and most men also seek long-term committed relationships. But men's shorter-view sexual psychology produces a mating market in which the sexual services of women are in top demand. In the modern environment, this gives women an opportunity to extract value from sex through prostitution, sexual barter, and ongoing mating relationships.

The Sexual Economy of Prostitution

I worked at a legal brothel in Nevada for approximately three years. I wasn't very good at it, by the way, having too much attitude for the clientele, but [I] managed to keep the job. . . . I do not necessarily includ[e] this time period as . . . relevant to my "sex life," as it was work. I didn't have anywhere else to go in life, and the other girls at the house became very much like family.

—predominantly heterosexual woman, age 36

Within the broader ambit of what motivates women to have sex, our goal is to understand the sexual psychology that drives women to prostitution. While we will not take an ideological stand on this topic, it is worth noting the spectrum of political and moral beliefs about prostitution, since the ability of a woman to gain resources from it is limited by laws, social mores, and religions.

On one end, there are people who argue that prostitution should be illegal and criminalized because it is degrading to women. It makes them vulnerable to being used and abused by men. It causes women to be treated as sex objects or commodities. And, according to some thinkers, it maintains men's political dominance over women. Some of these arguments have held sway. In fact, prostitution is illegal in some places, including most of the United States. Nonetheless, there are far more countries where prostitution is legal—including most of Europe, Mexico, most of South America, Israel, Australia, and New Zealand. Prostitution is also legal in some counties within the state of Nevada.

Even in countries in which prostitution is illegal, there are sometimes very large loopholes for circumventing the restrictions. In Iran, for example, prostitution is illegal, and it is a crime to advocate it, to assist a woman in becoming a prostitute, or to operate a brothel. Those found guilty can be—and often are—executed by firing squad or stoning. Yet historically Iran has allowed a practice called *mutia*, in which women become "temporary wives" for a few hours in an exchange of sex for money. In the Philippines, prostitution is illegal, but some employees of bars are given the euphemistic title "customer relations officer" and required to be tested for sexually transmitted diseases once a week. In Thailand and other countries, prostitution is illegal, but the laws are rarely enforced. Most countries that have legalized prostitution impose various restrictions. Some, such as England and Scotland, make it illegal to proffer or solicit sex on the streets but permit "outcall" sexual escort services, meaning that prostitution is okay as long as it remains private rather than public. In Canada, prostitution, brothels, and outcall escort services are fully legal, but "pressing and persistent" solicitation on the street is illegal.

With prostitution so common, even in countries in which it is mostly or wholly illegal, some people advocate that governments should not consider prostitution to be a crime and give women the right to use their bodies in any way they wish. As one former prostitute argued:

> A woman has the right to sell sexual services just as much as she has the right to sell her brains to a law firm when she works as a lawyer,

or to sell her creative work to a museum when she works as an artist, or to sell her image to a photographer when she works as a model, or to sell her body when she works as a ballerina. Since most people can have sex without going to jail, there is no reason except old-fashioned prudery to make sex for money illegal.

Dr. Jocelyn Elders, a surgeon general under President Bill Clinton, echoed this sentiment: "We say that [hookers] are selling their bodies, but how is that different from athletes? They're selling their bodies. Models? They're selling their bodies. Actors? They're selling their bodies."

Regardless of one's position on whether prostitution should be legal, it is important to understand the underlying motivations of women who enter into the "world's oldest profession." Because women's sexuality is so highly prized, it can be regarded as an asset that economists call fungible—it can be transposed or exchanged for many other kinds of resources. But how do women become prostitutes instead of finding other ways to take advantage, if they like, of their sexual value?

Slavery and Desperation

Prostitution is not a singular phenomenon—but it does almost singularly affect women, who comprise well over 90 percent of the world's prostitutes, while more than 99 percent of prostitutes' clients are men. Some girls and women become prostitutes because they are literally forced to become sex slaves.

The problem of sexual enslavement, also called sex trafficking, is particularly pernicious in Myanmar (Burma), Pakistan, India, Cambodia, and Thailand. Sex traffickers use a variety of tactics to enslave girls and women. They typically prey on those in extreme poverty. A common trick is to promise a well-paying job in another city or country; pay the girl's or woman's parents a sum of money to initiate her move; and then sell her sexual services to a brothel, often bribing police and border guards along the way.

The conditions in the brothels, some of which are operated openly, are often appalling. The women and girls are forced to have sex with dozens of men each day, paying most or all of their earnings to the brothel own-ers. Although some of their clients are Westerners, the largest clientele consists of men from local or neighboring Asian countries. The details of sex trafficking have been documented in several excellent books and are beyond the scope of this one. Although there are movements devoted to eliminating sex trafficking, the demand for prostitutes is so great and the money to be made by traffickers so lucrative that these efforts have met with little success. Suffice it to say that why women have sex in these cir-cumstances is obvious—they are forced to do so.

But there are also women who turn to prostitution because it is the best among strictly limited options for survival. Some women become prostitutes because they are unmarriageable in their cultural communi-ties. Women with dependent children often have difficulty attracting husbands. Among the Ganda of Uganda, for instance, women with chil-dren are actually forbidden by law to marry. Malays and Somalis histor-ically forbade women who have been divorced to remarry. Even when not strictly forbidden to remarry, divorced women sometimes have great difficulty attracting husbands, especially if they were divorced on the grounds of adultery. In Myanmar and Somalia, nonvirgin single women are considered to be "tarnished," making it extremely difficult for them to marry. In most cultures, men regard a woman who has children sired by other men as an onerous burden, which lowers these women's mate value. And women who suffer from disease or disfigurement often have difficulty attracting husbands. For these reasons, some women are essen-tially forced by circumstances to become prostitutes to support them-selves and their children.

In other cases, there are women whom many men would consider desirable as wives, but who choose not to marry because they perceive the eligible men to be of low quality or because they see prostitution as a better option than marriage. Indeed, some women even choose prosti-tution to avoid the drudgery of marriage. In Singapore, for instance, historically some Malay women reported becoming prostitutes to avoid the hard work expected of wives, which included gathering and carry-ing firewood and laundering clothes by hand. Among the Amhara and Bemba of Africa, prostitutes can earn enough money to hire men to do work for them—work that is normally expected of wives.

Hookers to Call Girls

There is a hierarchy of prostitutes ranging from low-priced street prostitutes, commonly called hookers, to high-priced call girls. Of course, the amount of money a woman is able or willing to receive in exchange for her sexual services varies greatly, depending on the location and competition, her level of attractiveness, and her degree of desperation. An attractive street prostitute might make two hundred dollars for an act of sex, while a desperate drug addict, blemished with needle marks and missing teeth, might take as little as twenty bucks. Street prostitutes are targeted by police more often than escorts or call girls since they are both visible and vulnerable.

Young girls and women who are homeless sometimes trade sex for money, food, shelter, or drugs. Often these are tragic cases in which adolescent girls have fled from homes riddled with emotional, physical, or sexual abuse. On the streets, they have sex as a strategy of survival. Some trade sex to support their boyfriends as well as themselves. As one put it, "Me and [my boyfriend] would pretty much leech off him for awhile [the man she was having sex with for money]. Pretty much I was using [the man] to get money for drugs or to get alcohol or drugs for me and [my boyfriend]."

One woman in our study described a similar motivation:

> *We both had a drug addiction at the time—the kind that keeps you up all night talking. I was never initially propositioned for anything but I knew if I stuck around and got him to fall in love with me then I could have all [the drugs] I wanted and I did just that.*
>
> —gay/lesbian woman, age 20

At the other end of the spectrum are high-priced call girls, as exemplified by Ashley Alexandra Dupré. In February 2008, Dupré allegedly charged Eliot Spitzer, then the governor of New York, $4,300 for a sexual encounter. When the media exposed the purported transaction, it brought to light a booming underground business of high-end sex clubs, including the one for which Dupré allegedly plied her trade, the Emperors Club VIP, located in New York City. According to news reports, call girls for the Emperors Club VIP typically charged between $1,000 and $3,000 per hour, depending on their sophistication and attractiveness. Although the escort agencies generally receive half of the money, it is not difficult to understand the lure of this quick cash, especially when compared to jobs such as waitressing, which pay a paltry seven to thirteen dollars an hour on average.

Although prostitution can be extremely lucrative, it can also be a psychologically stressful and physically risky means of making money. In addition to the risks of sexually transmitted diseases and the potential for violence at the hands of clients, many prostitutes suffer the emotional toll of living a double life. As one prostitute put it: "It's very stressful to lead two lives, to have to lie all the time—how is it that you can afford those great shoes, that $2,000 bag, the apartment? Of course you put up with it because you love the money and the control . . . but you do get lonely."

Sugar Babies and Their Sugar Daddies

Not all women who exchange sex for money view it as prostitution:

> I only [have sex for money] with my kid's father. Not a prostitute or anything and because I love him but nothing is free in this world.
> —heterosexual woman, age 32

A "sugar baby" is a woman who offers her time, company, and usually sex to a financially well-off man (her "sugar daddy"), who in turn takes care of the woman financially—covering many, and sometimes all, of her expenses. The women in these relationships are usually significantly younger than the men. No one knows how common these arrangements are, since they are usually kept secret. A study of more than one thousand urban Kisumu Kenyans revealed that 7.4 percent of women reported themselves to be in a relationship with a "sugar daddy," although systematic studies of this phenomenon in other cultures have not yet been conducted. A hint at the prevalence of sugar daddies within the United States comes from the modern proliferation of Web-based businesses specifically devoted to matching sexually attractive women with financially attractive men. The sites, billed as dating services, include Sugardaddie.com, SugarDaddyForMe.com, WealthyMen.com, Million aireMen.com, and MarryMeSugarDaddy.com. There is even a Web site devoted to rating the quality of sugar daddy / sugar baby Web sites!

When women seek out sugar daddies, they say their main motivation is financial. An Associated Press report about sugar babies notes that for some of the women, the relationship is a way to live the "high life" without enduring the drudgery of a nine-to-five job. The benefits, sometimes given in the form of gifts, range from spa and acrylic nail appointments to dinners at expensive restaurants, designer clothing, jewelry, exotic vacations, luxury cars, and even luxury apartments. One woman in our study found sex to be an equitable exchange for books:

> *I basically was a glorified "sugar baby" for one relationship. I slept with one of my professors. I received a lot of attention academically and the man gave me tens of thousands of dollars' worth of books. I didn't feel guilty or anything. To me, the books were a bonus and really, he would have given me items anyway because I was his research assistant and his friend. I always wondered why people believed that this was unethical and borderline illegal as prostitution. He was a great lover, so he didn't need to give me anything.*
>
> —gay/lesbian woman, age 25

But some women also seek more than the money. Another news article observed that what starts out as sex for resources can be transformed into a committed relationship marked by romance, loyalty, and even chivalry.

Not all sugar-daddy relationships end up happily, though, as illustrated by the experience of a woman in our study:

> *I was living out of a hotel, pregnant and with my eldest son and there was an ex-professional football player that wanted to be my "sugar daddy" and put my son and I into a house and financially take care of us in exchange for sex. He told me he would give me a*

car so I had sex with him. Later he wanted to have sex again before delivering the car and I began to feel "cheated" so I quit talking to him.

—predominantly heterosexual woman, age 21

Sexual Bartering

Unlike in prostitution and sugar-baby relationships, some forms of sexual bartering are implicit rather than overtly negotiated. Here is how a few women in our study describe the sex-resource exchange:

I love sex so there is no reason in the world not to have sex with someone who wants it with you if they are going to take the time out and buy you a nice meal.

—bisexual woman, age 45

This person was very powerful in his company and was pretty wealthy. It wasn't done at first for anything other than mutual attraction. But after he started giving me gifts, it felt like that was all I was having sex with him for at that point.

—heterosexual woman, age 29

I was seeing a man who was sixty-nine years old, twenty-two years older than me. He took me to an expensive steak and seafood restaurant. I was only seeing him because I was bored, new in town, had not met anyone else. We both lived with relatives so mostly parked in his car, a big Cadillac. He usually only wanted oral sex, so I did it. I figured, why not? He enjoyed it and I got a good meal.

—heterosexual woman, age 47

Often the sex-resource exchange is not as explicit as these examples imply. Nonetheless, most women are quite aware of the role of resources in being sexually attracted to a man. In one of the first comprehensive studies of tactics men use to attract women, the act "He bought me dinner at a nice restaurant" proved to be one of the most effective. The Buss Lab discovered that effective sexual inducements for women include:

- He spent a lot of money on me early on.
- He gave me gifts early on.
- He showed me that he had an extravagant lifestyle.

Moreover, women find stinginess in a man to be a huge sexual turnoff.

One study found that women shown photographs of different men are more sexually attracted to men who wear expensive clothing, such as three-piece suits, sports jackets, and designer jeans, than to men who wear cheap clothing, such as tank tops and T-shirts. Another study had the same men photographed wearing two different sets of clothes. One was a Burger King uniform with a blue baseball cap and a polo-style shirt. The other was a white dress shirt with a designer tie, a navy blazer, and a Rolex watch. Based solely on these photographs, women stated that they were not willing to consider dating or having sex with the men in the low-resource garb, but were willing to entertain the possibility of dating, sex, and even marriage with the men in the high-resource attire.

In the 1993 movie *Indecent Proposal*, the character Diana, played by Demi Moore, is motivated to have sex for a single night in exchange for a million dollars. The movie spurred debates across the country, with women discussing the hypothetical question of whether they would sleep with a stranger for the same amount of money. A joke circulated in which a woman was asked whether she would sleep with Robert Redford, who had played the propositioning sexual partner, for a million dollars. After a long pause, she replied: "Yes, but you'll have to give me some time to come up with the money!" The punch line highlights the fact that women, too, deem some men to be valuable sexual resources—high-status, handsome men, such as Robert Redford, who is a verifiable sex (and status) symbol.

Not surprisingly, women in our study reported having sex not only for money but also as a means of getting a job, a raise, or a promotion. This phenomenon is known as the "casting couch," a euphemism for a situation in which an actress trades sexual favors with a producer, director, or other executive with decision-making authority in return for a movie role. Marilyn Monroe admitted to having sex with powerful men to break into Hollywood and secure key starring roles, although these episodes apparently caused her great emotional anguish. After her sex sessions with studio bosses, she reputedly took hour-long showers to wash away the defilement she endured at the hands of "wrinkled old men." The casting couch is still alive in Hollywood today, as documented in Oscar winner Julia Phillips's book, *You'll Never Eat Lunch in This Town Again*. Nor is it limited to the United States. In India, the TV show *India's Most Wanted* documented casting-couch incidents in the country's blockbuster "Bollywood" musical film industry. And in 2006, the Chinese actress Zhang Yu released twenty graphic sex videos taken from a video camera she kept hidden in order to verify her claims that she had had to pay for many of her starring roles through sexual exchanges.

Although most women who trade sex for professional advancement suffer through rather than enjoy the sex act, this is not always the case. Some women willingly exchange sex for positions and privileges in the workplace. One woman, for example, reported that she did not consider the expectation that she have sex with the foreman at her workplace to be sexual harassment, since she was able to get "easy work" as a result.

Nor are the hallowed halls of academia exempt from the basic laws of sexual economics. Offering sex for a good grade was all too common during the 1960s and '70s, prior to the enactment and enforcement of sexual harassment rules on college campuses. The offers can come from either party—and can be consensual or threatening in nature. Perhaps the most flagrant case came to light when it was revealed that over a thousand women allegedly secured better grades from Italian professor Emanuele Giordano in exchange for their sexual favors.

Women's sexual attraction to a man is sometimes influenced by the nonmonetary resources he has at his disposal. One woman needed the help of a handyman:

> *A guy I dated would do handyman work around my house and instead of money, I paid with sex. When my common sense and dignity returned, I fired him and began doing my own handyman work. I have more pride in myself and achievements and respect for myself now.*
>
> —heterosexual woman, age 44

But cold, hard cash is another inducement:

A wealthy ex-boyfriend of mine knew that I was having some finan-cial troubles so he offered me $20 for a blow job. It was a very basic exchange of services; he helped me out, I helped him out. We're on friendly terms and have been for many years. Anytime I need money, he offers it again. It's more or less a joke between us at this point.
—predominantly heterosexual woman, age 24

As this example illustrates, there may be no crisp demarcation be-tween prostitution and gift giving. "Gift giving or even cash payment for sexual intercourse," one scholar writes, "cannot be used as criteria to define prostitution, for these occur in courtship or even in marital sit-uations." As the prominent evolutionary biologist Nancy Burley notes, "Since prostitution and courtship exist as a continuum, the vast major-ity of copulatory opportunities involve costs to males in terms of time and/or material goods."

A significant difference, however, is the psychological meaning that the women themselves attach to the gifts they receive. Women often in-terpret gifts not for their literal material value, but rather for the sym-bolic meaning behind them—as evidence that the sexual partner is interested in her for a deeper enduring relationship rather than a single moment of passion. That is why the thought that the person puts into the gift is often more important than its dollar value. And in some sex-ual transactions, neither money nor gifts are exchanged at all. Rather, what is exchanged is sexual pleasure, as occurs in relationships termed "friends-with-benefits."

Friends-with-Benefits, Booty Calls, and Hooking Up

Historically, people have viewed friendships as mutually beneficial nonsexual alliances, involving trust, loyalty, and mutual personal re-gard. But a sexual component has been added to some friendships in the modern world, particularly on university campuses and among young urban adults. Research reveals that roughly 60 percent of American col-lege students have engaged in a "friends-with-sexual-benefits" relation-ship at some point in their lives and that roughly 36 percent currently have a "sex buddy." Indeed, when women have casual sex, most prefer to have it with a friend (63 percent) than with a stranger (37 percent).

These sexual connections emerged in our study of why women want sex. One woman who had been separated from her boyfriend during her college years said she sought a friend-with-benefits "because life is too damn short to be waiting four years to have sex again." Another woman in our study described it this way:

> *I was attracted to the guy . . . and even though I couldn't see us together in the long term and didn't think he was really "Mr. Right" for me, I felt like having sex but didn't want to wait until Mr. Right came along, if Mr. Right was ever going to come along at all.*
> —heterosexual woman, age 21

Romantic relationships are typically characterized by high levels of passion, intimacy, and commitment. Friends-with-benefits, in contrast, have moderate levels of passion and intimacy, but low levels of commitment. Nonetheless, unlike traditional one-night stands, a friend-with-benefits relationship typically involves mutual respect, longevity, and some measure of affection. Although more women (18 percent) than men (3 percent) expect the beneficial friendship to turn into a romantic relationship, more than 80 percent expect no romance to be imminent.

Less emotionally connected and more sexually casual are "booty calls," a slang phrase made popular by the 1995 dance song "Booty Call" by Fast Eddie and the 1997 movie *Booty Call* starring Jamie Foxx. The label derives from the mode of initiation—typically, a phone call, e-mail, text message, or instant message made by either friend for the sole purpose of proposing sex. Booty calls are made to people with whom a person has already had a casual sexual relationship, although sometimes they occur with ex-mates or in the context of more serious relationships. One study found that among twenty-two potential reasons for accepting a booty call, women ranked second "because the person did *not* want more than just sex from me."

There are exceptions, of course. In our study, one woman implied that she hoped for more than just sex:

It was a relationship called "fuck buddy," someone that you are not dating but just have sex. . . . It was kind of living a secret life that no one knew about. . . . He did not want to date but wanted to have sex, so I had sex with him. I knew he was fucking other females other than me, but I still did it because he told me to and I wanted or hoped that it would turn around.

—heterosexual woman, age 23

So what motivates most women to have sex in these various friends-with-benefits relationships? The primary answer appears to be the reciprocal, trusting exchange of pleasure for pleasure among equals. Sexual pleasure is a major motivation for women's sexual activity, and sex with a friend provides women with a greater sense of trust, security, and safety than sex with a stranger. Many women said that low-commitment sex with a trusted person discharged them of the commitments, complexities, and entanglements typically entailed by a romantic relationship. Some women, perhaps those focusing heavily on school or a career, report that they do not have the time or inclination to form an emotionally committed romantic relationship. So a sex buddy provides a mutually beneficial sexual exchange that can meet a woman's sexual needs, and sometimes even her intimacy needs, without the time burden entailed by a long-term emotional bond.

Most women, though, do not generally view a friend-with-benefits relationship as an alternative to a more traditional romantic relationship. Some use these sexual exchanges as good-for-now interludes while in the process of searching for romance. Some use them as a sexual testing ground for evaluating what they might want in a long-term mate. And others have friends-with-benefits as a sexual supplement to an ongoing committed relationship.

Not all friends-with-benefits relationships result in unmitigated, mutually beneficial sexual bliss. Women who have these relationships also report some disadvantages. These include developing romantic feelings for the friend (65 percent), harming the friendship (35 percent), causing negative emotions (24 percent), and risking negative sexual side effects such as sexually transmitted diseases (10 percent). Interestingly, the vast majority of women, 73 percent, never explicitly discuss the ground rules or expectations for these relationships. Of those who did talk explicitly, 11 percent say they came to a mutual agreement about the sex-for-sex exchange, and only a tiny minority of women, 4 percent, indicated that they "set the rules," to which the friend agreed.

Only one scientific study has explored how sex-buddy relationships fare over time. That study, involving sixty-five women and sixty men, all college students, found that in 36 percent of the cases, the sex friends remained friends but stopped having sex. Another 28 percent remained sex buddies over a longer period of time. In 26 percent of the cases, the relationship ended entirely. And in 10 percent, the friend relationship blossomed into a romantic relationship—a happy outcome for this minority, but not the primary motivation for women who enter into a sex-for-sex exchange with a friend.

Still Trading After All These Years

Many exchanges of sex for resources are more subtle and unspoken, occurring implicitly in the context of ongoing relationships, as exemplified by this account from one woman in our study:

> My boyfriend bought me a car a few years back. I wasn't in the mood for sex, but he was, so we had sex whenever he asked . . . for at least a couple of weeks!
>
> —heterosexual woman, age 22

Or, following the adage that "time equals money," because not doing so would inconvenience the person:

> I wasn't that into him and he had driven five hours to come and visit me; I felt bad [that] he had come all that way to see me and that I realized I didn't like him as much as I thought I did so I figured what the heck.
>
> —heterosexual woman, age 24

In these cases, no explicit exchange of sex for resources occurred. Rather, the woman felt motivated to have sex not out of sexual desire, but rather out of a sense of reciprocity in repaying, or balancing out, a material or nonmaterial debt.

Here is how another woman described using a sexual exchange to build up a debt with her partner:

> *Sometimes in a relationship you do things because you know that if you please your partner they are happy, which helps jump-start a deeds process. For example, if the house really needs cleaning and you want some help, the person is more open to helping when they are in a good mood. Also, if you need a favor such as building something your partner is more likely to say yes if you return a favor in the most pleasurable of ways!*
> — heterosexual woman, age 25

Other women are more direct in their description of sexual economics:

> *[I have sex] to get my way or to persuade my husband into something I really want and he might be opposed to.*
> — heterosexual woman, age 31

> *I will often use sex as leverage in my relationship to get what I want.*
> — heterosexual woman, age 27

> *You know the situation with your spouse where you really want to please them sexually because you want to have your own way on something. Little things like choosing [where to eat] dinner.*
> — heterosexual woman, age 25

In hunter-gatherer societies, women are sexually attracted to men who have the ability to provide meat through hunting. This attraction occurs whether a woman wants to become a wife or a mistress. Among the Siriono of Bolivia, for example:

> Food is one of the best lures for obtaining extramarital sex partners, and a man often uses game as a means of seducing a

potential wife. Failures in this respect result not so much from a reluctance on the part of a woman to yield to a potential husband who will give her game, but more from an unwillingness on the part of the man's own wife to part with any of the meat that he has acquired, least of all to one of his potential wives.

Siriono women who become extramarital-affair partners often refuse to have sex with their paramours unless a regular supply of meat is delivered. Wives, however, supervise the main meat distribution, so that if part of a husband's catch is missing, they suspect their husband of carrying on an affair, provoking jealousy, outrage, and efforts at mate guarding. In the never-ending battle of the sexes, Siriono men try to circumvent their wife's mate guarding by sending a chunk of meat to their mistress through an intermediary before returning home with the main bounty.

Siriono women's sexual attraction to men who provide meat is dramatically illustrated by the case of a man who was an unsuccessful hunter. He suffered low status, experienced "hunting anxiety," and had lost a previous wife to a man who was a better hunter. The anthropologist Allan R. Holmberg felt sorry for him, so he gave him meat, and taught him how to hunt game using a shotgun. Before long, the man's status had risen considerably and he attracted a wife and several new sex partners. He also gained confidence and began to insult other men rather than being the butt of their insults.

These sexual economics occur repeatedly in nearly all well-studied traditional societies. Among the Hadza of Tanzania, a man "may find it difficult to marry a wife, or, once married, to keep a wife, if he is unsuccessful in hunting big game." Similar patterns occur among the Mehinaku of Brazil, the Sharanahua of eastern Peru, and the Yanomamö of Venezuela. Men are quite aware that women find meat provisioning to be sexually attractive. They use meat to attract long-term and short-term sexual partners, and they use meat to poach the mates of other men. One Yanomamö man described a potential rival to the anthropologist Raymond Hames: "He's not even a man [referring to his lack of hunting prowess]. She will leave him and come with me because he can't hunt and I can." From an evolutionary perspective, it is often a mutually beneficial exchange.

In modern Western cultures, these sorts of direct exchanges tend to be far less common, or at least less explicit. Nonetheless, sexual economics sometimes continues to influence why women have sex within marriage. The exchange of sex may not be for economic resources per se, but rather for reciprocal favors. In a therapy session, one woman described how she had a much lower sex drive than her husband but she agreed to have sex with him because he agreed to cut the lawn and take the garbage out—equally aversive tasks in her eyes!

The resources a husband brings in, or fails to bring in, can affect a woman's sexual motivation. A woman in our study said that her husband's performance at work influenced her inclinations to have sex:

> *My husband receiving a promotion and raise at work is a good indicator that we will be having sex. Perhaps it's a sort of reward for him, and also—he does look more attractive to me when he generates big bucks. I don't think it's so much the money as it is his accomplishment, that he is a winner in other people's eyes.*
>
> —heterosexual woman, age 48

But the motivation can also go the other way—increasing a woman's inclination to have sex with men other than her husband. Although women are motivated to have affairs for a variety of reasons—a husband's infidelity, his lack of interest in sex, verbal or physical abuse—one that also ranks high in research conducted by the Buss Lab is the failure of the husband to hold down a job. In these circumstances, the affair is most often motivated by a desire to switch mates, trading up to a partner better able to provide.

Sexual economics arises within marriages in yet another way—women's sexual refusals. Women who lack economic resources themselves and who are dependent on their husbands for financial support report feeling that they are less willing to refuse their husband's sexual advances, compared to married women who have their own source of income. Women who have resources have more power both to act on their sexual desires when they have them and to opt out of sex with their husbands when they lack sexual desire.

Sexual economics play out across cultures in many forms. On the mating market, women accrue significant power as a result of men's sexual psychology—their desire for sexual variety, their sex drive, their sexual overperception bias, their persistent sexual fantasies, and a brain wired to respond to visual stimulation. As the valuable resource over which men compete, women can, and some often do, exercise that power to exchange their sexual resources for benefits, including food, gifts, special favors, grades, career advancement, or entrée into the movie business. In some of these exchanges, there is no sharp line demarcating honest courtship, seduction, and prostitution. Nonetheless, there is a world of psychological distance between prostitution, which is explicitly quid pro quo, and honest courtship, where gifts are typically prized for their symbolic value as an indicator of commitment or the esteem in which the woman is held.

9. The Ego Boost

Body Image, Attention, Power, and Submission

☙✍

> *If sex and creativity are often seen by dictators as subversive activities, it's because they lead to the knowledge that you own your own body (and with it your own voice), and that's the most revolutionary insight of all.*
>
> —Erica Jong (b. 1942)

"Self-esteem" is a psychological term that refers to a person's sense of his or her value or worth. Self-esteem is typically measured by asking people about whether they are satisfied with themselves; whether they feel they have a number of good qualities and are able to do things as well as other people; and whether they are proud of themselves, feel successful, and have respect for themselves. Self-esteem has been related to personality features such as shyness, behavioral outcomes such as how well someone can perform a task under pressure, thought processes such as the likelihood of taking blame for failures, health behaviors such as using birth control and conducting breast self-exams, and clinical problems such as anxiety and depression.

A woman's self-esteem affects, and is affected by, her sexuality, her sexual experiences, and her sex appeal. Self-assurance is sexy. Blissful intimate episodes boost confidence. There are deep psychological connections between our sex lives and our sense of self in both sexes. Among men, for example, research reveals that those who experience a bout of impotence, or erectile dysfunction, suffer a tremendous blow to their self-esteem. There's an adaptive reason for this link: Failure to perform sexually, historically, would have jeopardized a man's reproductive success. Conversely, few things raise a man's self-esteem more than a fresh sexual conquest of an attractive woman. Among women, evolution has forged adaptive links between esteem and sexual success. Sometimes these links, as we will see, can go awry in the modern world.

Although some standards of female beauty are culturally variable—such as the preference for relative slenderness or plumpness—many are universal. Features that have universal sex appeal include clear, smooth skin, plump lips, clear, large eyes, good muscle tone, sprightly gait, symmetrical features, and a low waist-to-hip ratio—all of which are associated with fertility. Studies of how women feel about their bodies reveal that their body esteem, unlike that of men, is closely linked with their overall sexual attractiveness, as well as to their specific body attributes such as waist, thighs, and hips. Because a woman's appearance provides such a bounty of cues to her fertility, men have evolved mate preferences that, perhaps unfortunately, give tremendous importance to a woman's physical appearance. In some ways, it is a psychological fact of life that women are sometimes treated as sex objects, just as men are sometimes treated as status objects.

On the positive side, having sex can provide women with a rush of confidence. One woman in our study experienced a boost from sex that lasted for days:

> I had sex with someone who I felt close to because I was feeling alone and lonely. This man was kind and loving to me always and it made me feel better to have him with me, in bed, for a night. We had amazing sex and he would do anything I asked, always. I felt more confident and certainly sexier (as a woman) the following days. It helped boost my self-confidence a great deal.
>
> —heterosexual woman, age 39

At times women describe having sex because they believed doing so would improve their low self-esteem:

> To be honest, the reason I have slept with five out of the six men I have in my lifetime was because they were out of my league. I have

a weakness for [when] someone who is nice looking, employed, and of average intelligence likes me. Usually only toothless, ugly creepy guys like me.

—heterosexual woman, age 24

When it works, seeking sex for esteem can give women tremendous benefits—a boost from mood-altering hormones such as oxytocin; the assurance of her value as a human being; the confidence to trade up to a better partner; and a sense of sexual power in a world that sometimes tries to take it all away.

Feeling Attractive

In times of feeling less confident—overweight, unattractive, etc.—it has been nice to know that someone else found me attractive and "wanted" me.

—heterosexual woman, age 23

In part because of the evolutionary roots of women's sexual attractiveness, self-esteem is greatly influenced by how women feel about their bodies.

After finally losing enough weight where I . . . felt comfortable and sexy in my own skin, I saw my best male friend and he was blown away by my appearance. So I flirted extra, and was [more] friendly . . . and more aggressive [than usual], and let him know that after the bar we would be going to my apartment.

—predominantly heterosexual woman, age 22

What determines how a woman feels about her body, however, is not always objective. Although it is true that a woman's body image is affected by her actual physical characteristics—including weight and body shape—researchers have found that it is also greatly influenced by her own personal perceptions about her body and what it should look like. In fact, for women who are dissatisfied with their bodies—an alarming 55 percent of both married and single women in North America—their expectations of what their bodies should look like contribute more to their dissatisfaction than do their actual body characteristics.

Concerns about body image exist in women of all ages. In a nation-wide survey of thirty thousand individuals ranging in age from fifteen to seventy-four, 55 percent of women expressed dissatisfaction with their bodies. Among adolescent girls, body image is adversely affected by exposure to beauty magazines. Among women in their late fifties and older, body image tends to be linked more to their health than to how their bodies compare with the latest winner of *America's Next Top Model*. There are also cultural differences in how satisfied or dissatisfied women tend to be with their bodies, with media-saturated Western countries expressing more dissatisfaction. Even within the United States, studies find cultural differences: Black women were much more satisfied with their bodies than were women of other races or ethnicities.

Not surprisingly, body image concerns play a major role in propelling women to buy and try all the latest diet advice and supplements—a $50 billion industry, in North America alone. A poor body image causes some women to develop eating disorders, including anorexia nervosa (self-starvation) and bulimia nervosa (binge eating and purging). Less well known is the fact that how a woman feels about her body significantly impacts all aspects of her sexuality. Studies among U.S. college women reveal that those who rate themselves as unattractive are less likely to have a sexual partner, probably because women who are dissatisfied with their bodies are self-conscious and experience anxiety about someone viewing them naked. Consequently, they sometimes avoid rather than pursue sexual opportunities. Even among college students who are in sexual relationships, women with negative body images have less frequent sex and experiment less sexually than their positive-body-image peers.

Of course there are always exceptions. Some women with poor body images deliberately seek out sexual activity to try to make themselves feel better about their looks. Two women in our study exemplify this motive for having sex:

> *To be honest, I wanted the affection of another person, if only for a short time. The few times I have had sex for attention, I wasn't feel-*

ing attractive or sexy. I thought that if this man wanted to have intercourse with me, then he must find [me] somewhat attractive and sexually appealing. After the act was over, I felt empty, not used in any way, but still empty. I guess it was because I was realizing that just because a man had sex with me, it didn't make me any happier.
—heterosexual woman, age 23

I have never been skinny, but I am not obese. It is difficult for me to believe that anyone would want to have sex with me. Apparently that has not been the case, as I have had sex with what others would deem as "desirable" men. After my last long-term relationship ended (we were talking about marriage), I quickly took up with a very good-looking man who treated me like crap, but who I had sex with a lot because it made me feel good to know that someone this attractive and successful would want to have sex with me.
—heterosexual woman, age 32

Breaking Up with Barbie

In addition to altering how willing a woman is to engage in and experiment with sex, a negative body image can adversely affect a woman's actual sexual response. Women with poor body images have lower sex drives, more problems becoming aroused, and greater difficulty achieving orgasms. A study conducted in the Meston Sexual Psychophysiology Lab had eighty-five college women come into the lab one at a time and privately fill out questionnaires about their sexual functioning and their body image. The body image questionnaire asked how they felt about their weight and various aspects of their sexual attractiveness. Then, in rooms by themselves, the women read an erotic story and rated how "turned on" the story made them. Women who felt good about their bodies experienced much more sexual desire in response to the stories than did women who felt bad about either their weight or their level of attractiveness. The women with poorer body images also reported having lower desire in real-life situations with their partners.

If a woman's view of her body changes over time, it can also change her level of sexual desire and her body's response during sex. Dr. Patricia

Barthalow Koch and her colleagues at Pennsylvania State University assessed changes in the sexuality of more than three hundred middle-aged women across time. They found that over a period of ten years, approximately 57 percent of the women reported a lessening of sexual desire, 58 percent reported actually engaging in sex less often, 40 percent reported enjoying sex less, and 32 percent reported having more difficulty with orgasms. The researchers then looked to see what might explain the decreases in sexual functioning among so many women. Guess what? Body image played a major role. The more a so many woman perceived herself to be less attractive than she was ten years earlier, the more she reported a decrease in sexual functioning over the past ten years. The reverse was also true. The more a woman judged herself to be attractive, the more likely she was to report an increase in sexual response and sexual activity over the previous ten years.

When a woman is too focused on how her body looks during sex or how her partner may be evaluating her body, she becomes distracted from the pleasurable sensations that can help her to become aroused and have an orgasm. Training women to refocus their attention on pleasurable sensations during sex is a key part of many successful sex therapy techniques. Challenging the woman's often unfounded beliefs about what her body *should* look like and helping her to view her body in a more accurate and objective manner are also effective treatment techniques. A study of thirty-two clinically obese women who underwent a thirty-one-week weight-loss program demonstrated the link between body image and sexual functioning. In addition to losing a substantial amount of weight, women completing the program experienced huge improvements in body image and sex drive, and actually engaged in sex more frequently. When they were later asked why they thought their sexual functioning improved after the program, almost three-quarters of the women said that it was because they felt better about their bodies.

Much has been written about the media's role in contributing to women's dissatisfaction with their bodies. We seem to be on a first-name basis with women who are celebrated primarily for being thin and pretty, but does anyone know the name of the most recent woman to win a Pulitzer Prize for literature? (It was Geraldine Brooks, in 2006.) So let's take a closer look at the images against which women usually judge their bodies. Runway models are typically five foot ten or taller and average 120 to 124 pounds in weight. Many young (and not so young) women dream about looking like them. But the reality is that only about 5 percent of all women have the genetic makeup to achieve that body type—no matter how much they diet, exercise, undergo plastic surgery, or develop a health-destroying eating disorder. Pictures of waiflike movie stars, with shoulder blades poking through their sweaters, grace the gossip and fashion weeklies, looking, as one feminist Web site calls it, "impossibly beautiful." So impossibly beautiful, in fact, that photo-altering software programs are used to slim and tuck cheeks, arms, stomachs, and legs while magically expanding bra cup sizes. The ideal has become so pervasive in the entertainment industry that in some cases, photos have to be altered to make women's hip and collar bones less pronounced.

Even Barbie can be implicated. As it turns out, researchers have calculated that if Barbie were life-size, she would be five foot nine and her measurements would be 39-18-33. She would weigh no more than 110 pounds, which means she would have so little body fat that she would not menstruate. Ken and his plastic descendants should be forewarned of the risks her oh-so-shapely body has on her reproductive abilities. Perhaps the distorted bodies of the Bratz dolls, which feature oversized heads and tiny bodies that are truly physically impossible, will break the cycle.

Social Esteem

Building a healthy sense of self-esteem often comes from taking stock of your personal strengths and abilities and being content with who you are and what you have to offer the world. But instead of focusing inward on oneself as a person, some people focus outward on external comparison to create their sense of self-worth. In addition to comparing their bodies to the ones plastered on billboards, they analyze how much they earn compared to others, what neighborhood they live in (and how their houses stack up against the proverbial Joneses), and what social circles they are accepted into. Based on psychological calculations, people then assess how worthy they are—in their own eyes and in the eyes of others.

As anyone who has experienced junior high school knows, this comparative rating and ranking isn't just an adult pastime. Your friends affect how "popular" you are, even in grade school. For many young adults, self-esteem is closely linked to who their friends are and to their social standing among peers—a phenomenon captured in parent-frightening detail in sociologist Rosalind Wiseman's book *Queen Bees and Wannabes*. As Wiseman notes, "a girl in the popular clique can duck a reputation as a slut even if she's frequently having sex." In our study, many women recalled situations where they engaged in sex to try to gain friends and influence their social acceptance:

> *I had a friend in high school who was really assertive, and really rebellious. She made it seem as if the only way I could be "cool" with her was if I shunned everything I thought was right and went on this track of having sex just to do it. Before I became friends with her, I was really naïve. I really knew nothing about sex and so I trusted her that things such as daring friends to have sex, and cheating on their girlfriends, and sleeping with every guy who showed interest were normal things to do. I would have sex just so that she would have more respect for me, since I was really poor in high school and thus had very, very few friends. I hated every experience I was having, and it took me five years to feel validated as a moral person again after I stopped being friends with her.*
>
> —heterosexual woman, age 22

Some women had sex to induce people to like them:

> *[I was] just young I think and wanted to feel like I was "someone," [to] build my self-esteem through someone else. I thought I was a big shot and that this would make people in school like me. I realize now that I did use a lot of outside sources to try to make myself like-able . . . to fit in. And, at the time it didn't work . . . [it] made me feel worse really. . . . I just wanted to be like all the other girls . . . or at least what my version in my head thought they were like.*
>
> —heterosexual woman, age 41

Some had sex to fit into a certain social group:

> *I felt like being a virgin excluded me from my social circle. I didn't "get" things my sexually active friends did and felt I was often excluded from social activities for this reason. So, I had sex with someone older in order to gain acceptance into their social circle which consisted of older, highly educated individuals.*
>
> —heterosexual woman, age 26

As we've seen, women are often attracted to men of high status because with status come resources, a nice lifestyle, and myriad social benefits. From an evolutionary perspective, high status in a man might be a marker of good genes to pass along to children. But some women in our study sought out sex with a high-status partner for a completely different reason: They were not actually interested in pursuing a relationship with the person, or getting pregnant, or even reaping the material benefits that could follow. They simply wanted to raise their social status in the eyes of their friends by having sex with someone of high mate value:

> *The guy wasn't super famous, just in a very popular local band that is working on an album for a major company. It was fun, he was a good lover and everyone knew what happened because I lived in a dorm and he came there when we were intimate. I just did it to make other girls envious. . . . It made me look cool.*
>
> —heterosexual woman, age 22

For other women, having sex with a high-status partner caused them to feel more desirable. In these cases, they had sex not to impress their friends or raise their social status, but to raise their own sense of self-worth. Sometimes it did not go as well as hoped:

> *The person I had sex with was a very wanted guy in my college years and any girl would be proud to say she was his date, or so I thought. After a fun night of drinking at the local nightclub (it was*

ladies' night, we drank for free!), I was feeling courageous enough to approach him and to start flirting a bit. Well, one thing led to another and we wound up back at his place for a night of sex. I was definitely willing, mainly because the liquor I had in me gave me the courage to let my insecurities about my looks go for that one glorious night. That glorious night wound up giving me an STD, a reputation, and a horrid hangover! Never again was I so foolish!

—heterosexual woman, age 32

But other times, it went even better than planned:

When I first met my husband I considered him "out of my league." . . . I grew up very shy, nerdy, and hung out with the "skaters." And here comes Mr. All American Boy—muscles, tall, tan, great smile—exactly who would never have paid attention to me if we went to high school together. We got back to my apartment after dinner and he brought in his bag and I casually told him that he could either sleep on the couch or I didn't mind sharing my bed with him. He chose my bed and I didn't hold back. . . . We ended up getting married six months later. Every once in a while I will catch myself looking at him doing something and think damn, I can't believe he is my husband.

—heterosexual woman, age 24

The Attention Deficit

Although some people seem to be born blessed with healthy self-esteem, psychological research points to several significant influences during childhood, including parental attachment, support, and attention. One study of 16,749 adolescents, for example, found that higher parental support and parental monitoring were linked to higher self-esteem in their children. Children's *perceptions* of their parents' level of attention to them is especially critical—parents who keep a loving but watchful eye and who are ready to react on short notice if needed. Perhaps this parental monitoring gives children the confidence to explore the opportunities and dangers of their environment and enable them to grow into fully functioning adults. Not all women are happy beneficiaries of loving parental attention; some suffer from parental neglect. Low self-esteem sometimes causes women to make up for this attention deficit—seeking through sex the attention that they never got from their parents.

In our study, a number of women described having sex as a way to try to "make up" for something that was missing in their early home life. In many cases, this meant using sex to get attention and emotional connection. Some women reported that they used sex to feel the love, care, and attention that they did not get at home:

> *I was a teenager growing up in an abusive, poor household. I thought that if I was physical with guys it would lead to love, plus I liked the attention they gave me for my body, which was nice. It happened on several instances but one time I remember just laying there and staring up at the sky, waiting for it to be over. I wanted to feel good about it and pretended to be excited, but I really just wanted emotional closeness. I felt dirty, but continued doing it over and over, hoping.*
>
> —heterosexual woman, age 28

For others, having sex served the purpose of filling a void—but only temporarily:

> *I was raised in an abusive household. I grew up believing that there was something fundamentally wrong with me, for which I deserved to be abused. Sex was the first attention I got that, while it was not motivated in any long-term sense, while it was occurring, I felt truly appreciated, wanted, and loved.*
>
> —predominantly heterosexual woman, age 25

> *I was a teenager with low self-esteem. Having had parents who basically ignored me my whole life, I erroneously assumed that sex meant that the person cared about me. The attention from sex was nice, but ultimately, I found out that no, it doesn't actually mean that the person really cares about you.*
>
> —bisexual woman, age 24

And one woman shared an account of how an abusive past made her seek out sex because she simply wanted to *feel* something:

> *I was in a bad head space where I felt like life and doctors had used and abused me for their own purposes. For a while I didn't respect myself or my body and I figured, "What the hell, it's just flesh, nothing more." So I would completely flash anyone and everyone or behave in a raunchy manner just because after all it was just flesh and completely meaningless. I lost my virginity in the same mindframe. [It was] like, "What the hell, the opportunity presented itself." It lasted all of maybe forty-five minutes, [then] he fell asleep and I just got dressed, sat there for a while, like okay now what? [Then I] went off to find some friends to have lunch with. I guess I just wanted to feel something and to feel degraded was to feel something.*

> —heterosexual woman, age 24

Moving On

Just as some people look externally, assessing their resources and social standing to judge their own self-worth, some people determine how they feel about themselves by whether someone loves them romantically. Because there is no guarantee that any love will last forever, this puts their self-esteem in a rather precarious position. If a woman's entire self-esteem is based on another's love for her, then she risks feeling extremely depressed and worthless if that person's love ceases. Even for people who do not put all their self-esteem eggs in another's love basket, having someone stop loving you can be psychologically bruising.

Depending on the level of loss, most people who have suffered rejection go through a period of mourning during which they seek ways to comfort themselves. Some turn to friends for comfort, some rely on alcohol or chocolate, and, according to our study, some seek sex. As one woman in our study wrote, "The best way to get over someone is to get under someone else!" Many women in our study relayed stories about how they used sex to heal their love wounds. Their experiences were all unique.

For some women, having sex with someone else after a relationship ended helped restore their self-esteem:

> *Whenever I get hurt by someone I really care about I end up having sex with someone else. It helps me get over that person and move on. It also helps me feel better about myself, especially if the person left me for someone else. It makes me feel like I am still desirable and it wasn't me that made him leave for someone else.*
>
> —heterosexual woman, age 19

> *I had just gotten out of a really bad relationship, and was feeling pretty bad about myself. It was the typical post-relationship blues, feeling rather unlovable and unable to see a point where another person would want me or be attracted to me. When I met [this guy], I didn't particularly like him and wasn't particularly attracted to him. However, he showed some interest, so we started hanging out. Before long, we started having sex. I continued to lack any real feelings towards him, but enjoyed feeling like someone wanted me.*
>
> —heterosexual woman, age 24

For other women, having sex to restore their self-esteem after a break-up provided only a very short-lived fix:

> *My ex had unceremoniously dumped me on my birthday, opting to date someone his family would accept. I felt abandoned, unwanted, not good enough and, perhaps most importantly, undesired. Months of depression ensued. With time I began to feel a return in my self-esteem, but couldn't shake feeling unlovable. During the summer vacation I ran into a childhood friend who I knew had an intense decade-long crush on me. Perhaps it was the loneliness, perhaps it was the alcohol, but I became convinced being with him would erase the feelings of rejection installed by my ex. Surely he would have that type of power, after all he did manage to cultivate the*

ten-year crush on me. In the end, I temporarily felt a boost in my sense of self-worth, however the feelings of loneliness were replaced with guilt and shame. I tried to find a way to feel loved; instead I found a way to cease loving myself.

—heterosexual woman, age 24

And for some women, it did not serve the intended purpose at all:

I've actually had rebound sex several times. I thought it would help me forget about that other person, or even erase that person from my body by having another's imprint upon it. It didn't actually do that, of course, it was simply sex with another person. I still missed the old lovers just as much as I did before the act.

—heterosexual woman, age 23

Whereas some women have sex to make up for what is psychologically lacking or to restore a sense of self-worth after a breakup, others have sex to achieve a true sense of power.

Exerting Sexual Power

Sex for some women affords them a tremendous sense of power, and that feeling of command and dominance motivates them in the sexual realm. One woman in our study captured this theme eloquently:

It's mostly a matter of feeling capable of initiating sex and demonstrating power over the person you have sex with, even if that person is a long-term partner. In many ways sex is about power, power to give your partner pleasure and take it from them, and power to feel attractive and desirable. I don't think it's unusual to have sex at least partly for this reason.

—heterosexual woman, age 22

Power is not always an end in itself. Rather, it is a way that women can exert control and influence over a sexual partner. Sometimes the control occurs within the context of an existing romantic relationship:

*For a female, it's easy to keep a man in control through sex. You
can be equal, withhold it from him, etc. I was with a controlling
boyfriend, but we were equals when it came to sex, and I could
even tell him what to do when in most cases that wasn't an option.*
—heterosexual woman, age 19

In other cases, a feeling of supremacy comes from simultaneously commanding a sexual partner and beating out another woman for sexual attention:

*This happened shortly after my husband and I split up after he had
an affair. I engaged in a threesome with a man and a woman as a
way of getting back at him. He never found out and that was never
my intention. The threesome happened as a result of my wanting to
prove to myself that I was still desirable and could be wanted by
someone. I liked the idea of it being a taboo act and something I
had never tried before. I had no interest in the woman and we did
not interact with each other in any way, our attentions were both
focused solely on the male in this encounter. I experienced a feeling
of power when I was able to distract his attentions away from her
to have intercourse with me.*
—heterosexual woman, age 29

And sometimes the power comes not merely from outcompeting other
women, but from succeeding in sexually attracting a powerful high-status
man:

*He was the kind of guy all the women wanted to be with. He'd
walk into a room and all the attention was focused on him. When
he focused his eyes on you, you couldn't help but feel like the most
important person in the world. I'd known him all my life, but we
had never been more than acquaintances. But one day he focused
his gaze on me, and I couldn't resist him. The idea of him, the most
important person in my peer group, wanting me, a wallflower, generated a surge of power within. I felt important, like his equal.*
—heterosexual woman, age 24

Power may not simply come from dominating others. Some women have sex because they feel that it is a sphere of their life over which they can wield control:

> *For awhile while I was suffering with bulimia I was having serious control issues and it felt good to me at the time to have complete sexual control over someone, especially a man.*
>
> —heterosexual woman, age 23

> *The opportunity to breathe life into a dying man, once loved in youth, is a powerful exchange—a promise of immortality for the dying and elevation to a higher spiritual plane for the living.*
>
> —heterosexual woman, age 58

> *I had sex with a couple of guys because I felt sorry for them. These guys were virgins and I felt bad that they had never had sex before so I had sex with them. I felt like I was doing them a big favor that no one else had ever done. I felt power over them, like they were weaklings under me and I was in control. It boosted my confidence to be the teacher in the situation and made me feel more desirable.*
>
> —heterosexual woman, age 25

Power is a prominent thread in many erotic romance novels. Romance novels constitute a more than $1 billion industry, and this genre of fiction sells more copies of books than any other, including mysteries. In 2004, for example, romance novels constituted 55 percent of all paperback books sold in the United States. They are translated into dozens of languages and sell in more than one hundred international markets. And 95 percent of the consumers of romance novels are women, so the books provide a unique window into women's sexual psychology.

Although the love story between the heroine and the hero is the central plot driver in romance novels, it is fascinating to examine how the writers—almost exclusively women—portray women's sexuality. Readers identify with the heroine as a powerful and compelling object of male sexual desire. The heroine has sexual control because the hero's overwhelming passion for her ensures his sexual fidelity to her. In essence, the hero becomes dependent on the sexually powerful heroine. The heroine's sexual power is especially enhanced because of the nature of the hero who is mesmerized by her—he is typically ruggedly handsome; masculine in face, body, and behavior; exceptionally high in social status (a prince or an extraordinarily successful businessman); and fabulously wealthy. In short, he has all of the attractions that would have been critical to women across cultures and throughout human evolutionary history.

In many erotic romance novels, the hero uses some measure of physical force, "taking" the heroine sexually, despite her protestations and resistance. A few psychologists argue that because some women find these forceful sexual submission depictions to be arousing, they reflect psychological pathology or socially internalized gender scripts that urge women to link sex with submission to men. The actual scientific evidence, however, supports a different interpretation. Psychologist Patricia Hawley studied forceful sexual submission fantasies in a sample of nearly nine hundred women. She found that women who tended to have and to enjoy these sexual force fantasies, far from being submissive or pathological, in fact were more dominant, more independent, and higher in self-esteem than other women. Women who were less socially powerful had fewer sexual fantasies in which they were forced to sexually submit. Hawley concluded that the erotic allure of women's forceful submission fantasies reflects feminine power rather than weakness, since the man in the fantasy is provoked uncontrollably by her sexual attractiveness, allure, and irresistibility.

Sexual Submission

Although the heroine in romance novels holds sexual power over the high-mate-value hero, there is also, almost paradoxically, a way in which she yields or submits to his uncontrollable sexual passion for her. This fusion of sexual power and sexual irresistibility through submission occurs frequently in erotic romances, and was cited by women in our own study as a reason they have sex:

> *It's simply enjoyable to submit, when one has to be in control of one's life all the time. When I have to spend all day every day fulfilling*

responsibilities and obligations and taking care of business, it's nice
to just let go and give someone else complete and utter control. I
also love the idea of someone wanting me so much that they can't
resist, and I can only submit.

—bisexual woman, age 18

Another woman expressed how sexual appeal, sexual submission, and
sexual power were linked in her mind:

Sometimes being submissive turns me on. Not always. But I've
wanted to have sex a few times so that my partner could be in con-
trol. It made me feel sexy and wanted and in control in other ways.
I wanted him to be in control but it made me feel like I was in con-
trol too. Being submissive sometimes includes having my wrists tied
down with rope or having my partner hold my arms down.

—heterosexual woman, age 33

A plausible explanation is that being submissive can cause a woman to
feel sexually desirable, and her sexual desirability, in turn, gives her
power and control over her partner. Overall, we found that two reasons
women gave for having sex—"I wanted to submit to my partner" and "I
wanted to 'gain control' of the person"—were related; statistically, they
clustered together, suggesting that sexual submission can in fact be a
means of gaining control.

Perhaps this is one reason why sexual submission is a popular sexual
fantasy among women. A study of 141 married women discovered that
the fantasy "I imagine that I am being overpowered and forced to surren-
der" was the second most common fantasy out of the list of fifteen, exceeded only by fantasies of "an imaginary romantic lover." Other studies
verify that a substantial number of women experience pleasurable sexual
submission fantasies. One study found that 29 percent of the women participants had experienced sexually arousing submission fantasies, and another study found that 30 percent of women had experienced the sexual
fantasy "I'm a slave who must obey a man's every wish."

Other women enjoy being sexually submissive not because it necessarily gives them power, but simply because it gives them a change of pace from their usual style of interacting:

> *I act very outgoing and tend to take control of situations in my daily life. I really like sex where I am submissive because it is different than how I usually act. I trust my boyfriend to not take advantage of me so it's easier to let someone else be dominant over me and not worry about being in control.*
>
> —heterosexual woman, age 28

In fact, control can sometimes be a burden, and some women experience relief in relinquishing it. Some women say they became annoyed with men who do not take control—men who can't decide which restaurant they want to go to, what movie they want to see, what their life's goals are, and constantly ask the woman what she wants to do. The sense of freedom gained from submissive role-playing comes across in these women's accounts:

> *I wanted to display my submissiveness to my boyfriend as a role-playing game. We had been wrestling, and it started to get sexual. I had been in a submissive mood, and the thought and the physicality of him dominating me turned me on. He took four leather belts out of his closet and tied me to his bed. I felt completely out of control and like I didn't have to worry about anything; where to put my hands, what to say, what to do. I let him take over completely.*
>
> —predominantly heterosexual woman, age 22

> *I am a masochist and a sexual submissive. . . . I was always scolded growing up for masturbating, thus I think I have associated sex with embarrassment and humiliation at times. I enjoy being called a slut by my partner, although I don't really see . . . myself as needing embarrassment. It is a game, a way of getting out an urge.*
>
> —woman, age 31, sexual orientation not given

I am a submissive and enjoy being degraded in a scene. I only do this with trusted and respected partners. I would not seek to be degraded by someone wasn't a steady partner.

—heterosexual woman, age 53

In our study, we discovered that a small minority of women reported that they had sex because they wanted to be punished:

There are times where I feel like I deserve to be punished. If my boyfriend comes on to me and I don't want to have sex I won't stop him. I want to feel used.

—heterosexual woman, age 18

I felt guilty for emotionally hurting my long-time boyfriend. . . . I guess I kind of wanted to let him hurt me physically to absolve myself of the guilt of hurting him emotionally. I don't even remember what I did, to hurt him I mean, it was a long time ago. . . . I didn't face him while we were doing it, I turned away from him, just told him I liked it better that way. I think he knew something was wrong because I typically tend to crave closeness. Somewhere deep inside he was aware he was hurting me, but I just begged him to give it to me the way I liked it, told him what to do, and so he did it. I felt just a tiny bit better after it was over. Like him hurting me physically evened the playing field a bit.

—heterosexual woman, age 20

Having submissive sex as a means to punish oneself is much less common than submitting to sex because it is psychologically linked to their partner finding them sexually attractive and irresistible. But stories like these open the door to the darker sides of sex, including the experiences of women who agreed to have unwanted sex because they felt it was not their right to say no, or because they felt they somehow owed the person. As we will explore in the next chapter, when these women reflected on such experiences, many said that low self-esteem and feeling worthless played a role in their sexual choices.

10. The Dark Side

Sexual Deception, Punishment, and Abuse

⊂℞ℬ⊃

*Pleasure cannot be shared; like Pain, it can only be experienced
or inflicted, and when we give pleasure to our Lovers or bestow
Charity upon the Needy, we do so, not to gratify the object of
our Benevolence, but only ourselves. For the Truth is that we
are kind for the same reason as we are cruel, in order that we
may enhance the sense of our own Power.*
—Aldous Huxley (1894–1963)

Humans have dark and disturbing facets in their sexual psychology that we cannot ignore. An astonishingly large number of women sometimes have sex because men deceive them, drug them, verbally coerce them, or physically force them. In some ways, these may seem like odd topics to cover in a book about why women have sex. Indeed, some of our friends and colleagues wondered why we would discuss topics such as forced sex in this book at all, since many do not consider rape to be about sex but rather about power and violence.

We are sensitive to these concerns and deliberated much over them. In the end, though, we decided to defer to the voices of the women in our study. The fact is that many women, when asked what motivated them to have sex, *did* respond by saying they were deceived by a man, verbally coerced, plied with drugs or alcohol, or physically forced. These are not ways in which women *want* to have sex. But they are nonetheless some of the reasons women end up having sex.

There is another purpose in getting these darker reasons for sex out in the open. Highlighting these circumstances through the words of actual women who have suffered these experiences and framing these first-hand accounts with scientific studies of their impact provides readers with knowledge that they might be able to use in their own lives or in supporting loved ones. Although societal awareness of rape has increased through college campuses and other public education projects, there is still an uncomfortable, sensationalistic, and sometimes blaming manner in the way rape cases are discussed and portrayed. Further, the experience of forced sex can shape a woman's sexuality for a long time after the event, and the fear of forced sex can permanently alter a woman's sense of safety and security.

For all these reasons, we would be remiss to ignore forced sex and pretend that it does not feature in some women's sexual lives. We hope that by hearing directly from the women in our study, others who have experienced forced sex will learn that they are not alone in their experiences. And we hope that it gives women (and men) a few tools that will help to prevent these abhorrent acts from occurring to begin with. We start with a phenomenon that is astonishingly common: deception.

Deception in Dating

Tactics of deception are common throughout the animal world. Any organism that perceives can be deceived. Fishermen create lures that mimic tasty food, deceiving the fish into biting a hidden barb. Among scorpion flies, males lure females with dead flies, highly desired meals for female scorpion flies, for the purpose of gaining copulations, only to take the dead fly away after the male has ejaculated. Humans are no exception to the use of deception in the sexual battlefield.

A deeper, evolutionary understanding of why sexual deception and other dark sides of mating are so prevalent comes from *sexual conflict theory*. Whenever the evolutionary interests of a man and a woman differ, there is the potential for sexual conflict. Sexual conflict theory predicts that when these conflicts occur repeatedly over generations each sex will evolve adaptations designed to pull or manipulate the other closer to its own optimum. If women prefer to mate with men who have resources, for example, then it is sometimes in men's evolutionary interest to deceive a woman about his resource holdings if that tactic succeeds in luring a woman into a sexual encounter. It is also in women's interest to detect deception and focus on honest signals rather than unreliable or deceptive signals. And indeed, we will see that women have a veritable army of defenses to guard against sexual treachery at the hands of men.

Evolutionarily, women hold an extraordinarily valuable reproductive resource: the joys and burdens of nine months of pregnancy in order to produce a child. So evolution has favored male strategies that succeed in gaining access to this valuable reproductive resource. The most common sexual strategy is *honest courtship*. Many men show genuine interest in a woman, and they display a diverse array of tactics to attract a woman, even in casual encounters or the early stages of a relationship: displaying a good sense of humor, showing sympathy to her troubles, showing good manners, being well groomed, making an effort to spend a lot of time with her, offering to help her, buying her dinners, and giving her gifts. Most men, of course, try to put their best foot forward initially, and perhaps do some minor concealing of weaknesses and tweaking of the truth. Small forms of deception are surprisingly frequent in traditional dating, as well as online dating.

Online dating sites have become an increasingly common forum for meeting mates, so it's appropriate to enter the world of sexual deception through the lens of this modern mode of mating. One study estimated that 16 million Americans have used an online dating service, and of those, 3 million have entered into long-term relationships, sometimes marriage, with someone they met online. A recent study of online dating ads explored the extent to which men and women provide deceptive information about themselves. The researchers compared men's and women's advertised height, weight, age, and other characteristics with actual measured height and weight and independently verified age. Fifty-five percent of the men, compared with 41 percent of women, lied about their height. Women were somewhat more likely than men to shade the truth about their weight. Overall, an astonishing 81 percent of the sample engaged in some form of deception, be it about physical characteristics, income, habits such as smoking or drinking, or political beliefs.

As sexual conflict theory predicts, however, both sexes are well aware of the risks of deceptive online ads. Indeed, one study found that

86 percent of online daters believe that *others* deceive about their physical appearance, and cite deception as one of the largest disadvantages of online dating.

Despite the frequency of deception, most lies turned out to be modest embellishments. Men exaggerated their true height by only half an inch on average. Women underestimated their weight by roughly 8.5 pounds. Most online daters appear to deceive in ways that are "close enough to steal," rather than grossly mischaracterize themselves on qualities that would soon be discovered in a face-to-face date. There are always exceptions, though. One man said he was three inches taller and eleven years younger than he actually turned out to be. One woman said that she was thirty-five pounds lighter than her measured weight turned out to be. On the whole, though, the mischaracterizations told by most online daters were slight exaggerations rather than bold-faced lies.

Deception in dating is an equal opportunity tactic—both men and women do it. On qualities that are easily observable, such as height, weight, and attractiveness, people sometimes lie just a little. Outright lies, such as a short man claiming to be six feet tall or a heavyset woman claiming to be 125 pounds, will be easily detected, and the deception will backfire as soon as the two people meet. However, some deceptions are difficult to identify. Qualities such as income or social status are generally tougher to verify, which is why at least some Internet dating sites now contain investigative procedures that independently verify income, education, and other information. Some even check to see whether the person has a criminal history, a fact that some people may "inadvertently" omit from their dating profiles.

Sexual Deception

Most women seek some kind of emotional connection or emotional involvement with a man before consenting to sex. From an evolutionary perspective, this is emotional wisdom women have inherited from their successful maternal ancestors. A man's emotional involvement, particularly his genuine love, provides a powerful signal that he will stick with her through thick and thin, through health and sickness. Love provides the best chance that he will devote his commitment, provisions, and protection to one woman and her children. Men not in love feel freer to flit from woman to woman.

Men are sometimes baffled by women's desire for emotional involvement and love. Here is how one man expressed it:

> You would think saying "I love you" to a woman to thrill and entice her isn't necessary anymore. But that's not so. These three words have a toniclike effect. I blurt out a declaration of love whenever I'm in the heat of passion. I'm not always believed, but it adds to the occasion for both of us. It's not exactly deception on my part, I have to feel *something* for her. And what the hell, it usually seems like the right thing to say at the time.

In fact, studies by the Buss Evolutionary Psychology Lab reveal that emotional deception by men is an astonishingly common tactic for persuading women to have sex with them. In one study, we asked 240 women and 239 men to describe the ways in which they had been deceived by members of the opposite sex. We found that women reported having been deceived by men in the following ways:

- concealed a serious involvement with another woman (9 percent);
- lied about how attracted he was to other women (26 percent);
- concealed emotional feelings for another woman (25 percent);
- exaggerated his work ambitions (21 percent);
- exaggerated how kind and understanding he was (42 percent);
- misled her about how strong his feelings were for her (36 percent);
- concealed the fact that he was flirting with other women (40 percent);
- misled her about the depth of his feelings for her in order to get sex (29 percent); and
- misled her about the level of his long-term commitment to her (28 percent).

These percentages are likely to be underestimates of the actual rates of deception. In another study of 112 men, 71 percent admitted that they had sometimes exaggerated the depth of their feelings for a woman in order to have sex with her.

Many cases of deception from our own study are heart-wrenching:

While in college I went out and drank a lot. There was this one guy who I really liked. He fed me all the lies that we are told to know, but at the time I did not think about that. For example, he told me he was not like other guys and he would call me in the morning and he really was into me. He told me how pretty and smart I was and how lucky he would be if we were together. All I really thought was how much I liked the guy and how much I wanted him to like me. I completely bought into his lies. After a few more drinks we went upstairs and had sex. The next day he did not call me. Then I found out that he told all his friends how easy I was. I felt completely degraded.

—heterosexual woman, age 27

Like this woman, Sandra Hicks found out the hard way. Her husband, Ed Hicks, was by all accounts a good husband. He was handy at fixing things around the house, romantic in his manners, and generally fun to be around. Then one day Sandra Hicks discovered that their tax refund check, which she had been eagerly awaiting, had been diverted to pay off . . . a tax lien from Ed Hicks's marriage to another woman! In fact, Ed Hicks was married to two different women, neither knowing about the other. And he had been married to at least five other women previously, three times failing to get divorced before tying the knot with the next. After Ed Hicks got caught and jailed, he continued to charm women. He almost succeeded with one woman, until she was warned by three of his previous wives about his deceptive ways: " 'I know men,' said the woman who requested anonymity to protect her privacy. 'You usually pick up red flags. But him . . . God he talks good.' "

Some men are skilled at the art of sexual deception using tactics that play on the emotional heartstrings of women. Oxytocin, as we saw in chapter 3, is a powerful bonding hormone that increases significantly with orgasm in women—more so than in men. If having sex with someone is more likely to increase feelings of emotional attachment in women than in men, women are more vulnerable to the negative consequences of sexual deception. It is no surprise that people who fall prey to emotional con artists suffer greatly. Often, women who have experienced such deception later find it difficult to trust current or potential sexual partners; they may avoid physical intimacy or become anxious when the prospect of sexual intimacy arises.

Defending Against Deception

Although men sometimes succeed in deceiving women, it would be flat-out wrong to conclude that women are passive dupes in men's mating games. Women know that men have a powerful desire for casual no-strings sex. Women, in fact, have developed sophisticated means of identifying deceivers. Research shows that women are superior to men at *reading nonverbal signals* such as facial expressions and body movements. They decode facial expressions, evaluate vocal tones to assess sincerity, and gather information about a man's social reputation and sexual history. Some spend hours discussing specific conversations with their close friends, who help to evaluate a man's intentions: "He said X, and then I said Y, . . . but did he look you in the eye when he said Z?"

Another key tactic that some women use involves *insisting on a longer courtship* before consenting to sex than men typically desire. In one Buss Lab study, we asked women and men about the likelihood that they would have sex with someone whom they found attractive if they had known the person for varying lengths of time, ranging from one hour to five years. Whereas most men were likely to have sex after just one week, most women preferred a longer wait. Imposing a time delay before having sex allows a woman a greater window of assessment and evaluation, a strategy in part designed to weed out deceivers.

Women also have specialized *emotional defenses* that protect them from being deceived. Research from the Buss Lab shows that women become extremely angry and upset when they discover that men have deceived them about the depth of their feelings in order to have sex. These emotions cause women to etch those deceptive episodes in memory, attend more closely in the future to possible instances of deception, and ultimately avoid future occurrences of deception.

Evolutionary psychologist Martie Haselton discovered yet another defense women have to avoid being emotionally deceived by men: the *commitment skepticism bias.* To understand the commitment skepticism bias, consider a concrete example: On a second date, a man declares to a woman that he is deeply in love with her. Based on this cue, what is the correct inference about the man's true state of commitment to the woman? There are two possible errors of inference a woman can make. One error would be to infer that he is lying, when in fact he truly loves her. The other error would be to infer that he is telling the truth about his love, when in fact he is practicing the art of deception. Evolutionary logic suggests that being deceived would have been the more costly error to women over human history. Women deceived in these ways would have risked an unwanted or untimely pregnancy; being inseminated by a man with inferior genes; and possibly raising a child without the help of an investing father. So evolution has fashioned a particular psychology in women, according to this theory: a commitment skepticism bias designed to underinfer men's true level of commitment. The commitment skepticism bias serves an important function. It helps women not to be overly impressed with easy-to-fake signals, such as verbal declarations of depth of feeling. It requires men who are truly committed to display additional commitment cues over a greater length of time. And it causes men who are truly interested in just a "quick shag," as the British say, to soon tire of the delay and move on to more gullible, exploitable, or sexually accessible targets.

At this point in time, women and men are the end products of the perpetual arms race of deception strategies and deception detection defenses. Some women succeed and deflect deceivers; and some fall victim to men's deceptive charms.

Drugging, Coercion, and Rape

Most women have sex with the expectation that it will lead to positive outcomes, be it sexual pleasure, love and commitment, gaining revenge, lowering anxiety, or preventing a mate from straying. But sometimes the only positive expectation for a woman having sex is avoiding harm—psychological, physical, or both.

In chapter 6, we explored why women sometimes agree to have sex against their own desires in order to please their partners, to stop them from nagging, to maintain relationships, because they feel it is their "wifely duty," or because they do not know how to say no. Undeniably, sex under these conditions could be considered coercive. There is often a fine line between agreeing to have sex in order to keep a persistent partner quiet and being verbally pressured into having sex against one's will. But some situations are clear-cut. When a woman is forced to choose between having sex or ending the relationship, or is made to feel fearful, guilty, or bad about herself for saying no, or is given alcohol or drugs to lower her inhibitions and "give in," then sex moves into the realm of coercion. Some women in our study talked about these coercive pressures:

> *My first physical boyfriend pushed, and pushed and pushed. I had already set boundaries with him and thought he would respect them or not push too far past them. I didn't know where it was going at first. Later, like a lot of girls, I just couldn't say no. My [religious] background, which encouraged passivity and kept me naive about sex, was a major factor in this happening to me. Later, a second partner pushed me into sex. He used alcohol as an aid and spiked my drinks ... without me knowing. Again my [religious] background is an important factor in my inability to say no, naiveté about sexual interactions and also about alcohol (the room was spinning heavily, and I did not know I was drunk or what it meant to be drunk). He also used several made-up stories to get me feeling sorry for him, which was another important factor in my compliance. There are several more circumstances like this where persistence from a partner, emotional games, alcohol, passivity, and difficulties saying no were all important factors in sex. I felt nervous, unsure and confused. I didn't want to make the other person angry with me. I trusted them not to take advantage of me and remained passive, and when things didn't go the way I'd trusted them to I didn't know what to do. There was an element of non-reality to all these encounters and a passive loss of control. These experiences all occurred before age nineteen, after which I got stronger and wiser.*
> —predominantly heterosexual woman, age 23

I was very young and very naive, probably about fourteen years old. I met up with a guy (probably seventeen) and we went to hang out at his house. Everything was going fine up until a point. There was a little making out (kissing) but then I wanted to stop. Well he told me that if I didn't have sex with him he wouldn't take me home. Well I had lied to my father about where I was so I didn't think I could call him to pick me up. I was scared I'd get in trouble so I just did what he wanted me to do just to get it over with and get out of there. All I wanted was to get out of there and that seemed to be the fastest way.

—predominantly heterosexual woman, age 31

Sexual coercion and rape can and do occur between strangers. But more often than not, they take place within the context of either a potential or existing relationship. They occur in all cultures, across all levels of income, and at all ages. They occur among both men and women, but with a much higher frequency among women. According to the National Violence Against Women Survey of eight thousand women, approximately 15 percent of the women had been raped and 3 percent had experienced attempted rape. Sixty-two percent of the assaults were by a past or current partner, and the likelihood of physical injury was higher with intimate partners than with strangers.

Sexual Abuse and Young Women

In our study, a disturbing number of women described situations where they were sexually coerced or raped as young adolescents. Shocking statistics show that over one-third of high school girls experience sexual coercion or violence in dating relationships. Given that more than 70 percent of American adolescents report at least one serious romantic relationship before the age of eighteen, many young women experience traumatic sexual experiences at an early age.

Adolescents, compared with older women, are especially vulnerable to sexual coercion. This is because young women often lack the relationship knowledge that comes with dating experience. As a result, they are often uncertain of what is expected of them as a romantic partner, and may miss warning signs of forthcoming abuse.

Sexual coercion in young women is more likely to occur when there is a significant difference between partners in intelligence, social status, or age:

> When I was about seventeen, I dated a guy who was twenty-six. I wanted to date him, but he moved a little faster than I wanted. I didn't want to lose him, so when we would make out, he would force my head down for oral [sex]. He would hold my head there for a long time, even if I was crying. I continued the relationship and figured this was part of what I needed to do to be datable.
>
> —heterosexual woman, age 38

A man who is much older than a young woman is generally more sexually experienced and knowledgeable, and tends to be in a power position over her. These factors make it more likely that the younger woman will be pressured into having sex before she is ready. Young, sexually inexperienced women also often accept responsibility for the event. A woman sometimes feels at fault because she believes she "led him on," or should have known how to get out of the situation. One study found that between one-fourth and one-third of U.S. high school students think that it is acceptable for a boy to force a girl to have sex if she lets him touch her breasts, wears revealing clothing, agrees to go home with him, or had dated him for an extended period of time.

Sexual coercion or rape during adolescence may be more harmful than during adulthood. Adolescence is the stage of life when women are just beginning to develop their identity as a sexual person and their expectations for future relationships. If they learn at an early age that being pressured or forced to have sex is part of being in a relationship, then they may come to expect this type of behavior in future relationships, thus creating a potential cycle of violence.

Regardless of the age when sexual abuse occurs, the psychological consequences are far-reaching and can adversely affect almost all aspects of a woman's life. Coerced or forced sex by a dating partner often represents a monumental breach of trust. This betrayal can make it difficult for some women to trust or commit to future sexual partners. Many women who have been raped develop post-traumatic stress disorder, or PTSD, a syndrome marked by flashbacks reexperiencing the terrifying emotional aspects of the rape, being easily startled, experiencing sleep problems, and feeling emotionally numb or detached. One study compared forty adult women rape victims with an age-matched control group of thirty-two women who had experienced severe, nonsexual, life-threatening events such as physical attacks, major car accidents, or robberies. Ninety-five percent of rape victims experienced PTSD, versus 47 percent of the control group.

A full 90 percent of the rape victims also experienced post-rape sexual problems, such as absence of sexual desire (93 percent), aversion to sex (85 percent), or genital pain (83 percent). Many rape victims also developed eating disorders such as bingeing (68 percent) or purging (48 percent), as well as anxiety disorders apart from PTSD (38 percent). Some victims turn to alcohol or drugs, and many suffer from depression, anxiety, rage, disgust, confusion, feelings of helplessness, fear, or low self-esteem. The psychological aftermath of rape, in short, is typically extremely traumatic to victims.

Here is how one woman in our study described the effect early sexual abuse had on her life:

> When I was [very young], I was coerced into performing oral sex on a male at least twice. He was sixteen. I was confused and unsure of what was happening. When I grew old enough to know what had happened, I was sad and disgusted by this incident. I have gone through many counseling sessions with friends and professionals to come to terms with this event in my life and understand how it has affected my sexuality and sex life. I am sure it has affected me in ways I will never be able to detect or connect, but I can at least identify with the feelings of inadequacy, lack of pleasure in sexual situations, performance anxiety, and low self-esteem. I have come a long way in transcending these issues.
>
> —predominantly heterosexual woman, age 27

As they mature, most people develop an identity with and owner-ship over their bodies. But when people are sexually abused, particu-larly if it is early in life, they may come to believe that they are powerless over their body, that they have no physical boundaries that they own and are able to protect. Women often describe "mentally disconnect-ing" from the abusive experience while it is occurring. If the woman is unable to physically remove herself from the situation, her only way to "escape" is to dissociate mentally from her body. Some women who later enter into loving relationships then find it hard to connect and "be in the moment" during sex because they are so used to coping with sex by mentally escaping. If a woman learns that there is nothing she can do to protect her body from harm, she may become less vigi-lant of, or defensive in response to, danger cues. She may feel power-less in deciding whether sex will or will not occur whenever a partner wants it.

Some researchers believe that these consequences of abuse may partly explain why an unusually high proportion of women experience repeated incidents of sexual abuse. Estimates of the rates of revictimiza-tion in women range from 15 percent to 72 percent. One study found that women who were sexually abused in childhood were almost twice as likely to experience rape in adulthood as were women who had no history of childhood sexual abuse. Although high rates of sexual revic-timization in women have been well documented, the factors that con-tribute to this risk are not well understood. Alcohol and substance use have been shown to be risk factors in some cases, but they do not seem to explain the chances of revictimization. The characteristics of the abuse—such as abuse severity, the use of force, the duration of abuse, and whether the abuse involved a family member—have been found to increase the risk of revictimization. A recent study found that low sex-ual self-esteem, high levels of sexual concerns, and a willingness to en-gage in sexual behaviors outside a relationship also partly explain which sexually abused women were more vulnerable to repeated sexual as-sault.

Two women in our study described their experiences of revictimiza-tion:

I was raped at [age] fifteen by three boys in my class at school, on the way home from school. I was a virgin until that point. It was . . . behind the school where dozens of students were passing . . . They all heard my screams for help, but no one came. I only got away by biting one of them so hard I drew blood. This fact, along with the scratches and bruises on me and them (from my fighting back), helped the police convict them. They all got slaps on the wrist, and were told to be good for two years. I was continually raped by my first real "partner"—we lived as common-law spouses for eighteen months. I was raped by a guy who followed me out of a nightclub and forced me into an alleyway near the club. Dozens of people saw him, and heard me screaming, yet no one came to help. . . . Until I met my second (and current) husband, I didn't know that men could be kind and gentle and loving. I have had my faith in men restored by the actions of just one man.

—heterosexual woman, age 35

I [was] sexually abused as a child by a few relatives. In addition to that, I've also been raped a few times when I was a teenager. I've only told a few people and when I did I wasn't taken seriously, which is really sad. . . . I was a ward of the state from [an early age]. . . . I was sent to a children's shelter. I hated being there so I would get together with other girls who felt the same way and left with guys from the neighborhood. One particular time I was with a couple of neighborhood guys and a girl I knew. They all hated me and thought I was a whore because they heard that I slept with someone else. This was probably true because at this time of my life I had no respect for myself and didn't care what happened to me. Night fell and we found a laundry room in the basement of an apartment building. One of the guys without my permission forced me to have sex with him. I just lay there and mentally disconnected my mind from what was happening to me. I felt hurt and used—as if that was my only purpose.

—predominantly heterosexual woman, age 28

Sexual Abuse in Committed Relationships

My ex-husband was mentally and verbally abusive and coerced me into having sex most of our fifteen-year relationship. When I would refuse sex with him he would be angry and verbally abusive for as long as three days afterward. Eventually I stopped trying to say no to him because it was easier to give in and deal with fifteen minutes of sex than days of abuse.

—heterosexual woman, age 36

There is often a fine line between unwanted sex and rape. This is especially true when rape occurs in a long-term relationship, where the couple has engaged in consensual sexual intercourse in the past. Women who are sexually abused in marital relationships frequently define it as rape only if physical force or harm is involved. And research shows that when a woman is sexually abused in a committed relationship she is more likely to make excuses for her partner such as "He's only like that when he's drunk" or "I should know better than to provoke him." They also tend to minimize the situation by claiming things like "It's only happened a couple of times."

Women's reluctance to acknowledge being raped by their partners often stems from fear of reprisal, reputational damage, or physical harm. Indeed, sexual abuse and physical abuse frequently go hand in hand in abusive marital relationships. At a very basic level, forcing a wife to have sex is an assertion of power, and in many cases the assertion of power extends into other areas of the relationship. Abusive men often try to isolate their partners from contact with family and friends, undermine their self-esteem, and subordinate them in dozens of small ways. By doing so, they make their partners more dependent upon them and thus more compliant to their demands. Some men justify forcing a wife to stay at home by saying that their wives "cannot be trusted."

In a study of women who had been raped by their husbands, sociologists David Finkelhor and Kersti Yllo described three distinct types of marital rape. One type, which they called "battering rape," accounted for 40 percent of marital rapes. Battering rape occurs when husbands not only rape their wives but physically beat them as well—sometimes prior to and sometimes after sex. "Force only" rapes, in which husbands use only the minimum amount of force necessary to make their wives have sex with them, comprised another 40 percent. In the force-only category, husbands often want to engage in a particular type of sexual act against the wife's wishes.

The third type of marital rape is "obsessive rape." The least common but the most disturbing, it is characterized by husbands who are obsessed with sex and are willing to use almost any type of force to get it. Obsessive rapists often use sadistic acts, and the men's sexuality involves a need to humiliate, degrade, and dominate their wives. One woman in our study described this type of terrifying and humiliating experience:

> I was raped, repeatedly, both as a child, and during my first marriage. As a child, I had a gun pointed at my head and was told if I didn't do what I was told I would be shot. During my marriage, my first husband bartered me to his friends as a fuck toy. I was told if I didn't do what I was told, he would kill me in my sleep, and [he] kept a knife under his pillow to prove it.
>
> —predominantly homosexual woman, age 26

Many studies have been conducted in which the researchers describe different rape scenarios and then ask people to rate things such as the severity or harmfulness of the rape. Respondents often rate the rapes as less harmful to a woman when the perpetrator is her husband, not a stranger. Perhaps some of these attitudes about marital rape can be traced historically to the belief that it was a man's right to have sex with his wife, and rape within a marital context was not unlawful. Decades ago, the approach of Lord Hale, an eighteenth-century British jurist, was integrated into American rape statutes: "But the husband cannot be guilty of a rape committed by himself upon his lawful wife, for by their mutual matrimonial consent and contract the wife hath given up her self in this kind unto the husband which she cannot retract."

It was not until as recently as 1993 that all fifty U.S. states changed these long-standing laws and made marital rape a crime. Currently, marital clauses in the laws of thirty states still provide that a husband cannot be charged with rape under certain conditions, such as if his wife is unconscious, asleep, or mentally or physically impaired.

Still, today not all countries have laws that criminalize marital rape; in fact, a law recently passed in Afghanistan actually legalizes it. One clause stipulates that "as long as the husband is not traveling, he has the right to have sexual intercourse with his wife every fourth night." Another asserts that "unless the wife is ill or has any kind of illness that intercourse could aggravate, the wife is bound to give a positive response to the sexual desires of her husband." This law applies only to the Shiite community, which comprises 20 percent of the population of Afghanistan, a country with 30 million people. Sunnis in the country are exempt from the law. U.S. president Barack Obama called the law "abhorrent." International protests have called for its repeal, and they may succeed. Nonetheless, the controversial law highlights the problem of marital rape—a problem that affects millions of women worldwide, even in countries that criminalize it.

In addition to the many negative psychological consequences that often follow a history of sexual abuse, rape can disrupt a woman's sexual functioning in later consensual relationships. Research conducted in the Meston Sexual Psychophysiology Lab shows that many sexually abused women report sexual difficulties that persist for decades after the abuse. Some report having no desire for sex whatsoever, and others report the opposite—engaging in frequent indiscriminate and high-risk sexual activities. Some women report being so anxious and fearful about sex that they experience panic attacks when their partners initiate sex. Others report having difficulties becoming sexually aroused or having an orgasm, and some women experience intense pain during sexual intercourse with their partners. Some women develop vaginismus, a specific type of sexual pain disorder wherein the muscles surrounding a woman's vagina involuntarily tighten and make intercourse or even inserting a tampon impossible.

How effective treatment will be depends on the type of sexual abuse and whether it involved penetration or physical harm, the frequency of abuse, the age at which the abuse occurred, and who the abuser was. The hopeful news is that the past decade has seen great progress in

developing successful therapeutic techniques, such as Stress Inoculation Training and Prolonged Exposure, to treat women who have suffered sexually abusive experiences. Stress Inoculation Training involves
psychotherapy, role-playing, deep muscle relaxation and controlled
breathing exercises, coping skills, and thought-stopping techniques to
counter ruminative or obsessive thinking about the traumatic experience. Prolonged Exposure involves having the woman relive the assault
by imagining it as vividly as possible and describing it aloud, in the
present tense, to her therapist. The woman is asked to repeat the rape
scenario several times during each therapy session. She usually attends
ten therapy sessions and, in addition, listens to a tape recording of herself telling the assault story at least once a day for homework. In the
short term, the exposure to the rape image often increases anxiety, but
after a period of time anxiety is significantly diminished as the woman ha-
bituates to it. One study that compared nine biweekly ninety-minute
sessions of supportive counseling, Stress Inoculation Training, and Prolonged Exposure found that all three treatments produced substantial
improvements in rape-related distress, general anxiety, PTSD, and depression among women rape victims. But of the three types of treatment, Prolonged Exposure had the greatest long-lasting effects on PTSD
symptoms.

In our study, one woman explained how counseling helped restore
her sense of self-worth:

> When I was a freshman in college when I was seventeen years old,
> I went on a date with a friend. We had a nice time and went out
> for pizza and a walk around college. He came back to my room
> with me and climbed into my bed and we slept, which was not an
> uncommon occurrence for us, as we were friends. I woke up later
> in the night to him touching my genital regions and when I said no
> he continued to force me to have intercourse with him. He was
> much larger than me and I was afraid to fight back with more
> than my words because I was fearful that he was going to hurt me.
> In the morning when I kicked him out I felt ashamed and dirty
> and used. I sought help at the hospital but spent the next few

months in a deep depression. I received counseling and was able to get a better understanding that I was a worthy and beautiful person.

—heterosexual woman, age 23

The Meston Lab is conducting a five-year study to examine the effectiveness of a simple writing intervention in helping women with a history of early abusive experiences deal with current sexual and relational concerns. All of the women in our study previously had traumatic sexual experiences and are currently in consensual sexual relationships. In the study, the women write for thirty minutes, once a week for a minimum of five weeks, on how they view themselves as a sexual person. We encourage them to link their thoughts to past, current, and future sexual experiences or relationships, and to be as detailed as possible in their writing. So far the findings are encouraging. Many women who have completed the study show substantial improvement in their ability to enjoy sexual activities with their current partners. Enormously gratifying is the fact that a number of women have said that participating in our study has changed their lives.

We do not know exactly how writing about a traumatic event can have positive therapeutic effects, but there are several likely reasons. One is that writing allows a person to release negative feelings, in a safe environment, that may otherwise be inhibited or avoided. It provides a cathartic release of emotions. Another is that writing provides a way to psychologically reorganize the traumatic memory in a structured and coherent way. When you write about an event, as opposed to just thinking about it, you are naturally forced to give the event a beginning, a middle, and an end. This structuring puts the memory of abuse into the context of the past, and it may be more likely to "stay put" in the past where it belongs rather than constantly intruding into and disrupting present-day events. Finally, through the writing process, individuals receive repeated exposure to aversive thoughts and feelings. Although this may create a temporary increase in anxiety, repeated exposure to the aversive memory through repeated writing makes it have less and less of an emotional impact.

Women's Defenses Against Rape

There is good evidence that rape is not a recent phenomenon, but rather has a long and disturbing history. The anthropologist Peggy Sanday examined 156 tribal societies from a database known as the Standard Cross-Cultural Sample. She found that rape rates were particularly high in patrilocal cultures—those in which a married couple reside with or near the husband's parents. Other studies confirm that when women lack genetic kin in close proximity, rates of rape and spousal abuse increase. Sanday found higher rape rates in tribal societies in which intertribal feuding and warfare were common. Indeed, of the several factors that characterize cultures with high rape rates, including lack of female power and lack of female political decision making, cultures characterized by a male ideology that valorized toughness and fighting ability showed the highest rape rates.

The human historical record confirms the ubiquity of rape across cultures and over time. Biblical sources are replete with rules for rape and for dealing with rapists. An Assyrian law from the second millennium BCE carries this injunction: "If a seignior took the virgin by force and ravished her, either in the midst of the city . . . or at a city festival, the father of the virgin shall take the wife of the virgin's ravisher and give her to be ravished." In the King James Bible, Numbers 31:17–18 and 31:35 state: "Now therefore kill every male among the little ones, and kill every woman that hath known man by lying with him. But all the women children, that have not known a man by lying with him, keep alive for yourselves. . . . And thirty and two thousand persons in all, of woman that had not known man by lying with him." And in Genesis 34, a Hittite prince rapes Dinah, the daughter of Jacob: He "saw her . . . took her, and lay with her, and defiled her."

Historical records also show that rape was especially common in war. Some anthropologists have proposed that the sexual acquisition of women by force was the primary reason for going to war to begin with. The feared conqueror Genghis Khan (1162–1227) explicitly relished rape as one of the key benefits attained through warfare: "The greatest pleasure is to vanquish your enemies, to chase them before you, to rob them of their wealth, to see their near and dear bathed in tears, to ride their horses and sleep on the white bellies of their wives and daughters." Similar patterns of rape in war, amply documented by Susan Brownmiller in her book *Against Our Will,* continue in modern warfare. The Japanese invasion of Nanking during World War II, for example, resulted in an estimated twenty thousand rapes of young Chinese girls and women. The Russian assault on Germany in 1945 produced rapes of massive numbers of women, where "Soviet soldiers treated German women much more as sexual spoils of war." Even more recently, an estimated twenty thousand Bosnian Muslim women were raped by Bosnian Serbs in the mid-1990s. And in her confirmation hearings to become secretary of state in January 2009, Hillary Clinton listed widespread rape as a tool of war in the Congo as among the pressing foreign policy issues that would be facing the United States.

The human history of rape is even depicted in art and literature. The rape of the Sabine women, for example, narrated by Livy and Plutarch, depicts a legend in which the Romans invited the Sabines to a festival with the goal of killing off the men and abducting the women to make them wives. The legend produced a wealth of art during the Renaissance and was portrayed in the twentieth century by Pablo Picasso.

The key point of this brief historical review is simply to show that rape has been a recurrent horror for women across cultures and throughout human history. We do not need a formal theory to tell us that rape inflicts heavy costs on rape victims, but it is important to examine *why* rape is experienced as so traumatic. From an evolutionary perspective, the costs of rape include interference with women's mate choice, one of the cardinal features of women's sexual strategies. A raped woman risks an unwanted and untimely pregnancy with a man she has not chosen. Victims of rape risk being blamed or punished, resulting in damage to their social reputations and their future desirability on the mating market. And if a raped woman already has a boyfriend or husband, she risks being abandoned by him. Finally, raped women typically suffer psychological humiliation, anxiety, fear, rage, and depression, as we witnessed in the heart-wrenching descriptions from the women in our studies.

Given the appalling costs that rape inflicts on women, it would defy logic if women had not developed defenses designed to prevent its occurrence and to cope with its aftermath. Women in the fields of evolutionary psychology and evolutionary anthropology have been at the forefront of hypothesizing and investigating women's anti-rape defenses:

- The formation of alliances with males as special friends for protection (anthropologist Barbara Smuts)
- Mate selection based on qualities of men such as physical size and social dominance that deter other men from sexual aggression (psychologists Margo Wilson and Sarah Mesnick)
- The cultivation of female-female coalitions for protection (Barbara Smuts)
- The development of specialized fears that motivate women to avoid situations in which they might be in danger of rape (psychologists Tara Chavanne and Gordon Gallup)
- The avoidance of risky activities during ovulation to decrease the odds of sexual assault when women are most likely to conceive (Tara Chavanne and Gordon Gallup)
- Psychological pain from rape that motivates women to avoid rape in the future in similar circumstances (anthropologist Nancy Thornhill and biologist Randy Thornhill)

There is some scattered evidence of the effectiveness of all of these defenses, although in our view, women's anti-rape defenses have been sorely neglected by the scientific community and urgently warrant allocation of research funds.

To these potential anti-rape defenses, we propose three more. One is *maintaining physical proximity to close kin.* In ancestral conditions, women grew up within a small-group context, surrounded by genetic relatives—a father, brothers, uncles, grandfathers, mother, sisters, aunts, and grandmothers—all of whom could either deter potential rapists or inflict massive costs on them. In the modern environment, however, women often leave the protective envelope of close kin to go to college or to take jobs in large urban areas, making them more vulnerable to potential rapists. We would never discourage women from attending college or taking jobs in large cities, of course. Rather, we wish to point out that one key anti-rape defense that almost certainly helped to protect ancestral women from rape is no longer available to many modern women. Women who lack genetic kin in close proximity likely have to activate other anti-rape defenses, such as cultivating female-female coalitions or male "special friends" who offer protection and deter potential rapists.

From an evolutionary perspective, another potential anti-rape defense is the occurrence of *rape fantasies*—fantasies that involve the three key elements of force (or threat of force), sex, and nonconsent. An astonishing number of women—between 31 percent and 57 percent—have experienced rape fantasies at some point in their lives. These are almost certainly underestimates, given that rape fantasies are perceived as socially undesirable and hence are potentially embarrassing for women to admit to, even on a seemingly anonymous questionnaire.

How could rape fantasies possibly serve as an anti-rape defense? It turns out that women's rape fantasies come in at least two major varieties. The first is *erotic rape fantasies*. These are quite different from the images that normally come to mind when people think about rape. In erotic rape fantasies, the male is typically attractive, dominant, and overcome with sexual desire for the woman. Although she signals nonconsent in her fantasy, the fantasized self typically offers little resistance. The dominant, attractive man simply "takes" her sexually. Although woman who have erotic rape fantasies experience low to moderate levels of fear, the fantasy typically contains no realistic violence. These forms of sexual fantasy, which as we saw are present in many romance novels, arouse women both through stress, which we will discuss in a more healthful context in the next chapter, and the imagination of an idealized mate.

Aversive rape fantasies have an entirely different nature and function. In contrast to erotic rape fantasies, in aversive fantasies the male is likely to be a stranger rather than familiar, older rather than younger, and decidedly unattractive. These fantasies contain considerable coercion and painful violence. An example might be a rapist grabbing the woman, throwing her to the ground, and ripping off her clothes while the victim fights mightily to prevent the rapist from penetrating her. Women who have aversive rape fantasies tend to be more fearful than other women of actual rape, and some have been sexually abused as children. Although speculative, it is possible that aversive rape fantasies function as anti-rape defenses by creating a fear that motivates women to be particularly cautious.

Whether this speculation turns out to be correct, it should be abundantly clear that there is absolutely no evidence that women actually want to get raped, and a mountain of evidence that they do not. Women find actual rape aversive and traumatizing—just about the most cost-inflicting act that can be perpetrated on them short of murder. Because some people have terrifying dreams or fantasies of falling does not mean that they actually want to experience a fall to their death; precisely the opposite. Similarly, the fact that some women experience rape fantasies does not mean that they actually want to be raped. These aversive fantasies may help to protect them from rape by motivating caution, as occurred in this example coming from a study by the Buss Lab:

> I thought he wanted to rape me. My friend and I were walking to a movie theater in a bad part of town late at night, and he started following us for no apparent reason . . . and when we started running, I guess he gave up. I just thought that the person was going to take my friend and I with a weapon of some sort, take us to some hidden place (there were a lot of places he could've taken us), and rape us and then kill us with the weapon. We may have been imagining things, but we were scared and we just ran to the movie theater. We knew if we ran, we would get to the well-lit place before he could attack us. I have no idea whether he wanted to rape us, but we weren't taking any chances.

A final way that women might defend against rape is through developing *specialized fear of rape by strangers*. Many rapes throughout human history occurred in the context of warfare, in which the victorious group forced themselves on the unprotected women of the defeated group. At least some of women's rape-avoidance strategies were probably designed primarily to make them sexually wary of strange males, despite the fact that many modern rapes occur at the hands of a woman's acquaintances or even partners.

It is possible that women's fear of stranger rape in fact continues to be effective in the modern environment, lowering rates of stranger rape compared to the rates that would exist without this psychological defense. Deeper understanding of women's anti-rape psychology and how it plays out today could help to reduce the rates of this horrific crime. Studies are urgently needed to determine which anti-rape strategies are effective in contemporary society and which might backfire. Such studies of strategic effectiveness should in no way blame victims of the crime of rape. Rather, they should be designed to equip women and those who care about them with the best scientific knowledge of self-defense. Women's ancient sexual psychology now operates in a modern world, and in some ways is ill equipped to deal with the threats of this new world—which cannot be said about the subject of our final chapter: how the healing qualities of sex serve the needs of women today.

11. Sexual Medicine

The Health Rewards of a Sex Life

⧉

> *If the menstrual discharge coincides with an eclipse of the moon or sun, the evils resulting from it are irremediable . . . congress with a woman at such a period being noxious [and] attended with fatal effects to the man.*
>
> —Pliny the Elder (AD 23–79)

So far, we have discussed some of the better-known reasons why women have sex: to give or get love, to feel emotionally connected, and to enjoy the pleasures of sexual attraction and the sensations of sexual arousal and orgasm. We have explored ways that women strategize to have sex in order to attain specific goals—be they resources, revenge, or to capture or keep a mate. We have analyzed why some women have sex out of feelings of obligation, duty, or pressure, or because they are emotionally manipulated or physically forced. We have also examined women who have sex to enhance their self-esteem, gain experience, get rid of their virginity, or satisfy a nagging curiosity. But there is also a collection of utilitarian reasons for having sex that center on a woman's physical and psychological health, often with a multitude of benefits.

Better than Ibuprofen

Everyone has heard (or perhaps used—only under exceptional circumstances, of course) the timeworn dodge "Not tonight dear, I have a headache." It is true, and not just a convenient excuse, that sex can exacerbate, or even bring on, a headache. Head and neck muscles often tighten during sexual activity, and blood pressure can increase during orgasm, causing blood vessels in the brain to dilate, a condition technically named "coital cephalgia." However, in our study, we discovered that some women have sex with the goal of getting *rid* of a headache:

> *I suffer from migraine headaches and although the attacks are few and far between and are generally mild, I find that when I have sex during my headaches, especially when I have a great over the top climax, it goes away before I know it.*
>
> —heterosexual woman, age 42

One woman reported that her doctor actually prescribed having sex as a way to relieve migraines:

> *My neurologist recommended reaching orgasm as a way to deal with the pain of migraines. I have tried this and sometimes it does work. Often after taking migraine meds and darvacet I will reach a relaxed state I call the "fuck me stage." The pain may be still [be] hanging on in the back of my head but having sex and a nice orgasm will end the pain. I would rather do this with a partner, but I have used a vibrator to reach orgasm in an attempt to keep migraines from rebounding. Using orgasm to end the migraine keeps the rebounds at bay.*
>
> —heterosexual woman, age 43

As far back as the seventeenth century, the "father" of neurology, Thomas Willis, noted the increased sexual appetite of his patient Lady Catherine when she was plagued with a headache.

How can sex serve as both a headache catalyst and cure? During sexual activity, something therapeutic happens: When the body releases its oxytocin surge, the high level of the hormone triggers the release of endorphins, the brain chemicals that bear a remarkably close resemblance to morphine. Many people associate endorphins with a "runner's high," the feel-good "brain burst" that occurs after vigorous athletic activity. Endorphins serve as powerful pain relievers as well. Women's bodies release low levels of endorphins throughout the day. Without them, even minor aches and pains we experience would be much more intense. (Morphine and heroin addicts get so used to receiving synthetic pain relievers that after a while they stop producing the real thing. If the drug is taken away, they are left with little or no pain relief, real or synthetic.)

The release of endorphins during sexual activity can relieve headaches—and quite effectively for many women, according to a study conducted at the Headache Clinic at Southern Illinois University. In this study of fifty-eight women migraine sufferers who had engaged in sex during a headache, almost half reported at least some headache relief through orgasm. Only three women found that having an orgasm made their migraine worse. Better yet, orgasms provide relief within minutes and are free! Compare this to highly effective migraine medications such as triptans. When triptans are injected, which is the fastest possible way to get a drug into a person's system, it takes about fifteen minutes before most women report relief and up to an hour for others, and the cost is approximately seventy dollars per dose. (The medication provides relief in about 80 percent of cases.)

Some headache researchers believe that there is a "headache generator" in a specific area of the brain and that orgasms might somehow "switch off" this generator. This would explain why the headache relief from orgasms is usually permanent, as opposed to lasting only a few hours, as might be the case if endorphin release was the sole cause. Researcher Beverly Whipple of Rutgers University found that stimulation of the G-spot, the nickel-sized area on the inside front wall of the vagina, raised pain thresholds by an astonishing 40 percent. And during orgasm itself, women were able to tolerate an amazing 75 percent more pain.

It is not surprising, then, that sexual activity has been reported not only to relieve headache pain but to provide at least temporary relief for all sorts of aches and pains from arthritis to whiplash to muscular dystrophy to back pain:

> It was about ten years ago. I hurt my back and I literally couldn't move. I was on some very strong painkillers. I had read a study

that implied that orgasm releases powerful chemicals in the brain that relieve pain. I thought "why not?" My husband offered to test the study. I couldn't move so he had to work around my back injury. All I could do was lay there. It worked! I kid you not. Orgasm worked just as well as Tylenol III.

—woman, age and orientation not given

The Period for Sex

Sex can also ease the pain of menstrual cramps. In a premenopausal woman, each month the lining of the uterus produces hormones called prostaglandins. These hormones stimulate the contractions that move tissue and menstrual blood out of the uterus, but they also cause menstrual cramps. Sexual activity has a significant impact on how prostaglandins affect the body, and this explains why some women in our study reported deciding to have sex to relieve cramps:

The physical pleasure of sex is one of the best ways for me to relieve menstrual cramping. I've had sex for this reason many times as a comfort-based motivation.

—heterosexual woman, age 47

During orgasm, a woman's uterus contracts, and in the process, those excess (some might say "evil") cramp-causing prostaglandins are used up—relieving cramps. An added benefit is that having sex during menstruation can also lead to a shorter menstrual cycle. Some women report their period comes to an abrupt end within a day of having intercourse, leading them to wonder whether intercourse somehow "jammed it all up there until the next month." To the contrary, the increased number of uterine contractions during orgasm helps expel menstrual blood more quickly—ending the menstrual period more efficiently. In the mid-1960s, the sex researchers William Masters and Virginia Johnson directly observed women having orgasms in the laboratory in order to document the physiological changes that took place. With the help of a speculum device, they could actually see the pressure of sex causing menstrual fluid to squirt out of the cervical canal during the final stages of orgasm.

Sex can also decrease the chances that a woman will suffer from endometriosis, a common gynecological condition that occurs when uterine tissue grows outside the uterus in areas such as the ovaries or fallopian tubes. This growth can cause pain during sex, pelvic pain, and sometimes infertility. Researchers at Yale University School of Medicine found that women who regularly engaged in sexual intercourse or masturbation during menstruation were one and a half times less likely to develop endometriosis than women who abstained from sexual activities during their periods. (Curiously, tampon use also decreases a woman's chances of having endometriosis.)

In a way, sexual activity serves as the vagina's maid service. Menstrual blood often contains bits of endometrial tissue that can flow backward into the pelvic area. This phenomenon, called "retrograde menstruation," increases a woman's risk of developing endometriosis, so having intercourse during menstruation could decrease the risk by sweeping the vagina clear of menstrual debris. Orgasm, either through intercourse or masturbation, could further decrease the risk of endometriosis because the orgasmic contractions can help push menstrual debris out of the uterus. On a related note, in the same Yale School of Medicine study, women who used only menstrual pads were more than twice as likely to develop endometriosis as were women who used only tampons. This suggests that tampons remove menstrual fluid and debris more efficiently than pads. Douching, either when menstruating or not, was unrelated to endometriosis risk.

So, sex during menstruation can relieve cramps, shorten the menstrual cycle, and decrease the risk of endometriosis. Clearly, scientific evidence was not available when Pliny the Elder made *his* list of the consequences of intimacy during menstruation. According to Pliny, contact with menstrual blood turned new wine sour, rendered crops barren, dulled the edge of steel and the gleam of ivory, drove dogs mad, and even caused tiny ants to turn in disgust from grains of corn that tasted of menstrual blood.

The "Chill Out" Effect

[Sex] is a stress reliever, and let's face it, most of the time men don't care why, they're just happy to help along.
> —predominantly heterosexual woman, age 22

Everyone knows how feeling angry or anxious can change how we experience things. Negative thoughts can occupy, even take over, our minds and prevent us from noticing pleasant things in the immediate environment. Sometimes, as we've seen, in sexual situations the negative thoughts are so distracting that they prevent us from focusing on sexually arousing cues such as the pleasurable sensations of a partner's touch or positive emotions toward our mates. Masters and Johnson termed this "spectatoring" because instead of being fully engaged in the sex act, it is as if the sexual participant is a "third person," removed psychologically from the experience. Obviously, if you are thinking about what a jerk your boss was that day, or you are lying there making a list of the forty-two things you need to do by tomorrow rather than becoming aware of and turned on by any genital response, it is not going to help you to become sexually aroused or have an orgasm. This is the side of stress that sometimes causes women not to enjoy sex or not to want to have sex.

But there is also a whole host of physical changes that occur in the body during a stressful situation that lead many women to *want* to engage in sexual activity. When a person is feeling stressed out, the branch of the nervous system known as the sympathetic nervous system, or SNS, becomes activated. The SNS is responsible for increasing heart rate and blood pressure, for stimulating sweat to get rid of excess water in our bodies, for relaxing the bladder muscles (which is why some people or animals urinate uncontrollably when they are frightened), for decreasing digestion, and for stimulating the liver to release glucose for energy. SNS activation also releases norepinephrine, a brain chemical that has a molecular structure similar to the stimulant amphetamine. All of these changes speed up the body so that we can react quickly when we are confronted with a physical threat or a compromising situation, the quintessential "fight or flight" response. The SNS is meant to be active only during a limited critical period—until we deal with the stressor by either fighting back or running away. If the activation persists because, for whatever reason, we are unable to resolve the stress efficiently, then it becomes distracting psychologically and makes us feel extremely uncomfortable physically.

No one would dispute that it is hard to relax or to concentrate on work when you are sweating and shaking and your heart is pounding at 110 beats per minute. Prolonged activation of the SNS can lead to all sorts of cardiovascular, immune system, and nervous system disorders. Many people who frequently experience excess nervous system arousal take beta-blockers or other anti-anxiety drugs, such as Clonazapam or Xanax, to get rid of the symptoms. In our study, some women reported that having sex can also do the trick:

> *There have been days when life is difficult, usually because of work-related stress, and you just want to let out some steam. So, coming home and fucking passionately really is a good release under those circumstances.*
>
> —heterosexual woman, age 44

> *I suppose it is more accurate to say that I had sex to relieve aggression brought on by boredom. Sometimes when I'm with my partner I recognize that I'm feeling irritable, and that leads to aggressiveness. Usually it is just because I am feeling bored. So, I have sex 'cause it's easier than fighting. Plus it gives me something to do.*
>
> —predominantly heterosexual woman, age 27

> *On occasion, when I am feeling frustrated and angry I need a physical outlet for this extra energy. I have found that having sex is a positive way to deal with these negative emotions and can calm me down. Other forms of physical exertion (e.g., exercise) can have a similar effect, but don't always.*
>
> —heterosexual woman, age 23

For a lot of women in our study, having sex when they were stressed also helped clear their minds so that they could focus better on their goals, or approach a problem more objectively:

School sometimes really frustrates me. Whenever I have a difficult problem that seems almost impossible to solve, I'll take a break from it and have sex with my boyfriend. Usually afterward I find it easier to solve the problem because I've taken a break from it and gotten out my frustrations by having sex.

—heterosexual woman, age 19

And for some, this applied to having sex after a fight with their partner:

I was in a long-term relationship at a very young age. . . . I think that I believed that sex after fighting made everything better. Honestly, it usually did, albeit briefly. . . .

—heterosexual woman, age 25

Having sex during or after a fight with one's partner can sometimes help resolve relationship differences. Because sex can release built-up anger and frustration, which in turn allows our bodies to return to normal levels of arousal, it can help clear our minds, at least temporarily, of the negative thoughts that caused the fight. While sex does not actually *solve* the underlying problem that triggered the fight, it can better equip women to confront a problem rationally instead of angrily and emotionally:

Make-up sex is always more passionate and fun. However, I find it does not solve everything. . . . [But] you can sort of just take all the emotions and bad energy and channel it into passion and lust and good things and you come out feeling a hundred times less stressed.

—heterosexual woman, age 24

For couples who have a strong foundation, having sex after a fight can also serve as a reminder of the commitment they truly feel toward each other. And, for all the reasons described in chapter 3 on love and emotional bonding, "make-up" sex can help people to reconnect.

The Sleep Aid

Chronic stress of the human variety can wreak havoc on the body in many ways. Difficulty falling or staying asleep affects more than 20 million Americans—twice as many women as men. An even greater number of people experience occasional insomnia brought on by excitement or stress or from drinking too much caffeine or alcohol, favorite "home remedies" for dealing with stress shocks. Typical recommendations for people who have trouble sleeping include going to sleep and waking up at the same time each day; avoiding caffeine, nicotine, alcohol, and big meals late in the day; using your bed only for sleeping and sex; getting regular exercise; and keeping your bedroom dark, quiet, and cool.

The many testimonies from women in our study suggest that having sex should also be added to the list of sleep remedies:

> Getting close to finishing my graduate degree I fought insomnia and stress. I was running to control these things, I was working hard, but I grew to also need the euphoria and ability to shut down my brain that orgasm brought, as well as the flood of endorphins that gave me enough peace to rest. I rarely had anyone near me at my beck and call, however, so often as not I would use a dildo or two to get myself off, which had the added advantage of being completely selfish [and] without guilt.
>
> —predominantly heterosexual woman, age 29

If you follow this recommendation, one bit of advice: Highly active sex that gets your heart pumping can make a woman more energized than sleepy. So if you're using sex as a sleep aid, you might consider saving "aerobic" sex for earlier in the day and pursue a more subdued "sleepy-time" sex.

Endorphins released during orgasm can help induce sleep by relaxing the mind and the body. But probably more important, during orgasm the hormone prolactin is released—and there is a strong link between that hormone and sleep. Prolactin levels are naturally higher when we sleep, and studies conducted in animals show that prolactin injections make animals intensely sleepy. Prolactin release has also been associated with feelings of satiety. In men, prolactin is partly responsible for the refractory period. In women, prolactin does not have the same inhibitory effect as it does in men, which may explain why so many more heterosexual women than men seem to complain that their partners fall asleep right after sex.

Interestingly, research has shown that there is a 400 percent greater increase in prolactin from orgasms that occur from intercourse than from masturbation. From an evolutionary perspective, this makes sense: If orgasms from intercourse make women feel more fulfilled than orgasms from masturbation, then women would be more inclined to engage in partnered sex, which, unlike masturbation, can serve a direct reproductive function. To the extent that prolactin induces sleepiness in women, it would be more important that sleepiness occur following intercourse than masturbation as it would induce the woman to lie still, which could facilitate sperm transport to the egg.

Stress as a Sexual Stimulant

Although sex can help rid a person of feelings of anxiety, anxiety can also enhance a woman's genital sexual response. Some women in our study reported having sex because anxiety made them feel more "turned on":

> When I am overstressed or worried, I often respond by becoming increasingly horny. . . .
> —heterosexual woman, age 20

> Oh, how I loved my [husband]. We were married sixty-four years and never spent a day apart all those years. We had so much fun. Oh, sure, we fought, but the makin' up part was fun too!
> —heterosexual woman, age 86

The effects of anxiety on sexual arousal have been measured using vaginal photoplethysmography technology, which was described in chapter 2. In one study, women watched a travel documentary that created no stress. Immediately afterward, they watched a film of a couple engaging in foreplay, oral sex, and intercourse. On another occasion, the women watched a film designed to elicit an SNS response before watching a similar erotic film. Women showed much greater vaginal engorgement from the erotic films on the day they viewed the anxiety-evoking film first, even though there were no scenes in the anxiety films that could have provoked sexual thoughts in the women. Therefore, the most compelling explanation is that the SNS activation caused by the anxiety-evoking film increased the women's sexual arousal.

In the Meston Sexual Psychophysiology Lab, we decided to look at exercise, which also increases SNS activity. The women visited the lab on two separate days. On one of the days, they simply watched a travel documentary followed by an erotic film. On the other day, they exercised for twenty minutes on a stationary cycle or a treadmill just before watching a similar film sequence. They exercised at 70 percent of their maximum heart rate, which is a pretty intense workout for most people. On both days, a vaginal photoplethysmograph measured the women's sexual arousal while they watched the films. As it turned out, on the days the women exercised before viewing the films, they showed a much greater increase in vaginal engorgement from the sexual films. In fact, their sexual arousal to the film was a whopping 150 percent greater on the days they exercised. So, in addition to preparing our bodies for the "fight or flight" response, activation of the SNS prepares a woman's body for sexual arousal.

This finding is quite different from what research has found in men. Activation of the SNS impairs a man's ability to get an erection, especially if he is concerned about his sexual abilities. The finding from the Meston Lab suggests just the opposite for women—that activation of the SNS might help women who have sexual problems. If a women is "into" having sex psychologically, but her body is not responding, she might try doing something energizing—chase her partner around the block (or better yet, have the partner chase her), go dancing, or watch a scary movie together. Many self-help books tell women who have problems becoming sexually aroused or having an orgasm to do the opposite—relax the body by listening to soothing music, take a bubble bath, or do some quiet meditation. Certainly these calming techniques are helpful for clearing and relaxing the mind, but research from the Meston Lab suggests they would not "jump-start" the woman's body for sex as effectively as an invigorating activity would.

Love at First Fright

A few years ago, the Meston Lab research team went to several theme parks in Texas to examine whether riding a roller coaster, which increases SNS activity, might be another way to enhance sexual responses. Having women insert vaginal probes at a family-oriented amusement park was obviously not an option, so the team was unable to measure women's genital sexual arousal directly. Instead, they measured sexual attraction. So for several days, the research team interviewed heterosexual women who were waiting in line to ride a roller coaster and women who had just gotten off the ride. The post-ride women were still in a state of heightened SNS arousal. The researchers asked the women to look at a photograph of a man and then fill out a brief questionnaire that asked how attractive they thought the man was, how much they would like to kiss him, and how willing they would be to go on a date with him. Even though all the women viewed the same photograph of an average-looking man, the women who had just gotten off the roller coaster rated the man as being more attractive and having higher dating potential than did the women who were waiting in line to take the ride. It appears that attraction increased as a result of residual SNS activation from the roller coaster ride.

Pragmatic daters and maters may wonder whether the findings from the roller coaster study mean they would have a better chance of attracting a mate if they frequented locales that offered dancing instead of lounging, or if they hung out at a gym instead of a coffee shop. The answer is not straightforward. In real-life dating situations, it depends on whether there is at least some initial level of attraction. If so, then yes, perhaps. But if the woman does not find her pursuer in the least bit appealing, then even having her run a marathon would not make her want to go on a date, much less have sex with the person.

This notion that SNS activation can increase sexual arousal and attraction for women is a new concept for most people today. Some clever men, however, figured this out long ago. As far back as AD 550, recordings of the Roman circus noted:

> Women stood up in the stands drumming with their fists on the backs of people in the seats before them and screaming hysterically: "Kill!, Kill!, Kill!" Even before the games started, smart young men could spot women who would give way to this madness and make a point of sitting next to them. While in the grip of hysteria, the women were unconscious of everything else and the boys could play with them while they screamed and writhed at the bloody spectacle below them.

The Sunnier Side of Sex

Worldwide studies confirm that women experience depression twice as often as men. Over a lifetime, approximately 20 percent of women and 10 percent of men become depressed. Differences in the release of sex hormones partially explains why more women than men are depressed. Evidence for this includes the fact that girls are more susceptible to depression than boys—but only after they begin menstruating and experiencing the associated hormonal changes of puberty. In men, testosterone levels fluctuate slightly throughout the day, with levels being the highest in the morning. But in women, levels of sex hormones such as estrogen and progesterone vary tremendously across the menstrual cycle. A woman's menstrual cycle is usually twenty-eight days, and if you count the first day of a woman's menstrual period as day one, then estrogen peaks around day twelve (just before ovulation) and progesterone is highest around days nineteen through twenty-two.

Women's sex hormones also change dramatically with life events such as puberty, pregnancy, delivery and post-pregnancy, and perimenopause. Such radical shifts in sex hormones negatively impact a number of brain chemicals and physiological processes that cause depression. This can also explain why as many as 5 percent of women experience symptoms of depression and anxiety the week before their menstrual period, a condition known as premenstrual dysphoric disorder. And it helps to explain why such a high proportion of women become depressed at times when they are experiencing dramatic changes in their sex hormones.

Sex differences in the production of the hormone melatonin can explain why women are three times more likely than men to experience seasonal affective disorder, or SAD—a form of depression that results from seasonal changes in the availability of natural light. Our bodies respond to decreases in daylight by secreting melatonin from the pineal gland, a small structure that resides deep in the brains of mammals. Melatonin creates a sense of sleepiness (which is why many people with insomnia take melatonin supplements). As morning approaches and light hits the retinas of the eyes, melatonin levels decrease, which in turn increases alertness or wakefulness. Given that nights are longer in winter than in summer, humans and other mammals secrete more melatonin in the winter. And because winter is when most people with SAD become depressed, scientists believe that SAD may be caused by too much melatonin.

If all mammals increase melatonin production in the winter, why is SAD so much more common in women than in men? Researcher Thomas Wehr and his colleagues at the National Institute of Mental Health have shown that it may be because women are more physiologically responsive to changes in exposure to light than are men. In our everyday life, we are exposed to lots of artificial light during the evenings, and one would think that this would affect melatonin production by "tricking" the brain to act as if it is daytime. When the researchers tested this hypothesis, they found an interesting gender difference: Regardless of the amount of artificial light they were exposed to, women much more than men were somehow still detecting and being influenced by the natural light. So, for women, the amount of melatonin secreted was greater in winter than in summer. For men, the artificial light seemed to compensate and they did not show the same degree of seasonal differences in melatonin secretion.

Prolonged stress that disrupts the body's delicate hormonal equilibrium can also cause depression in both men and women. The brain uses neurotransmitters to chemically communicate information that controls our thoughts and behaviors. There are many different types of neurotransmitters in the brain, but three in particular have been linked closely with mood: serotonin, norepinephrine, and dopamine. If the production of these neurotransmitters is somehow compromised, it can cause a region in the brain's limbic system to malfunction. The limbic system controls our emotions, appetite, sleep, certain thought processes, and sex drive—all of which are impaired when a person is depressed.

Stress also causes the adrenal glands, which sit on top of the kidneys, to secrete more cortisol. Cortisol is a hormone that increases the body's metabolism. Under normal levels of stress, cortisol levels increase and then gradually return to normal. Prolonged stress, however, can cause extended cortisol secretion, and this may be another cause of depression. We now know that cortisol levels are abnormally high in about half of all severely depressed people. As it turns out, estrogen, which is produced in much higher quantities in women than in men, can not only increase cortisol secretion, but it can impair the body's ability to shut down cortisol production post-stress. This could provide yet another explanation why more women than men suffer from depression and anxiety disorders. Also, given that sexual arousal and orgasm have been associated with decreases in cortisol, elevated cortisol could impair women's sexual response. In a recent study conducted in the Meston Lab, women who had higher levels of cortisol in response to viewing an erotic film were more likely to experience sexual desire and arousal problems than were women who showed the expected decrease in cortisol while viewing the film. On the flip side, having sex could help, at least temporarily, alleviate anxiety and depression by decreasing cortisol levels.

Many studies have shown that when women are depressed, they frequently experience sexual problems such as decreases in sexual desire and arousal. As we discussed in chapter 2, a number of drugs used to treat depression can impair sexual functioning. So, for women who are being treated with drugs for depression, it is sometimes hard to know whether the sexual problems are caused by depression or by the medication used to treat the depression. In another study conducted in the Meston Lab, close to one hundred college women who were in sexual relationships filled out a questionnaire that measured depression as well as sexual functioning. An anonymous and confidential code number assured the women that no one would know which response was theirs, making them more likely to answer the questions openly and honestly.

None of the women in the study were taking antidepressant medications. When the sexual functioning answers from moderately depressed women were compared to those of the nondepressed women, the researchers found that the depressed women experienced less vaginal lubrication and more pain during sex, had a harder time reaching orgasm, and felt less overall sexual satisfaction and pleasure than the nondepressed women did. The study also revealed a new and surprising finding: The depressed women masturbated much more often than the nondepressed women.

Why did depressed women find masturbation more rewarding than sex with a partner? One explanation is that the depressed women were masturbating as a "self-help" treatment—trying to feel better by having an orgasm. The endorphins released during orgasm create a temporary, but intense, sense of well-being. Because depressed women may find very little pleasure in their lives, even the short-term feel-good experience brought on by orgasm provides a meaningful mood-enhancing escape. Most women, even if they are not depressed, find it easier to have an orgasm through masturbation than with a partner—they know just the right places to touch and the amount of pressure that feels best. Also, having sex with another person requires a certain degree of social interaction—something that depressed people tend to avoid. And having sex solo would be unlikely to create "performance anxiety" or fear of being evaluated in the way that having sex with another person sometimes does.

The Mood Elixir

At times masturbation may provide benefits over partnered sex, but research conducted by psychologist Gordon Gallup of the State University of New York in Albany suggests there might also be benefits to having sex with a partner—a male partner, that is. In the study, 293 college women filled out a depression inventory and also a questionnaire about their sex lives that asked things such as how often they had intercourse, how long it had been since their last sexual activity, and what type of birth control they used. As it turned out, the women in the study who had sex *without* using condoms (but may have used oral contraceptives) were significantly less depressed than the women who had intercourse and used condoms as a regular form of birth control. They were also happier than the women who reported not having any sex at all. Perhaps the most shocking results came from the question on whether the women had ever attempted suicide. Over 13 percent of the women who said they always used condoms had attempted suicide in the past, compared with only 5 percent of women who said they never used condoms.

These findings suggest that there is something in semen that helped "cure the blues," something that women who used condoms or abstained from intercourse were not getting. It has been known for a long time that semen contains nutritional substances that help sperm make the journey through a woman's fallopian tube to capture that coveted egg. What fewer people know is that semen contains hormones including testosterone, estrogen, follicle-stimulating hormone, luteinizing hormone, prolactin, and several types of prostaglandins. All of these hormones have potential mood-altering abilities and can be absorbed into a woman's bloodstream through the vaginal walls. In fact, some of the hormones have been detected in women's blood within only hours of exposure to semen. Of the various semen-carrying candidates, estrogen and prostaglandins seem most likely to be the mood elevators. Both of these hormones have been shown to be lower than normal in depressed people, and estrogen has been shown to have mood-enhancing effects among postmenopausal women. Among younger women, there have been a few reports showing that certain estrogen-based contraceptives have mood-elevating properties.

In the same study, the researchers found that women who had been having regular intercourse without condoms felt more depressed the longer it had been since they stopped having sex. However, this was not the case with the condom-using women who had stopped having regular intercourse. The researchers suggested this might mean that the women who had not been using condoms went through some sort of "drug withdrawal" when they stopped having regular vaginal contact with semen. In chapter 2 we discussed the many evolutionary explanations for why orgasms may have evolved in women, one being that they feel good so they "reward" women for having sex. Physiologist Roy Levin has suggested that the mood-enhancing effects of semen could have evolved as a way to make sex rewarding for women even when they do not have orgasms.

In addition to showing that semen can enhance a woman's mood, these provocative findings have far-reaching implications for women's sexuality. As we saw earlier, low testosterone levels can account for low sex drive in some women, and testosterone is absorbed through the vagina even more quickly than through the skin. So, to the extent that semen-borne testosterone can seep into a woman's bloodstream, it could potentially have a beneficial effect on her sexual desire. Using duplex ultrasonography, researchers have shown that prostaglandin E_1, one of the magic substances found in semen, significantly increased the amount of blood flow to women's genitals. And in a later study, it was found that women with sexual arousal dysfunction who applied a cream that contained prostaglandin E_1 to the vulvar area prior to intercourse became significantly more sexually aroused. Women who applied a cream with a placebo instead of prostaglandin E_1 did not show the same beneficial effects. So to the extent that semen-borne prostaglandin E_1 can enter the woman's bloodstream, it could have a beneficial impact on her sexual arousal.

Further studies obviously need to be conducted before physicians start prescribing vials of semen as the new generation of antidepressant medication! However, these findings do offer a physiological explanation for why many women in our study reported having sex to "get rid of depression" and to "feel better."

One Is the Loneliest Number

Sometimes, I just crave the weight of another person on top of me.
—predominantly heterosexual woman, age 20

Loneliness is a common cause of depression. People differ widely in the amount of contact they want or need from other people. At one end of the spectrum are the social butterflies who thrive from social interactions, and at the other end are the social recluses who rarely wish to leave their homes. But for most people, a certain amount of contact with others is desired, or even needed, to have a sense of well-being and connectedness. A lack of social contact and, at a deeper level, a lack of intimacy lead to loneliness over time. Feeling lonely and lacking intimacy are problems that are especially apparent for heterosexual women in their elderly years. Because women more often marry men who are older and because men have a shorter life expectancy than women, women generally outlive their husbands. Because elderly single women outnumber elderly men, it is harder for them to find a mate.

In our study, women of all ages and sexual orientations described situations in which they had sex in an attempt to combat loneliness:

> *If I am lonely, I am more likely to be interested in talking to someone and possibly having sex with them. I really think that romantic and sexual involvement all boils down to loneliness. The only reason to engage in intimate behavior with someone else is to feel a human connection and physical pleasure. Physical pleasure can be found alone, so the biggest reason for sex is the human connection. The need for human connection results from loneliness.*
> —predominantly heterosexual woman, age 27

Feelings of loneliness can be so debilitating that they lead some women to make unwise relationship choices simply out of the fear of being alone:

> *I had sex in my last relationship so I would not feel so damned lonely and unlovable. It was a stupid thing because it ended up worsening the feelings for me. I had only seen the guy for a month or so. We were doing some heavy petting after a pretty serious discussion on where we were heading in our relations. He said he wanted to "fuck" and I obliged so someone would be next to me for a little while, so I'd feel like my body was more than a blob of gelatinous fat. I regret it now because we didn't really know each other very well and were not really sure where we were going. . . . Such is life.*
> —heterosexual woman, age 31

> *For the majority of my relationship with my ex-husband I thought sex would help keep him with me. Sex was all about him and keeping him happy. I was too young to know it, but he was not able to*

satisfy me because he lacked any sexual skills. He also lacked any love and compassion and genuine interest in me. He was/is a wholly selfish person. I received no gratification in our sexual encounters. It was always about him and trying to keep him happy so I would not have to be alone.

—predominantly heterosexual woman, age 39

One woman in our study described a situation in which the fear of being without an intimate partner led her to desperate and unhealthy measures:

I was always a "good girl" and never slept around much. One day I discovered I'd been given herpes from a guy I was no longer dating. I was devastated. It was in the seventies, when that was pretty much the worst thing a girl could get. I thought it meant that I could never have children, and I was certain that it meant no man would want me. So, I started having sex indiscriminately to try to find a husband. I purposely had sex when I had an outbreak because I wanted to give them herpes so that we would be in the same boat. It wasn't that I was trying to seek random revenge for what happened to me, it was that I was terrified of being alone. I thought that if someone else had the same disease as I did, we'd be connected, and he'd never leave me because of it.

—heterosexual woman, age 49

Sex, as we know, sometimes leads to a deep sense of emotional connectedness. But this occurs almost always when it is accompanied by feelings of love or affection, caring and tenderness, a shared history, or, at the very least, the hope for a shared future. This is not to say that a "one-night stand" cannot be immensely pleasurable and exciting for some women. What it does mean is that when the primary motive for having sex is to cure feelings of loneliness, casual sex is often disappointing:

I was feeling lonely at the time, [and I] knew that this guy would have sex with me . . . so we did. It really only allowed me to feel loved at the time . . . as soon as he left I felt lonely all over again.

—heterosexual woman, age 24

As one woman in our study eloquently described, needing to have sex is a part of needing intimacy and connection, but sex alone is not the cure:

> *I had a one-night stand a month or so after breaking off a three-year relationship. It was a complex combination of freedom, new ability to be adventurous, loneliness, sadness at intimacy lost, and a hope that there was something better out there. It didn't work in terms of making the loneliness go away, though. The other people weren't there for the same reasons, and afterwards I felt shame and worries that I didn't want to deal with. The sex wasn't particularly good because I didn't know them well and there was a lot of alcohol involved, and it served to teach me that sex wouldn't fix loneliness, it was a symptom of intimacy but it couldn't create it.*
>
> —predominantly heterosexual woman, age 29

But not all women in our study who had sex to avoid loneliness described it as a negative experience. Some women said that it helped them get through the night, kept them from engaging in self-destructive behaviors, or boosted their self-confidence.

The Sex Diet

> *My boyfriend and I were on a diet and felt we were not getting enough exercise so we decided to have a little fun and burn a few extra calories a few times a day by having sex. It was fun and really helped us to feel the burn.*
>
> —predominantly heterosexual woman, age 25

Depending on which report you read, a sexual session can burn anywhere from 100 to 250 calories. Clearly the range is related to the level of athleticism during sex. Ballet maneuvers and handsprings during sex will burn more calories than will the "lie back and wait for the royal treatment to arrive" technique. Also in the equation is whether the event is a noontime "quickie" or an extended night of erotic pleasure. According to a survey of 152 heterosexual Canadian couples, the average lovemaking session for women lasts 18.3 minutes. This consists of 11.3 minutes of foreplay and 7 minutes of intercourse. (Interestingly, the male halves of these same couples reported that foreplay lasted 13.4 minutes—considerably longer than what their female counterparts claimed.)

Women's ideal durations of foreplay and intercourse, as opposed to what they're actually having, were considerably longer—19 minutes of foreplay and 14 minutes of intercourse. According to a survey of over 1,400 women aged eighteen to fifty-nine years, American women have sex about 6.3 times per month. The average is somewhat higher among twenty- to thirty-year-olds (7.5 times per month) and somewhat lower among fifty- to sixty-year-olds (four times per month).

Given that a pound of fat is equivalent to 3,500 calories, the average American woman burns 3.78 pounds of fat a year having sex. So if American women all suddenly stopped having sex, in ten years they would all be thirty-eight pounds heavier. Viewed another way, if women had sex four times a week instead of twice, or managed to extend the session from 18.3 minutes to 36.6 minutes per romp, women would lose an extra four pounds of fat a year. Or they could remain the same weight and consume an extra seventeen chocolate sundaes, twenty-three sugar-glazed doughnuts, and fourteen champagne truffles a year—definitely food for thought.

Do It Till You Drop

"Sexercise" not only burns calories, like other forms of cardiovascular exercise, but supplies a host of other health benefits. It can increase metabolic rate, stretch muscles and increase flexibility, increase energy, help tip the good/bad cholesterol balance in the good direction, increase blood circulation to all parts of the body including the brain, and maybe even lower the risk of having a heart attack and extend life expectancy. One study that questioned men and women repeatedly over a twenty-five-year period found that sex was, indeed, a significant predictor of longevity. But there were also interesting gender differences.

For men, frequency of sex was related to longevity—the more sex they had, the longer they lived. For women, it was the quality of sex that mattered—the more they had enjoyed intercourse in the past, the longer they lived. A recent study of nearly 2,500 elderly Taiwanese men and women found that, over fourteen years, both men and women who had sex at least once per month lived longer than men and women who had sex less than once a month or not at all. In fact, women aged sixty-five and older who had sex more than once a week were almost twice as likely to still be alive fourteen years later than women who had sex only infrequently or not at all. One study showed that nuns, who presumably abstain from sex completely, have a 20 percent greater risk for breast cancer compared to the general U.S. population of women. However, women who do not experience pregnancy have the same increased risk of breast cancer. Thus, it is impossible to know whether the nuns were more likely to have an increased risk for breast cancer because they abstained from sex or because they had never experienced pregnancy.

Scientists do not know for certain why sex and longevity are related. There are so many lifestyle factors in addition to sex that could affect how long you live (for example, diet, exercise, genetics, stress) that it is virtually impossible to parse the pieces. The link between sex and longevity, however, likely has at least something to do with the fact that regular sexual activity increases levels of testosterone and estrogen. Both of these hormones have been described as protective factors against heart disease. Premenopausal women are less than half as likely to suffer from coronary heart disease as are men. But once a woman goes through menopause and her ovaries radically slow down the production of her sex hormones (estrogen, progesterone, testosterone), her risk for coronary heart disease catches up to that of men. Even younger women who have had both of their ovaries removed due to cancer are at a greater risk for developing coronary heart disease. In contrast, there is an abundance of research showing that postmenopausal women who take estrogen supplements have a lower risk of coronary heart disease. Some women, of course, choose not to take estrogen replacement therapy because they are afraid that the synthetic form of estrogen could increase their risk of breast cancer. The jury is still out on the true effect of hormone replacement therapy on a woman's risk of breast cancer. Because sex causes the body to produce its own natural estrogen (as opposed to the "polyester" version), regular sex could potentially help decrease the risk of heart disease without increasing the risk of breast cancer.

Booster Shots and Fringe Benefits

Another way that sex could increase longevity is that moderate levels of sex (with a sexually healthy partner, of course) can boost immune system functioning. This might explain why some women in our study reported having sex simply to "keep healthy" or to "live longer." Immunoglobulin A (IgA) is an antibody that binds to pathogens when they enter the human body. These antibodies help form a barrier against diseases such as the flu or the common cold. Levels of IgA, which is found in saliva and mucosal linings, indicate how robust our immune systems are. Studies show that exposure to enjoyable music or to pets can significantly increase IgA levels within a very short period of time—twenty to thirty minutes. Romantic relationships can also have an enormous impact on immune function—both good and bad. Overall, married people experience less disease and have better outcomes after various disease diagnoses than do single people. But men and women in poor relationships show substantial deficits in immune function.

To examine whether how often a person has sex could also influence immune system functioning, psychologists Carl Charnetski and Francis Brennan asked 112 college students, most of whom were women, how often they had sex during the past month. They also collected saliva samples from all the participants to assess IgA levels. Students who had sex infrequently (less than once a week) had slightly higher levels of IgA than students who had completely abstained from sex. However, students who had sex regularly (once or twice a week) had 30 percent higher levels of IgA than all other students—suggesting better immune system function. It may be that frequent sex made the students more relaxed and happy—both of which are known to increase IgA levels. The increase in opioid peptide release that occurs with orgasm may lead to increased immune system function.

The finding that was hard to explain was that students who had engaged in even more frequent sex—three or more times per week—had the lowest IgA levels of all students, lower even than the abstainers. This suggests there is an optimal frequency of sexual activity for keeping the body's defenses strong. Studies show that a moderate level of opioid peptide release enhances the immune system, but one study found that too much opioid peptide release can actually suppress immune system functioning.

Finally, women in our study described other health benefits that motivated them to have sex. In addition to inducing sleepiness, prolactin causes stem cells in the brain's smell center, the olfactory bulb, to develop new neurons. So, technically, sex can improve one's sense of smell. Another side benefit to regular sex is that it can improve bladder control by working and strengthening the same muscles that are used during urination. And for postmenopausal women, regular sex can help prevent vaginal atrophy that is often a consequence of aging-related decreases in sex hormones. One study found that postmenopausal women who had sexual intercourse at least three times a month had less vaginal atrophy than those who had intercourse less than ten times per year. Having sex can increase the presence of estrogen and testosterone; a burst of the body's own testosterone is thought to help fortify bones and muscles, and estrogen promotes healthy vaginal tissue, soft skin, and shiny hair. Perhaps this explains why Joan Crawford is quoted as once saying, "I need sex for a clearer complexion."

Much to our amusement, several lesser-known men's magazines and Web sites listed even more reasons why "women should have sex." These included assertions such as that kissing stimulates salivation, which cleans "gunk" stuck between your teeth, and that sex can help your nose run so that you are not so stuffed up afterward. Although there may be evidence somewhere to support these claims, we aren't convinced they are good selling points for motivating a woman to have sex. But more to the point, none of the women in our study mentioned even one of them.

CONCLUSION
Women's Sexual Complexities

Why women have sex is surely one of the most fascinating, complex, and enigmatic questions facing the psychology of human motivation. Throughout this book, we have explored many motives—from the frantic desperation to regain some measure of dignity after being spurned to the soaring heights of the consummation of true love; from the altruistic motive of boosting a partner's self-esteem to the selfish motive of exacting revenge; from the thrill of adventure to the dark side of deception; from the mundane motive of relieving a headache to the spiritual aspiration to get closer to God.

Although for economy and clarity of communication, we have parsed the reasons why women have sex into discrete motivations, it's important to acknowledge that what drives a woman to have sex is often more complex and multifaceted, containing varying combinations of motivations. A woman might have sex to gain status among her peer group *and* because she wonders what all the fuss is about. A woman might have sex because a prospective partner's appearance ignites her desire *and* because she's unhappy with her current relationship. A woman might have sex because she wants to relieve her own stress *and* boost her lover's self-confidence *and* become emotionally closer to her partner.

We must recognize too that women's sexual motivations sometimes conflict with one another. A woman may crave the oxytocin rush of an orgasm on a first date, yet also be motivated to delay sex so as not to appear "too easy." Another might be torn between her desire to have sex with an exciting new lover and her vow to fulfill her commitment of fidelity to her husband. A woman may even experience a conflict between a yearning to relinquish all control and feel the rush of sexual submission and her wish to take charge of the encounter and give full flower to her sexual power.

We have tried to examine the magnificent diversity of women's sexual motivations through several theoretical lenses. One is placing women's sexuality within an evolutionary perspective, framing it in the context of the bewildering variety of adaptive problems ancestral women have repeatedly confronted over eons of deep time. A second is physiological, which shows how features of hormones and brain chemicals, blood flow, and anatomy provide a foundation for women's sexuality. A third is a clinical lens, providing insight into the difficulties women encounter as they grapple with and sometimes successfully solve the sexual concerns of desire, arousal, and orgasm. A fourth is psychological, tapping into the rapidly expanding reservoir of scientific knowledge about the mental states that affect women's sexuality, and which in turn are altered by women's sexual experiences. We hope that the unique confluence of these multiple lenses has revealed many more facets of women's sexual motivation than would any single conceptual lens.

We also hope that beyond these theoretical lenses, the multiplicity of sexual motivation has sprung to life through the experiences directly and eloquently described by the women who graciously agreed to participate in our study. A woman recounting sex with her partner as "the fullest flower of the blossom of our love" may capture more of the true experience than the abstract triangular theory of love. The women who described suffering feelings of humiliation and degradation after being sexually deceived by a man brings the phenomenon of sexual exploitation to life more than our theoretical analysis of why sexual deception is so prevalent in the human species. The woman who highlighted her ecstatic experience when a man who was a good dancer *literally danced while having sex* provides an illuminating complement to describing the importance of biomechanical efficiency and smooth motor movements in sexual attraction.

We learned much about human sexuality from the women in our study, and we hope that you have, too.

NOTES

INTRODUCTION

xiv For instance, penile erection monitors: Rosen, R. C., and Beck, J. G. (1988). *Patterns of Sexual Arousal: Psychophysiological Processes and Clinical Applications* (New York: Guilford Press), 17–18.

xiv In the early 1970s, two doctors: Abrams, R. M., and Stolwijk, J. A. J. (1972). "Heat Flow Device for Vaginal Blood Flow Studies," *Journal of Applied Physiology* 33:143–46.

xix The survey itself was hosted: A small number of women elected to e-mail or mail their responses to us directly instead of using the online form.

1. WHAT TURNS WOMEN ON?

3 Back in the 1930s: Brossard, J. (1932). "Residential Propinquity as a Factor in Marriage Selection," *American Journal of Sociology* (September): 288–94.

3 With alphabetical seating: Segal, M. W. (1974). "Alphabet and Attraction: An Unobtrusive Measure of the Effect of Propinquity in a Field Setting," *Journal of Personality and Social Psychology* 30:654–57.

3 One study found that: Saegert, S., Swap, W., and Zajonc, R. (1973). "Exposure, Context, and Interpersonal Attraction," *Journal of Personality and Social Psychology* 25(2): 234–42.

3 Attraction increased as the number: Moreland, R. L., and Beach, S. (1992). "Exposure Effects in the Classroom: The Development of Affinity Among Students," *Journal of Experimental Social Psychology* 28:255–76.

4 The effect of mutual eye gaze: Williams, G. P., and Kleinke, C. L. (1993). "Effects of Mutual Gaze and Touch on Attraction, Mood, and Cardiovascular Activity," *Journal of Research in Personality* 27:170–83.

4 Participants again reported deep attraction: Huston, T. L., and Levinger, G. (1978). "Interpersonal Attraction and Relationships," *Annual Review of Psychology* 29:115–56.

4 As one woman said in her sexual memoir: Slater, L. (2008). "Overcome," in P. Derrow (ed.), *Behind the Bedroom Door* (New York: Bantam Dell), 55.

5 Psychologist Daryl Bem sums it up: Bem, D. J. (1996). "Exotic Becomes Erotic: A Developmental Theory of Sexual Orientation," *Psychological Review* 103:320–35.

5 Indeed, in college classes: Buss, D. M. (2009). Unpublished data.

5 Using an instrument called: Herz, R. S., and Cahill, E. D. (1997). "Differential Use of Sensory Information in Sexual Behavior as a Function of Gender," *Human Nature* 8:275–86.

6 The first clue came: Doty, R. L., et al. (1981). "Endocrine, Cardio-vascular, and Psychological Correlates of Olfactory Sensitivity Changes During the Human Menstrual Cycle," *Journal of Comparative and Physiological Psychology* 95:45–60.

6 In a revealing study: Santos, P. S. C., et al. (2005). "New Evidence that the MHC Influences Odor Perception in Humans: A Study with 58 Southern Brazilian Students," *Hormones and Behavior* 47:384–88.

7 University of New Mexico evolutionary psychologist: Garver-Apgar, C. E., Gangestad, S. W., et al. (2006). "MHC Alleles, Sexual Responsivity, and Unfaithfulness in Romantic Couples," *Psychological Science* 17:830–35.

8 In one study, men wore white cotton T-shirts: Thornhill, R., and Gangestad, S. W. (2008). *The Evolutionary Biology of Human Female Sexuality* (New York: Oxford University Press).

8 When women have extramarital affairs: Gangestad, S. W., and Thornhill, R. (1997). "The Evolutionary Psychology of Extra-Pair Sex: The Role of Fluctuating Asymmetry," *Evolution and Human Behavior* 18:69–88.

9 One study found that frequent: Cutler, W. B., et al. (1980). "Sporadic Sexual Behavior and Menstrual Cycle Length in Women," *Hormones and Behavior* 14:163–72.

9 Another study showed that women: Veith, J. L., et al. (1983). "Exposure to Men Influences Occurrence of Ovulation in Women," *Physiology and Behavior* 31(3): 313–15.

9 Dr. Winnifred Cutler, the director: Cutler, W. B., Friedmann, E., and McCoy, N. L. (1998). "Pheromonal Influences on the Sociosexual Behavior of Men," *Archives of Sexual Behavior* 27(1): 629–34.

10 Men who indicated: Sugiyama, L. S. (2005). "Physical Attractiveness in Adapta-tionist Perspective," in D. M. Buss (ed.), *Evolutionary Psychology Handbook* (New York: Wiley), 292–343.

10 Women prefer tall men: Buss, D. M., and Schmitt, D. P. (1993). "Sexual Strate-gies Theory: An Evolutionary Perspective on Human Mating," *Psychological Review* 100:204–32; Greiling, H., and Buss, D. M., unpublished data.

10 Women even take height: Scheib, J. E. (1997). "Female Choice in the Context of Donor Insemination," in P. A. Gowaty (ed.), *Feminism and Evolutionary Biol-ogy: Boundaries, Intersections and Frontiers* (New York: Chapman & Hall), 489–504; Scheib, J. E., Kristiansen, A., and Wara, A. (1997). "A Norwegian Note on Sperm Donor Selection and the Psychology of Female Mate Choice," *Evolution and Human Behavior* 18:143–49.

10 In Western cultures, tall men: For summaries of these studies, see Ellis, B. J. (1992). "The Evolution of Sexual Attraction: Evaluative Mechanisms in Women," in J. Barkow, L. Cosmides, and J. Tooby (eds.), *The Adapted Mind* (New York: Oxford University Press), 267–88; Buss, D. M. (2008). *Evolution-ary Psychology: The New Science of the Mind,* 3rd ed. (Boston: Allyn & Bacon).

11 Most women show a distinct preference: Hughes, S. M., and Gallup, G. G. (2003). "Sex Differences in Morphological Predictors of Sexual Behavior: Shoulder to Hip and Waist to Hip Ratios," *Evolution and Human Behavior* 24:173–78.

11 Potential rivals with a high shoulder: Dijkstra, P., and Buunk, B. P. (2001). "Sex Differences in the Jealousy-Evoking Nature of a Rival's Body Build," *Evolution and Human Behavior* 22 (5):335–41.

12 One study compared the muscularity: Frederick, D. A., and Haselton, M. G. (2007). "Why Is Male Muscularity Sexy? Tests of the Fitness Indicator Hypoth-esis," *Personality and Social Psychology Bulletin* 33:1167–83.

12 After viewing repeated: Olivardia, R. S. (2001). "Mirror, Mirror on the Wall . . . Are Muscular Men the Best of All? The Hidden Turmoils of Muscle Dysmor-phia," *Harvard Review of Psychiatry* 9:254–59.

12 "feels like Clark Kent": Frederick, D. A., Buchanan, G. M., et al. (2007). "Desir-ing the Muscular Ideal: Men's Body Satisfaction in the United States, Ukraine, and Ghana," *Psychology of Men & Masculinity* 8:103–17.

13 Women's sexual desires for testosterone-fueled: Penton-Voak, I. S., Perrett, D. I., et al. (1999). "Female Preference for Male Faces Changes Cyclically," *Nature* 399: 741–42. Roney, J. R., and Simmons, Z. L. (2008). "Women's Estradiol Predicts Preferences for Facial Cues of Men's Testosterone," *Hormones and Behavior* 53:14–19.

14 They are more likely to be the risk-taking: Jonason, P. K., Li, N. P., et al. (2009). "The Dark Triad: Facilitating Short-Term Mating in Men," *European Journal of Personality* 23:5–18.

14 They interpret this cultural difference: Penton-Voak, I. S., Jacobon, A., and Trivers, R. (2004). "Population Differences in Attractiveness Judgments of Male and Female Faces: Comparing British and Jamaican Samples," *Evolution and Human Behavior* 25:355–70.

15 They discovered that the infants: Langlois, J. H., et al. (1990). "Infants' Differential Social Responses to Attractive and Unattractive Faces," *Developmental Psychology* 26:153–59; Langlois, J. H., et al. (1994). "What's Average and Not Average About Attractive Faces?" *Psychological Science* 5:214–20.

16 Attractiveness is moderately linked: Langlois, J. H., Kalakanis, L., et al. (2000). "Maxims or Myths of Beauty? A Meta-Analytic and Theoretical Review," *Psychological Bulletin* 126:390–423.

16 The first scientific evidence: Puts, D. A., Gaulin, S. J. C., and Verdolini, K. (2006). "Dominance and the Evolution of Sexual Dimorphism in Human Voice Pitch," *Evolution and Human Behavior* 27:283–96.

16 Moreover, women in the fertile phase: Puts, D. A. (2005). "Mating Context and Menstrual Cycle Phase Affect Women's Preferences for Male Voice Pitch," *Evolution and Human Behavior* 26:388–97.

17 One hint as to why: Trivers, R. (1985). *Social Evolution* (Menlo Park, Calif.: Benjamin Cummings).

17 Psychologist Susan Hughes: Hughes, S. M., Dispensa, F., and Gallup, G. G., Jr. (2004). "Ratings of Voice Attractiveness Predicts Sexual Behavior and Body Configuration," *Evolution and Human Behavior* 25:295–304.

17 A second study, of the Hadza: Apicella, C. L., Feinberg, D. R., and Marlow, F. W. (2007). "Voice Pitch Predicts Reproductive Success in Male Hunter-Gatherers," *Biology Letters* 3:682–84.

18 One study had women view digitally masked: Grammer, K., Fink, B., et al. (2002). "Female Faces and Bodies: N-dimensional Feature Space and Attractiveness," in G. Rhodes and L. A. Zebrowitz (eds.), *Facial Attractiveness: Evolutionary, Cognitive and Social Perspectives* (Westport, Conn.: Greenwood).

18 In a fascinating experiment, psychologist Meghan Provost: Provost, M. P., Troje, N. F., and Quinsey, V. L. (2008). "Short Term Mating Strategies and Attraction to Masculinity in Point-light Walkers," *Evolution and Human Behavior* 29:65–69.

19 Evolutionary psychologist Karl Grammer: Grammer, K., Renninger, L., and Fischer, B. (2004). "Disco Clothing, Female Sexual Motivation, and Relationship Status: Is She Dressed to Impress?" *Journal of Sex Research* 41:66–74.

21 And studies from the Buss Evolutionary Psychology Lab: Buss, D. M. (1988). "The Evolution of Human Intrasexual Competition: Tactics of Mate Attraction," *Journal of Personality and Social Psychology* 54:616–28.

22 Indeed, studies have found: Comins, H., May, R. M., and Hamilton, W. D. (1980). "Evolutionarily Stable Dispersal Strategies," *Journal of Theoretical Biology* 82:205–30.

22 "Some guys just seem": Cloyd, J. W. (1976). "The Market-place Bar: The Inter-relation Between Sex, Situation, and Strategies in the Pairing Ritual *Homo Ludens*," *Urban Life* 5(3): 300.

23 Men scoring high on self-confidence: Twenge, J. M. (2002). "Self-Esteem and Socioeconomic Status: A Meta-Analytic Review," *Personality and Social Psychology Review* 6:59–71.

23 Another study, for example, discovered that only men: Kiesler, S. B., and Baral, R. L. (1970). "The Search for a Romantic Partner: The Effects of Self-Esteem and Physical Attractiveness on Romantic Behavior," in K. H. Gergen and D. Marlow (eds.), *Personality and Social Behavior* (Reading: Addison-Wesley), 155–65.

24 The Buss Lab found: Hill, S. E., and Buss, D. M. (in prep.). "The Multiple Determinants of Self-esteem." Unpublished manuscript, Department of Psychology, University of Texas, Austin.

26 "Balance," according to social psychologists: Hummert, M. L., Crockett, W. H., and Kemper, S. (1990). "Processing Mechanisms Underlying the Use of the Balance Schema," *Journal of Personality and Social Psychology* 58:5–21.

27 By pairing paced copulation with an almond scent: Coria-Avila, G. A., et al. (2005). "Olfactory Conditioned Partner Preference in the Female Rat," *Behavioral Neuroscience* 119:716–25.

2. THE PLEASURE OF IT

30 In a study conducted in the Meston: Levin, R., and Meston, C. M. (2006). "Nipple/Breast Stimulation and Sexual Arousal in Young Men and Women," *Journal of Sexual Medicine* 3:450–54.

33 Certain herbal formulas such as ephedrine: Meston, C. M., and Heiman, J. R. (1998). "Ephedrine-Activated Physiological Sexual Arousal in Women," *Archives of General Psychiatry* 55:652–56.

33 yohimbine plus L-arginine glutamate: Meston, C. M., and Worcel, M. (2002). "The Effects of Yohimbine plus L-Arginine Glutamate on Sexual Arousal in Post-menopausal Women with Sexual Arousal Disorder," *Archives of Sexual Behavior* 31:323–32.

33 ginkgo biloba extract: Meston, C. M., Rellini, A. H., and Telch, M. (2008). "Short-term and Long-term Effects of Ginkgo Biloba Extract on Sexual Dysfunction in Women," *Archives of Sexual Behavior* 37:530–47.

33 For example, a study conducted in the late 1980s: Atwood, J. D., and Gagnon, J. (1987). "Masturbation Practices of Males and Females," *Journal of Sex Research* 10:293–307.

33 . . . percentages almost identical to those reported by Alfred C. Kinsey: Kinsey, A. C., Pomeroy, W. D., and Martin, C. E. (1948). *Sexual Behavior in the Human*

Male (Philadelphia: W. B. Saunders Company), 628; Kinsey, A. C., Pomeroy, W. D., Martin, C. E., and Gebhard P. H. (1953). *Sexual Behavior in the Human Female* (Philadelphia: W. B. Saunders Company), 628.

33 Among college students, the Meston Lab: Meston, C. M., Trapnell, P. D., and Gorzalka, B. B. (1996). "Ethnic and Gender Differences in Sexuality: Variations in Sexual Behavior between Asian and Non-Asian University Students," *Archives of Sexual Behavior* 25:33–72.

35 Recently, researchers at the University of L'Aquila: Gravina, G. L., et al. (2008). "Measurement of the Thickness of the Urethrovaginal Space in Women With or Without Vaginal Orgasm," *Journal of Sexual Medicine* 5:610–18.

36 "the abrupt cessation": Kinsey, A. C., et al. (1953). *Sexual Behavior in the Human Female*.

37 "sensation of suspension or stoppage": Masters, W. H., and Johnson, V. (1966). *Human Sexual Response* (Boston: Little, Brown and Co.).

37 By 2001, there were no: Mah, K., and Binik, Y. M. (2001). "The Nature of Human Orgasm: A Critical Review of Major Trends," *Clinical Psychology Review* 21:823–56.

37 "An orgasm in the human female": Meston, C. M., et al. (2004). "Women's Orgasm," in T. F. Lue et al. (eds.), *Sexual Medicine: Sexual Dysfunctions in Men and Women* (Paris, France: Health Publications), 783–850.

38 Masters and Johnson claimed: Masters, W. H., and Johnson, V. (1966). *Human Sexual Response*.

38 Some theorists have postulated: Levin, R. J. "The Physiology and Pathophysiology of the Female Orgasm," in Goldstein, I., Meston, C. M., Davis, S. R., and Traish, A. M. (eds.) (2006). *Women's Sexual Function and Dysfunction* (London: Taylor & Francis Group), 231.

42 In a survey of over 1,600: Laumann, E. O., et al. (1994). *The Social Organization of Sexuality: Sexual Practices in the United States* (Chicago: University of Chicago Press).

45 Mangaian men who fail: Marshall, D. S. (1971). "Sexual Behavior on Mangaia," in Marshall D. S., and Suggs, R.C. (eds.), *Human Sexual Behavior: Variations in the Ethnographic Spectrum* (New York: Basic Books), 103–32.

46 These women had met for: Heinrich, A. G. (1976). "The Effect of Group and Self-Directed Behavioral-Educational Treatment of Primary Orgasmic Dysfunction in Females Treated Without Their Partners," Ph.D. dissertation, University of Colorado, Boulder, Colo.

47 The book *Becoming Orgasmic*: Heiman, J. R., LoPiccolo, L., and LoPiccolo, J. (1976). *Becoming Orgasmic: A Sexual Growth Program for Women* (Englewood Cliffs, N.J.: Prentice-Hall).

47 Early theorists hypothesized: Laqueur, T. (1990). *Making Sex: Body and Gender from the Greeks to Freud* (Cambridge, Mass.: Harvard University Press).

47 However, studies have now shown: Levin, R. J. (2002). "The Physiology of Sexual Arousal in the Human Female: A Recreational and Procreational Synthesis," *Archives of Sexual Behavior* 31:405–11.

48 One study found: Thornhill, R., Gangestad, S. W., and Comer, R. (1995). "Human Female Orgasm and Mate Fluctuating Asymmetry," *Animal Behavior* 50:1601–15.

48 One interesting and rather controversial: Baker, R. R., and Bellis, M. A. (1995). *Human Sperm Competition: Copulation, Masturbation and Infidelity* (London: Chapman and Hall).

48 If a woman has an orgasm: Ibid.

48 This in turn helps to facilitate: Reyes, A., et al. (1979). "Effect of Prolactin on the Calcium Binding and/or Transport of Ejaculated and Epididymal Human Spermatozoa," *Fertility and Sterility* 31:669–72.

3. The Thing Called Love

51 Romantic love is something: As cited in Hatfield, E., and Rapson, R. L. (2007). "Passionate Love and Sexual Desire: Multidisciplinary Perspectives," in J.P. Forgas (ed.), *Personal Relationships: Cognitive, Affective, and Motivational Processes,* 10th Sydney Symposium of Social Psychology, Sydney, Australia.

52 For example, Hatfield reports: As cited in Hatfield, E., and Rapson, R. L. (2009). "The Neuropsychology of Passionate Love," in D. Marazziti (ed.), *Neuropsychology of Social Relationships*, Nova Science.

54 Sternberg has identified: Sternberg, R. J. (1999). *Love Is a Story: A New Theory of Relationships* (New York: Oxford University Press).

55 Neuroscientist Niels Birbaumer: Birbaumer, N., et al. (1993). "Imagery and Brain Processes," in N. Birbaumer and A. Öhman (eds.), *The Structure of Emotion* (Göttingen, Germany: Hogrefe & Huber Publishers).

55 In 2003, a decade after: Bartels, A., and Zeki, S. (2000). "The Neural Basis of Romantic Love," *Neuroreport* 11 (November 27): 3829–34.

56 The "love is a drug": Liebowitz, M. R. (1983). *The Chemistry of Love* (Boston: Little, Brown).

57 To test their hypothesis: Marazziti, D., et al. (1999). "Alteration of the Platelet Serotonin Transporter in Romantic Love," *Psychological Medicine* 29(3):741–45.

58 The women believe that after: Jankowiak, W. (1995). *Romantic Passion: A Universal Experience?* (New York: Columbia University Press).

58 Susan Sprecher and her colleagues: Sprecher, S., Aron, A., et al. (1994). "Love: American Style, Russian Style, and Japanese Style," *Personal Relationships* 1:349–69.

58 Studies examining love in other: Jankowiak, W. R., and Fisher, E. F. (1992). "A Cross-Cultural Perspective on Romantic Love," *Ethnology* 31:149–55.

58 In the most massive study: Buss, D. M., Abbott, M., et al. (1990). "International Preferences in Selecting Mates: A Study of 37 Cultures," *Journal of Cross-Cultural Psychology* 21:5–47.

59 In a study on the link: Levine, R., Sato, S., et al. (1995). "Love and Marriage in Eleven Cultures," *Journal of Cross-Cultural Psychology* 26:554–71.

59 Clearly, in nations where: As cited in Hatfield, E., and Rapson, R. L. (2007). "Passionate Love and Sexual Desire."

59 Psychologists who have studied: Ibid.

59 A study that assessed 231 college dating couples: Rubin, A., Peplau, L. A., and Hill, C. T. (1981). "Loving and Leaving: Sex Differences in Romantic Attachments," *Sex Roles* 8:821–35.

62 Inscribed on the four-thousand: Arsu, S. (2006). "The Oldest Line in the World," *New York Times*, February 14, 1.

63 Women who are most open: Shaver, P. R., and Mikulincer, M. (2008). "A Behavioral Systems Approach to Romantic Love Relationships: Attachment, Caregiving, and Sex," in R. Sternberg and K. Weis (eds.), *The New Psychology of Love* (New Haven, Conn.: Yale University Press).

63 In the Meston Sexual Psychophysiology Lab: Meston, C. M., Trapnell, P. D., and Gorazalka, B. B. (1998). "Ethnic, Gender, and Length of Residency Influences on Sexual Knowledge and Attitudes," *Journal of Sex Research* 35:176–88.

63 Psychologist David Schmitt: Schmitt, D. (2008). Unpublished data.

63 With these people in mind: Buss, D. M. (1988). "Love Acts: The Evolutionary Biology of Love," in R. Sternberg and M. Barnes (eds.), *The Psychology of Love* (New Haven, Conn.: Yale University Press).

66 "Now when their nature": Plato (1991). Trans. with comment by R. E. Allen. *The Symposium* (New Haven, Conn.: Yale University Press).

67 In a study conducted: McCall, K. M., and Meston, C. M. (2006). "Cues Resulting in Desire for Sexual Activity in Women," *Journal of Sexual Medicine* 3:838–52.

68 Kissing between romantic or sexual partners: Eibl-Eibesfeldt, I. (1970). *Love and Hate: On the Natural History of Behavior Patterns* (New York: Methuen).

68 Human lips are densely packed: Walter, C. (2008). "Affairs of the Lips," *Scientific American* (February/March):24–29.

68 Whereas 53 percent of men: Hughes, S. M., Harrison, M. A., and Gallup, G. G. (2007). "Sex Differences in Romantic Kissing among College Students: An Evolutionary Perspective," *Evolutionary Psychology* 5:612–31.

69 There has not been a lot of research: Kosfeld, M., Heinrichs, M., et al. (2005). "Oxytocin Increases Trust in Humans," *Nature* 435:673–76.

71 The attachment-prone, faithful prairie voles: Insel, T. R., and Shapiro, L. E. (1992). "Oxytocin Receptor Distribution Reflects Social Organization in Monogamous and Polygamous Voles," *Proceedings of the National Academy of Science* 89:5981–85.

71 Very recently, it has also been discovered: Edwards, S., and Self, D. W. (2006). "Monogamy: Dopamine Ties the Knot." *Nature Neuroscience* 9:7–8.

72 They found that they could: Lim, M. M., and Young, L. J. (2004). "Vasopressin-Dependent Neural Circuits Underlying Pair Bonding in the Monogamous Prairie Vole," *Neuroscience* 125:35–45.

72 When they used a harmless virus: Lim, M. M., Wang, Z., et al. (2004). "Enhanced Partner Preference in a Promiscuous Species by Manipulating the Expression of a Single Gene," *Nature* 429:754–57.

73 In sharp contrast, the nonmonogamous: Meston, C. M., and Hamilton, L. D. (2009). Unpublished data.

76 Hands down, women: Buss, D. M., Shackelford, T. K., et al. (1999). "Jealousy and Beliefs About Infidelity: Tests of Competing Hypotheses in the United States, Korea, and Japan," *Personal Relationships* 6:125–50.

77 For this reason, some researchers believe that concealed ovulation: Others have argued for other functions of concealed ovulation, such as preventing men from mate guarding them when they are most fertile, which opens an option for securing benefits from extra-pair copulations.

4. The Thrill of Conquest

79 "The women always succeed": Viewer comment from the Internet Movie Database: www.imdb.com/title/tt0313038/usercomments.

79 When we think of competing: Lincoln, G. A. (1994). "Teeth, Horns, and Antlers: The Weapons of Sex," in R. V. Short and E. Balaban, *The Differences Between the Sexes* (New York: Cambridge University Press), 241.

79 "It's that he's an alpha": Somaiya, R. (2009). "It's the Economy, Girlfriend," *New York Times*, January 27, A21.

79 In fact, male-male competition: Buss, D. M. (2003). *The Evolution of Desire: Strategies of Human Mating* (New York: Basic Books).

81 The premium men place: Buss, D. M. (1989). "Sex Differences in Human Mate Preferences: Evolutionary Hypotheses Testing in 37 Cultures," *Behavioral and Brain Sciences* 12:1–49.

82 Harvard psychologist Nancy Etcoff: Etcoff, N. (1999). *Survival of the Prettiest: The Science of Beauty* (New York: Doubleday).

83 "many women said that": Allon, N., and Fishel, D. (1979). "Singles Bars," in N. Allon (ed.), *Urban Life Styles* (Dubuque, Ia.: William C. Brown), 152.

84 Evolutionary psychologist Kristina Durante: Durante, K. M., Li, N. P., and Haselton, M. G. (2008). "Changes in Women's Choice of Dress Across the Ovulatory Cycle: Naturalistic and Laboratory Task-Based Evidence," *Personality and Social Psychology Bulletin* 34:1451–60.

84 Another group of researchers: Haselton, M. G., Mortezair, M., et al. (2007). "Irrational Emotions or Emotional Wisdom? The Evolutionary Psychology of Emotions and Behavior," in J. P. Forgas (ed.), *Hearts and Minds: Affective Influences on Social Cognition and Behavior* (New York: Psychology Press), 21–40.

84 One study created a simulated: Durante, K. M., Li, N. P., and Haselton, M. G. (2008). "Changes in Women's Choice of Dress," *Personality and Social Psychology Bulletin.*

85 Women report more desire: Haselton, M. G., and Gangestad, S. W. (2006). "Conditional Expression of Women's Desires and Men's Mate Guarding Across the Ovulatory Cycle," *Hormones and Behavior* 49:509–18.

85 They even judge other women: Fisher, M. (2004). "Female Intrasexual Competition Decreases Female Facial Attractiveness," *Proceedings of the Royal Society of London, Series B* (Supplemental) 271:S283–85.

85 It is the phase in which: Buss, D. M., and Shackelford, T. K. (2008). "Attractive Women Want It All: Good Genes, Economic Investment, Parenting Proclivities, and Emotional Commitment," *Evolutionary Psychology* 6:134–46.

86 "I've heard that she slept": Buss, D. M., and Dedden, L. A. (1990). "Derogation of Competitors," *Journal of Social and Personal Relationships* 7:395–422.

86 "it was the girls themselves": Campbell, A. (2002). *A Mind of Her Own: The Evolutionary Psychology of Women* (Oxford: Oxford University Press), 197.

87 "The most risky confidences center": Lees, S. (1993). *Sugar and Spice: Sexuality and Adolescence* (London: Penguin Press), 80.

87 Being branded with derogatory: Campbell, A. (2002). *Mind of Her Own*, 198.

88 Such offers of immediate sex: Symons, D. (1979). *The Evolution of Human Sexuality* (New York: Oxford University Press); Buss, D. M. (2003). *Evolution of Desire.*

90 "calm and connection system": Moberg, K. U. (2003). *The Oxytocin Factor: Tapping the Hormone of Calm, Love, and Healing* (New York: Da Capo Press).

92 She claims to have shared: "Pamela Des Barres: Her Latest Book Celebrates the Outrageous, Unsung Exploits of Her Fellow 'Band-Aids,' " *The Independent,* September 23, 2007.

93 The practice of mate poaching: The phrase "mate poaching" was first coined in Buss, D. M. (1994), *Evolution of Desire;* the first study of human mate poaching: Schmitt, D.P., and Buss, D. M. (2001). "Human Mate Poaching: Tactics and Temptations for Infiltrating Existing Mateships," *Journal of Personality and Social Psychology* 80:894–917.

94 Evolutionary psychologist David Schmitt: Schmitt, D. P., et al. (2004). "Patterns and Universals of Mate Poaching Across 53 Nations: The Effects of Sex, Culture, and Personality on Romantically Attracting Another Person's Partner," *Journal of Personality & Social Psychology* 86:560–84.

95 "Friends" frequently end up: Bleske, A. L., and Shackelford, T. K. (2001). "Poaching, Promiscuity, and Deceit: Combating Mating Rivalry in Same-Sex Friendships," *Personal Relationships* 8:407–24.

95 A particularly insidious form: Buss, D. M. (2003). *Evolution of Desire.*

96 This point became apparent: Buss, D. M. (2005). *The Murderer Next Door: Why the Mind Is Designed to Kill* (New York: Penguin Press).

96 Research has documented: Kenrick, D. T., Gutierres, S. E., and Goldberg, L. (1989). "Influence of Erotica on Ratings of Strangers and Mates," *Journal of Experimental Social Psychology* 25:159–67.

97 men who frequently view sexual pornography: Zillman, D., and Bryant, J. (1988). "Pornography's Impact on Sexual Satisfaction," *Journal of Applied Social Psychology* 18:438–53.

97 "Do not read beauty magazines": Mary Schmich, "Wear Sunscreen," *Chicago Tribune,* June 1, 1997.

5. GREEN-EYED DESIRE

100 "Jealousy is not a barometer": Mead, M. (1935). *Sex and Temperament in Three Primitive Societies* (New York: Dell Publishing), as cited in Hatfield, E., Rapson, R. L., and Marlet, L. D. (2007). "Passionate Love," in S. Kitayama and D. Cohen (eds.), *Handbook of Cultural Psychology* (New York: Guilford Press).

100 Other researchers have joined her: Bringle, R. G., and Buunk, B. (1986). "Examining the Causes and Consequences of Jealousy: Some Recent Findings and Issues," in R. Gilmour and S. Duck (eds.), *The Emerging Field of Personal Relationships* (Hillsdale, N.J.: Erlbaum), 225–40.

100 At the other end of the spectrum, evolutionary psychologists: Symons, D. (1979). *The Evolution of Human Sexuality* (New York: Oxford University Press); Daly, M., Wilson, M., and Weghorst, S. J. (1982). "Male Sexual Jealousy," *Ethology and Sociobiology* 3: 11–27; Buss, D. M. (2000). *The Dangerous Passion: Why Jealousy Is as Necessary as Love and Sex* (New York: Free Press).

100 In romantic relationships, threats can come from: Buss, D. M. (2003). *The Evolution of Desire: Strategies of Human Mating* (New York: Basic Books); Schmitt, D. P., and Buss, D. M. (2001). "Human Mate Poaching: Tactics and Temptations for Infiltrating Existing Mateships," *Journal of Personality and Social Psychology* 80:894–917.

100 In general, the more insecure: Berscheid, E., and Fei, J. (1977). "Romantic Love and Sexual Jealousy," in G. Clanton and L. D. Smith (eds.), *Jealousy* (Englewood Cliffs, N.J.: Prentice-Hall).

102 Compared to the other countries: Buunk, B., and Hupka, R. B. (1987). "Cross-cultural Differences in the Elicitation of Sexual Jealousy," *Journal of Sex Research* 23:12–22.

102 Cross-cultural studies of jealousy: Hupka, R. B., and Ryan, J. M. (1990). "The Cultural Contribution to Jealousy: Cross-cultural Aggression in Sexual Jealousy Situations," *Behavior Science Research* 24:51–71.

102 The situations of two tribes: Hatfield, E., Rapson, R. L., and Marlet, L. D. (2007). "Passionate Love."

102 They were obsessed with painful: Salovey, P., and Rodin, J. (1985). "The Heart of Jealousy," *Psychology Today* 19:22–29.

102 "One Christmas Eve": Buss, D. M. (2000). *The Dangerous Passion: Why Jealousy Is as Necessary as Love and Sex* (New York: Free Press).

103 Some psychologists propose: Buss, D. M. (2003). *Evolution of Desire.*

103 "Othello's mistake was not": Ekman, P. (2003). *Emotions Revealed: Recognizing Faces and Feelings to Improve Communication and Emotional Life* (New York: Times Books).

103–4 It is far more common for men to abuse: Daly, M., and Wilson, M. (1988). *Homicide* (Hawthorne, N.Y.: Aldine); Buss, D. M. (2005). *The Murderer Next Door: Why the Mind Is Designed to Kill* (New York: Penguin Press).

106 In fact, women report evoking jealousy: Buss, D. M. (2000). *Dangerous Passion,* 73.

107 In sharp contrast, when the woman: Ibid.

109 Studies from the Buss Evolutionary Psychology Lab: Buss, D. M., and Schmitt, D. P. (1993). "Sexual Strategies Theory: An Evolutionary Perspective on Human Mating," *Psychological Review* 100:204–32.

110 *Mate guarding* refers to: These have been discussed in detail in Buss, D. M. (2003). *Evolution of Desire.*

110 "Wives are never happy": Symons, D. (1979). *Evolution of Human Sexuality,* 117.

114 And in a study of eighty-nine cultures: Betzig, L. (1989). "Causes of Conjugal Dissolution," *Current Anthropology* 30:654–76.

115 According to one study, most men's motivations: Glass, S. P., and Wright, T. L. (1985). "Sex Differences in the Type of Extramarital Involvement and Marital Dissatisfaction," *Sex Roles* 12:1101–19; Glass, D. P., and Wright, T. L. (1992). "Justifications for Extramarital Relationships: The Association Between Attitudes, Behaviors, and Gender," *Journal of Sex Research* 29:361–87; Thompson, A. P. (1983). "Extramarital Sex: A Review of the Literature," *Journal of Sex Research* 19:1–22.

116 Studies from the Buss Lab on the motivations: Buss, D. M. (2000). *Dangerous Passion.*

6. A SENSE OF DUTY

117 "While the urge to eat": As cited in Impett, E. A., and Peplau, L. (2003). "Sexual Compliance: Gender, Motivational, and Relationship Perspectives," *Journal of Sex Research* 40:87–100.

119 One study found that college women: Cohen, L. L., and Shotland, R. L. (1996). "Timing of First Sexual Intercourse in a Relationship: Expectations, Experiences, and Perceptions of Others," *Journal of Sex Research* 33:291–99.

121 This holds true for college students: Beck, J. G., Bozman, A. W., and Qualtrough, T. (1991). "The Experience of Sexual Desire: Psychological Correlates in a College Sample," *Journal of Sex Research* 28:443–56.

121 middle-aged people: Pfeiffer, E., Verwoerdt, A., and Davis, G. (1972). "Sexual Behavior in Middle Life," *American Journal of Psychiatry* 128:1262–67.

121 eighty- and ninety-year-olds: Bretschneider, J. G., and McCoy, N. L. (1988). "Sexual Interest and Behavior in Healthy 80- to 102-Year-Olds," *Archives of Sexual Behavior* 17:109–30.

121 whether measured among married persons: Julien, D., Bouchard, C., et al. (1992). "Insiders' Views of Marital Sex: A Dyadic Analysis," *Journal of Sex Research* 29:343–60.

121 couples in the early stages: McCabe, M. P. (1987). "Desired and Experienced Levels of Premarital Affection and Sexual Intercourse During Dating," *Journal of Sex Research* 23:23–33.

121 In a study of 1,410 American: Laumann, E. O., Gagnon, J. H., et al. (1994). *The Social Organization of Sexuality: Sexual Practices in the United States* (Chicago: University of Chicago Press).

122 This fits well with: Symons, D. (1979). *The Evolution of Human Sexuality* (New York: Oxford).

123 Many studies find that women: Meston, C. M., Trapnell, P. D., and Gorzalka, B. B. (1996). "Ethnic and Gender Differences in Sexuality: Variations in Sexual Behavior Between Asian and Non-Asian University Students," *Archives of Sexual Behavior* 25:33–72. Cawood, E. H., and Bancroft, J. (1996). "Steroid Hormones, the Menopause, Sexuality and Well-being of Women," *Psychological Medicine* 26:925–36.

123 Interestingly, when sexually compulsive men: Berlin, F. S., and Meinecke, C. F. (1981). "Treatment of Sex Offenders with Anti-Androgenic Medication: Conceptualization, Review of Treatment Modalities and Preliminary Findings," *American Journal of Psychiatry* 138:601–7.

125 Women who lack sufficient testosterone: Leiblum, S. R., and Sachs, J. (2002). *Getting the Sex You Want: A Woman's Guide to Becoming Proud, Passionate, and Pleased in Bed* (New York: Crown), 181.

125 Sandra Leiblum, a sex researcher: Ibid.

127 High levels of estrogen may: Leiblum, S. R., and Sachs, J. (2002). *Getting the Sex You Want*, 91.

128 Indeed, in traditional cultures: Sugiyama, L. (2005). "Physical Attractiveness in Adaptationist Perspective," in D. M. Buss (ed.), *Evolutionary Psychology Handbook* (New York: Wiley), 292–343.

129 Oral contraceptives that have: Leiblum, S. R., and Sachs, J. (2002). *Getting the Sex You Want.*

129 An estimated 96 percent: Clayton, A., Keller, A., and McGarvey, E. L. (2006). "Burden of Phase-specific Sexual Dysfunction with SSRIs," *Journal of Affective Disorders* 91:27–32.

129 Up to one-half: Rosen, R. C., Lane, R. M., and Menza, M. (1999). "Effects of SSRIs on Sexual Function: A Critical Review," *Journal of Clinical Psychopharmacology* 19:67–85.

130 Anti-anxiety medications, such as Valium: Leiblum, S. R., and Sachs, J. (2002). *Getting the Sex You Want,* 175–79.

131 Because overweight partners: LoPiccolo, J., and Friedman, J. M. (1988). "Broad-spectrum Treatment of Low Sexual Desire: Integration of Cognitive, Behavioral, and Systemic Therapy," in S. R. Leiblum and R. C. Rosen (eds.), *Sexual Desire Disorders* (New York: Guilford Press), 125–26.

131 "The wife's dreams of romance": Rubin, H. (1941). *Eugenics and Sex Harmony* (New York: Herald Publishing), 123–24.

133 Psychologist Lorraine Dennerstein: Dennerstein, L., Smith, A., Morse, C., et al. (1994). "Sexuality and the Menopause," *Journal of Psychosomatic Obstetrics and Gynaecology* 15:59–66.

134 Often, it goes both: LoPiccolo, J., and Friedman, J. M. (1988). "Broad-spectrum Treatment of Low Sexual Desire."

134 These couples have such: Nichols, M. (1988). "Low Sexual Desire in Lesbian Couples," in S. R. Leiblum and R. C. Rosen (eds.), *Sexual Desire Disorders,* 398.

136 One study of married couples: Carlson, J. (1976). "The Sexual Role," in F. I. Nye (ed.), *Role Structure and Analysis of the Family* (Beverly Hills, Calif.: Sage Publications), 101–10.

136 Researcher Lucia O'Sullivan: O'Sullivan, L. F., and Allgeier, E. R. (1998). "Feigning Sexual Desire: Consenting to Unwanted Sexual Activity in Heterosexual Dating Relationships," *Journal of Sex Research* 35:234–43.

137 Agreeing to unwanted sex: Impett, E. A., and Peplau, L. (2003). "Sexual Compliance: Gender, Motivational, and Relationship Perspectives," *Journal of Sex Research* 40:87–100.

137 Research has not directly addressed: Wieselquist, J., Rusbult, C. E., et al. (1999). "Commitment, Pro-Relationship Behavior, and Trust in Close Relationships," *Journal of Personality and Social Psychology* 77:942–66.

138 "Individual differences being what": Rainer, J., and Rainer, J. (1959). *Sexual Pleasure in Marriage* (New York: Julian Messner), 62–63.

139 Caretakers—whether mothers, fathers, nannies: Daniluk, J.C. (1998). *Women's Sexuality Across the Lifespan* (New York: Guilford Press).

142 In fact, one study found: O'Sullivan, L. F., and Allgeier, E. R. (1998). "Feigning Sexual Desire."

7. A SENSE OF ADVENTURE

146 One study tracked the importance: Buss, D. M., Shackelford, T. K., et al. (2001). "A Half Century of American Mate Preferences: The Cultural Evolution of Values," *Journal of Marriage and the Family* 63:491–503.

147 Several studies recorded: Laumann, E. O., Gagnon, J. H., et al. (1994). *The Social Organization of Sexuality: Sexual Practices in the United States* (Chicago: University of Chicago Press), 368–74.

149 A study conducted in the Meston: Meston, C. M., Trapnell, P. D., and Gorzalka, B. B. (1996). "Ethnic and Gender Differences in Sexuality: Variations in Sexual Behavior Between Asian and Non-Asian University Students," *Archives of Sexual Behavior* 25:33–72.

149 A study just completed: Meston, C. M., and Ahrold, T. (in press). "Ethnic, Gender, and Acculturation Influences on Sexual Behavior," *Archives of Sexual Behavior.*

149 Among Chinese women living: See http://english.peopledaily.com.cn/200311/08/eng20031108_127861.shtml.

150 At the other end of: Buss, D. M. (1989). "Sex Differences in Human Mate Preferences: Evolutionary Hypotheses Tested in 37 Cultures," *Behavioral and Brain Sciences* 12:1–49.

153 Women who have sex with women: Richters, J., Visser, R., et al. (2006). "Sexual Practices at Last Heterosexual Encounter and Occurrence of Orgasm in a National Survey," *Journal of Sex Research* 43:217–26.

154 According to a study by sex researchers: Masters, W. H., and Johnson, V. (1979). *Homosexuality in Perspective* (Boston: Little, Brown).

155 Psychologist Russell Eisenman: Eisenman, R. (2001). "Penis Size: Survey of Female Perceptions of Sexual Satisfaction," *BMC Women's Health* 1:1.

159 A more recent study on: Schmitt, D. P, Shackelford, T. K., et al. (2002). "Is There an Early-30's Peak in Female Sexual Desire? Cross-Sectional Evidence from the United States and Canada," *Canadian Journal of Human Sexuality* 11:1–18.

159 According to one study, approximately 25 percent: Laumann, E. O., Gagnon, J. H., et al. (1994). *The Social Organization of Sexuality*, 178–79.

163 This test has been done in both women: Laan, E., and Everaerd, W. (1995). "Habituation of Female Sexual Arousal to Slides and Film," *Archives of Sexual Behavior* 24:517–41.

163 and men: O'Donahue, W. T., and Geer, J. H. (1985). "The Habituation of Sexual Arousal," *Archives of Sexual Behavior* 14:233–46.

164 A woman's personality: Schmitt, D. P., and Shackelford, T. K. (2008). "Big Five Traits Related to Short-Term Mating: From Personality to Promiscuity Across 46 Nations," *Evolutionary Psychology* 6:246–82.

165 But an even greater predictor: Buss, D. M., and Shackelford, T. K. (1997). "Susceptibility to Infidelity in the First Year of Marriage," *Journal of Research in Personality* 31:193–221.

165 In the Meston Lab: Seal, B., and Meston, C. M. (Oct. 2004). "Perfectionism and Emerging Patterns of Sexuality," paper presented to the Annual Meeting of the International Society for the Study of Women's Sexual Health (ISSWSH), Atlanta, Ga.

165 David Schmitt came to: Schmitt, D. P. (2003). "Universal Sex Differences in the Desire for Sexual Variety: Tests from 52 Nations, 6 Continents, and 13 Islands," *Journal of Personality and Social Psychology* 85:85–104.

166 In the widely discussed book: Levy, A. (2006). *Female Chauvinist Pigs: Women and the Rise of Raunch Culture* (New York: Simon and Schuster).

8. Barter and Trade

167 "I think me and the": "Student Auctions Off Virginity for Offers of More than £2.5 Million," *The Telegraph* (London), January 12, 2009.

167 Stephanie Gershon yearned to explore: See www.cnn.com/2008/LIVING/personal/08/25/sex.for.stuff.

168 Although Natalie Dylan's: Kruger, D. J. (2008). "Young Adults Attempt Exchanges in Reproductively Relevant Currencies," *Evolutionary Psychology* 6:204–12.

168 "It's more about getting what": See www.cnn.com/2008/LIVING/personal/08/25/sex.for.stuff.

169 The gifts were identified: Symons, D. (1979). *The Evolution of Human Sexuality* (New York: Oxford University Press), 257–58.

170 "In the course of every": Sahlins, M. (1985). *Islands of History* (Chicago: University of Chicago Press; Malinowski, B. (1929). *Sexual Savages in North-western Melanesia: An Ethnographic Account of Courtship, Marriage, and Family Life Among the Natives of the Trobriand Islands, British New Guinea* (London: G. Routledge & Sons), 319.

170 "Whether men prove their virility": Siskind, J. (1973). *To Hunt in the Morning* (New York: Oxford University Press), 234.

172 Men are four times as: Ellis, B. J., and Symons, D. (1990). "Sex Differences in Sexual Fantasy: An Evolutionary Psychological Approach," *The Journal of Sex Research* 27:527–55.

172 Although there may be some reporting bias: Buss, D. M. (2003). *The Evolution of Desire: Strategies of Human Mating* (New York: Basic Books); Ellis, B. J., and Symons, D. (1990). "Sex Differences in Sexual Fantasy."

172 Men possess another psychological tic: Haselton, M. G., and Buss, D. M. (2000). "Error Management Theory: A New Perspective on Biases in Cross-sex Mind Reading," *Journal of Personality and Social Psychology* 78:81–91.

172 As a consequence, women: Buss, D. M. (2003). *Evolution of Desire.*

172 Research has also found: Symons, D. (1979). *Evolution of Human Sexuality.*

173 Several other gender differences: Ibid.

174 And, according to some thinkers: Dworkin, A., and Levi, A. (2006). *Intercourse* (New York: Basic Books).

174 "A woman has the right": French, D., and Lee, L. (1988). *Working: My Life as a Prostitute* (New York: W. W. Norton).

175 "We say that [hookers]": See www.sexwork.com/coalition/whatcountrieslegal .html.

175 The problem of sexual enslavement: Burley, N., and Symanski, R. (1981). "Women Without: An Evolutionary and Cross-cultural Perspective on Prostitution," in R. Symanski, *The Immoral Landscape: Female Prostitution in Western Societies* (Toronto: Butterworths), 239–74.

176 Although some of their clients: Brown, L. (2000). *Sex Slaves: The Trafficking of Women in Asia* (London: Virago Books).

176 The details of sex trafficking: Ibid.

176 Some women become prostitutes: Burley, N., and Symanski, R. (1981). "Women Without."

177 Street prostitutes are targeted: Salmon, C. (2008). "Heroes and Hos: Reflections on Male and Female Sexual Natures," in C. Crawford and D. Krebs (eds.), *Foundations of Evolutionary Psychology* (New York: Erlbaum).

177 Young girls and women: Tyler, K. A., and Johnson, K. A. (2006). "Trading Sex: Voluntary or Coerced? The Experiences of Homeless Youth," *Journal of Sex Research* 43:208–16.

177 "me and [my boyfriend]": Ibid., 212.

178 "It's very stressful": See www.salon.com/mwt/feature/2008/08/05/call_girls/.

178 A study of more than one thousand: Luke, N. (2005). "Confronting the 'Sugar Daddy' Stereotype: Age and Economic Asymmetries and Risky Sexual Behavior in Urban Kenya," *International Family Planning Perspectives* 31:6–14.

179 An Associated Press report about sugar babies: See www.associatedcontent .com/article/376288/how_to_get_a_sugar_daddy_sugar_daddies.html?cat—41.

179 Another news article observed: See www.articlepros.com/relationships/ Relationship-Advice/article-74309.html.

180 In one of the first: Buss, D. M. (1988). "The Evolution of Human Intrasexual Competition: Tactics of Mate Attraction," *Journal of Personality and Social Psychology* 54:616–28.

180 The Buss Lab discovered: Buss, D. M., and Schmitt, D. P. (1993). "Sexual Strategies Theory: An Evolutionary Perspective on Human Mating," *Psychological Review* 100:204–32.

181 Based solely on these photographs: Townsend, J. M. (1998). "Sexual Attractiveness Sex Differences in Assessment and Criteria," *Evolution and Human Behavior* 19(3):171–91.

182 "wrinkled old men": DiMaggio, J. (2006). *Marilyn, Joe, and Me* (New York: Penmarin Books).

182 And in 2006, the Chinese actress: See www.npr.org/templates/story/story.php ?storyId—6924667.

182 One woman, for example: Buss, D. M. (2003). *Evolution of Desire.*

182 Perhaps the most flagrant case: See http://austriantimes.at/index.php?id—7935.

183 "Gift giving or even cash": Gebhard, P. H. (1971). "The Anthropological Study of Sexual Behavior," in D. S. Marshall and R. C. Suggs (eds.), *Human Sexual Behavior* (New York: Basic Books), 257–58.

183 "Since prostitution and courtship": Burley, N., and Symanski, R. (1981). "Women Without."

183 Women often interpret gifts: Symons, D. (1979). *Evolution of Human Sexuality,* 258–59.

183 Research reveals that roughly 60: Bisson, M. A., and Levine, T. R. (2007). "Negotiating a Friends with Benefits Relationship," *Archives of Sexual Behavior* 38:66–73.

184 Indeed, when women have casual: Welsh, D. P., Grello, C. M., and Harper, M. S. (2006). "No Strings Attached: The Nature of Casual Sex in College Students," *Journal of Sex Research* 43:255–67.

184 "because the person did *not*": Jonason, P. K., Li, N., and Cason, M. (2009). "The 'Booty Call': A Compromise between Men's and Women's Ideal Mating Strategies," *Journal of Sex Research* 46:1–11.

185 These include developing romantic feelings: Bisson, M. A., and Levine, T. R. (2007). "Negotiating a Friends with Benefits Relationship."

186 Only one scientific study: Ibid.

187 "Food is one of the best lures": Holmberg, A. R. (1950). *Nomads of the Longbow* (Washington, D.C.: Smithsonian Institution Press), 64.

188 "may find it difficult": Washburn, S. L., and Lancaster, C. (1968). "The Evolution of Hunting," in R. B. Lee and I. DeVore (eds.), *Man the Hunter* (Chicago: Aldine), 293–303.

188 "He's not even a man": Symons, D. (1979). *Evolution of Human Sexuality,* 162.

189 Although women are motivated: Greiling, H., and Buss, D. M. (2000). "Women's Sexual Strategies: The Hidden Dimension of Extra-Pair Mating," *Personality and Individual Differences* 28:929–63.

189 Women who lack economic resources: Blumstein, P. and Schwartz, P. (1983). *American Couples: Money, Work, Sex* (New York: Morrow).

9. THE EGO BOOST

191 Among men, for example, research reveals: Althof, S. E., et al., (2003). "Treatment Responsiveness of the Self-Esteem and Relationship Questionnaire in Erectile Dysfunction," *Urology* 61(5):888–92.

191 Failure to perform sexually: Greiling, H., and Buss, D. M. (2000). "Women's Sexual Strategies: The Hidden Dimension of Extra-Pair Mating," *Personality and Individual Differences* 28:929–63.

192 Features that have universal sex appeal: Sugiyama, L. S. (2005). "Physical Attractiveness in Adaptationist Perspective," in D. M. Buss (ed.), *Evolutionary Psychology Handbook* (New York: Wiley), 292–343.

192 Studies of how women feel about their bodies: Franzoi, S. L., and Shields, S. A. (1984). "The Body Esteem Scale: Multidimensional Structure and Sex Differences in a College Population," *Journal of Personality Assessment* 48:173–78.

192 Because a woman's appearance provides such a bounty: Buss, D. M. (2003). *The Evolution of Desire: Strategies of Human Mating* (New York: Basic Books).

194 In a nationwide survey of thirty thousand individuals: Cash, T. F., Winstead, B. A., and Janda, L. H. (1986). "The Great American Shape-up," *Psychology Today* 20:30–37.

194 Among adolescent girls, body image: Jones, D. E., Vigfusdottir, T. H., and Lee, Y. (2004). "Body Image and the Appearance Culture Among Adolescent Girls and Boys: An Examination of Friend Conversations, Peer Criticism, Appearance Magazines, and the Internalization of Appearance Ideals," *Journal of Adolescent Research* 19:323–39.

194 Even within the United States: Cash, T. F., Morrow, J. A., et al. (2004). "How Has Body Image Changed? A Cross-sectional Investigation of College Women and Men 1983–2001," *Journal of Consulting and Clinical Psychology* 72:1081–89.

195 Women with poorer body images also reported: Seal, B., Bradford, A., and Meston, C. M. (under review). "The Association Between Body Image and Sexual Desire in College Women."

195–96 Dr. Patricia Barthalow Koch: Koch, P. B., Mansfield, P. K., et al. (2005). " 'Feeling Frumpy': The Relationships Between Body Image and Sexual Response Changes in Midlife Women," *Journal of Sex Research* 42:215–23.

196 A study of thirty-two: Werlinger, K., King, T. K., et al. (1997). "Perceived Changes in Sexual Functioning and Body Image Following Weight Loss in an Obese Female Population: A Pilot Study," *Journal of Sex and Marital Therapy* 23:74–78.

197 Pictures of waiflike movie stars: See http://shakespearessister.blogspot.com/2009/02/impossibly-beautiful.html.

198 "a girl in the popular clique can duck": Wiseman, R. (2003). *Queen Bees and Wannabes: Helping Your Daughter Survive Cliques, Gossip, Boyfriends, and Other Realities of Adolescence* (New York: Three Rivers Press).

200 One study of 16,749 adolescents: Parker, J. S., and Benson, M. J. (2004). "Parent-adolescent Relations and Adolescent Functioning: Self-esteem, Substance Abuse, and Delinquency," *Adolescence* 39:519–30.

206–7 In essence, the hero becomes dependent: Ellis, B. J., and Symons, D. (1990). "Sex Differences in Sexual Fantasy: An Evolutionary Psychological Approach," *Journal of Sex Research* 27:527–55.

207 Psychologist Patricia Hawley studied forceful sexual submission: Hawley, P. H., and Hensley, W. A., IV. (in press, 2009). "Social Dominance and Forceful Submission Fantasies: Feminine Pathology or Power?" *Journal of Sex Research*.

207 Women who were less: Salmon, C., and Symons, D. (2001). *Warrior Lovers: Erotic Fiction, Evolution and Female Sexuality* (London: Weidenfeld & Nicolson).

208 A study of 141 married women: Leitenberg, H., and Henning, K. (1995). "Sexual Fantasy," *Psychological Bulletin* 117: 469–96.

10. THE DARK SIDE

212 A deeper, evolutionary understanding of why sexual deception: Parker, G. A. (1979). "Sexual Selection and Sexual Conflict," in M. S. Blum and A. N. Blum (eds.), *Sexual Selection and Reproductive Competition among Insects* (London: Academic Press), 123–66; Parker, G. A. (2006). "Sexual Selection over Mating and Fertilization: An Overview," *Philosophical Transactions of the Royal Society* B, 361:235–59; Buss, D. M. (2001). "Cognitive Biases and Emotional Wisdom in the Evolution of Conflict between the Sexes," *Current Directions in Psychological Sciences* 10:219–53.

213 The most common sexual strategy: Buss, D. M. (2003). *The Evolution of Desire: Strategies of Human Mating* (New York: Basic Books).

213 One study estimated that 16 million Americans: Madden, M., and Lenhart, A. (2006). "Online Dating: Americans Who Are Seeking Romance Use the Internet to Help Them in Their Search, but There Is Still Widespread Public Concern about the Safety of Online Dating," Pew Internet & American Life Project, www.pewinternet.org/pdfs/PIP_Online_Dating.pdf.

213 The researchers compared men's and women's advertised height: Toma, C. L. Hancock, J. T., and Ellison, N. B. (2008). "Separating Fact from Fiction: An Examination of Deceptive Self-Presentation in Online Dating Profiles," *Personality and Social Psychology Bulletin* 34(8):1023–36.

214–15 Indeed, one study found that 86 percent of online daters: Gibbs, J. L., Ellison, N. B., and Heino, R. D. (2006). "Self-Presentation in Online Personals: The Role of Anticipated Future Interaction, Self-Disclosure, and Perceived Success in Internet Dating," *Communication Research* 33:1–26; Madden, M., and Lenhart, A. (2006). "Online Dating."

214 Love provides the best chance: Buss, D. M. (2006). "The Evolution of Love," in R. J. Sternberg and K. Weis (eds.), *The New Psychology of Love* (New Haven, Conn.: Yale University Press), 65–86.

215 "You would think saying": Cassell, C. (1984). *Swept Away: Why Women Confuse Love and Sex* (New York: Simon & Schuster), 155.

215 In one study, we asked 240 women: Haselton, M., Buss, D. M., Oubaid, V., and Angleitner, A. (2005). "Sex, Lies, and Strategic Interference: The Psychology of Deception between the Sexes," *Personality and Social Psychology Bulletin* 31:3–23.

215 We found that women reported having been deceived: Buss, D. M., and Haselton, M. G. (2005). "The Evolution of Jealousy," *Trends in Cognitive Science* 9:506–7.

216 " 'I know men,' said the woman . . . ' ": See www.washingtonpost.com/wp-dyn/content/article/2005/06/30/AR2005063001734.html.

217 Evolutionary psychologist Martie Haselton: Haselton, M. G., and Buss, D. M. (2000). "Error Management Theory: A New Perspective on Biases in Cross-sex Mind Reading, *Journal of Personality and Social Psychology* 78: 81–91.

220 According to the National Violence Against Women Survey: Tjaden, P., and Thoennes, N. (2000). *Full Report of the Prevalence, Incidence, and Consequences of Violence Against Women: Findings from the National Violence Against Women Survey* (Washington, D. C.: National Institute of Justice and Centers for Disease Control and Prevention).

220 Shocking statistics show that over one-third: Buzy, W. M., McDonald, R., et al. (2004). "Adolescent Girls' Alcohol Use as a Risk Factor for Relationship Violence," *Journal of Research on Adolescence* 14:449–70.

221 Sexual coercion in young women is more likely: Craig, M. E. (1990). "Coercive Sexuality in Dating Relationships: A Situational Model," *Clinical Psychology Review* 10:395–423.

221 One study found that between one-fourth and one-third: Davis, T. C., Peck, G. Q., and Storment, J. M. (1993). "Acquaintance Rape and the High School Student," *Journal of Adolescent Health* 14:220–23.

221 If they learn at an early age: Koss, M. P. (1985). "The Hidden Rape Victim: Personality, Attitudinal, and Situational Characteristics," *Psychology of Women Quarterly* 1:193–212.

222 One study compared forty adult women rape victims: Faravelli, G., et al. (2004). "Psychopathology after Rape," *American Journal of Psychiatry* 161:1483–85.

222 Some victims turn to alcohol or drugs: Russell, D. E. H. (1975). *The Politics of Rape: The Victim's Perspective* (New York: Stein and Day).

223 One study found that women who were sexually abused: Messman-Moore, T. L., and Brown, A. L. (2004). "Child Maltreatment and Perceived Family Environment as Risk Factors for Adult Rape: Is Child Sexual Abuse the Most Salient Experience?" *Child Abuse and Neglect* 28:1019–34.

223 A recent study found that low sexual self-esteem: Bruggen, L. K., Runtz, M. G., and Kadlec, H. (2006). "Sexual Revictimization: The Role of Sexual Self-esteem and Dysfunctional Sexual Behaviors," *Child Maltreatment* 11:131–45.

225 And research shows that when a woman is sexually abused: Lloyd, S. A., and Emery, B. C. (1999). *The Darkside of Dating: Physical and Sexual Violence* (Thousand Oaks, Calif.: Sage Publications).

225 In a study of women who had been raped by their husbands: Finkelhor, D., and Yllo, K. (1985). *License to Rape: Sexual Abuse of Wives* (New York: Holt, Rinehart & Winston).

226 Respondents often rate the rapes: Monson, C. M., Byrd, G., and Langhinrichsen-Rohling, J. (1996). "To Have and To Hold: Perceptions of Marital Rape," *Journal of Interpersonal Violence* 11:410–24.

227 in fact, a law recently passed in Afghanistan: See http://www.nydailynews.com/news/us_world/2009/04/17/2009-04-17_afghanistan_president_hamid_karzai_backpedals_on_afghan_marital_rape_law.html.

228 But of the three types of treatment, Prolonged Exposure: Foa, E. B., Rothbaum, B. O., Riggs, D. S., and Murdock, T. B. (1991). "Treatment of Posttraumatic Stress Disorder in Rape Victims: A Comparison between Cognitive-behavioral Procedures and Counseling," *Journal of Consulting and Clinical Psychology* 59:715–23.

230 The anthropologist Peggy Sanday examined 156 tribal societies: Sanday, P. (1981). "The Sociocultural Context of Rape: A Cross-cultural Study," *Journal of Social Issues* 37:5–27.

230 Other studies confirm that when women lack genetic kin: Figueredo, A. J. (1995). *Preliminary Report: Family Deterrence of Domestic Violence in Spain*, Department of Psychology, University of Arizona.

230 "If a seignior took the virgin by force": Quoted in Scholz, S. (2005). " 'Back Then It Was Legal': The Epistemological Imbalance in Readings of Biblical and Ancient Near Eastern Rape Legislation," *Bible and Critical Theory* 1 (22):36.

230 Historical records also show that rape: Symons, D. (1979). *The Evolution of Human Sexuality* (New York: Oxford University Press); Chagnon, N. A. (1983). *Yanomamö: The Fierce People* (New York: Holt, Rinehart and Winston); Ghiglieri, M. P. (1999). *The Dark Side of Man: Tracing the Origins of Male Violence* (Reading, Mass.: Perseus Books).

230 "The greatest pleasure is to vanquish your enemies": Quoted in Royle, T. (1989). *Dictionary of Military Quotations* (New York: Simon & Schuster).

231 "Soviet soldiers treated German women": Beevor, A. (2002). *Berlin: The Downfall, 1945* (New York: Viking Press), 326–27.

231 Given the appalling costs that rape inflicts: Buss, D. M. (2003). "Sexual Treachery," *Australian Journal of Psychology* 55:36.

233 From an evolutionary perspective, another potential anti-rape: Critelli, J. W., and Bivona, J. M. (2008). "Women's Erotic Rape Fantasies: An Evaluation of Theory and Research," *Journal of Sex Research* 45:57–70.

233 An example might be a rapist grabbing the woman: Kanin, E. J. (1982). "Female Rape Fantasies: A Victimization Study," *Victimology* 7:114–21., 117.

234 Women find actual rape aversive and traumatizing: Buss, D. M. (1989). "Conflict Between the Sexes: Strategic Interference and the Evocation of Anger and Upset," *Journal of Personality and Social Psychology* 56:735–47.

234 "I thought he wanted to rape me": Duntley, J. D., and Buss, D. M., unpublished data.

234 A final way that women might defend: Buss, D. M. (2005). *The Murderer Next Door: Why the Mind Is Designed to Kill* (New York: Penguin Press).

11. Sexual Medicine

238 The release of endorphins: Couch, J., and Bearss, C. (1990). "Relief of Migraine with Sexual Intercourse," *Headache* 30:302.

238 Some headache researchers believe: Weiller, C., May, A., et al. (1995). "Brain Stem Activation in Spontaneous Human Migraine Attacks," *Natural Medicine* 1:658–60.

238 And during orgasm itself: Whipple, B., and Komisaruk, B. R. (1985). "Elevation of Pain Threshold by Vaginal Stimulation in Women," *Pain* 21:357–67.

239 With the help of a speculum device: Cited in Levin, R. (2007). "Sexual Activity, Health and Well-being—The Beneficial Roles of Coitus and Masturbation," *Sexual and Relationship Therapy* 22:135–48.

240 Researchers at Yale University School of Medicine: Meaddough, E. L., Olive, D. L., et al. (2001). "Sexual Activity, Orgasm and Tampon Use Are Associated with a Decreased Risk for Endometriosis," *Gynecologic and Obstetric Investigation* 53:163–69.

240 According to Pliny: Cited in O'Dowd, M. J., and Philipp, E. E. (2000). *The History of Obstetrics and Gynecology* (New York: Pantheon Group), 291–92.

241 Masters and Johnson termed this "spectatoring": Masters, W., and Johnson, V. E. (1970). *Human Sexual Inadequacy* (Boston: Little, Brown).

245 Interestingly, research has shown that there is a 400 percent: Brody, S., and Kruger, T.H.C. (2006). "The Post-orgasmic Increase Following Intercourse Is Greater than Following Masturbation and Suggests Greater Satiety," *Biological Psychology* 71:312–15.

245 In one study, women watched a travel documentary: Palace, E. M., and Gorzalka, B. B. (1990). "The Enhancing Effects of Anxiety on Arousal in Sexually Dysfunctional and Functional Women," *Journal of Abnormal Psychology* 99:403–11.

246 In the Meston . . . Lab, we decided to look: Meston, C. M., and Gorzalka, B. B. (1995). "The Effects of Sympathetic Activation on Physiological and Subjective Sexual Arousal in Women," *Behaviour Research and Therapy* 33:651–64.

247 A few years ago, the Meston Lab research team: Meston, C. M., and Frohlich, P. F. (2003). "Love at First Fright: Partner Salience Moderates Roller Coaster–Induced Excitation Transfer," *Archives of Sexual Behavior* 32:537–44.

248 "Women stood up in the stands drumming": Mannix, D. P. (1958). *Those About to Die* (New York: Ballantine Books), 91.

248 Over a lifetime, approximately 20 percent: Weissman, M. M., and Olfson, M. (1995). "Depression in Women: Implications for Health Care Research," *Science* 269:799–801.

249 Researcher Thomas Wehr and his colleagues: Cited in Leibenluft, E. (1998). "Why Are So Many Women Depressed?" *Scientific American,* summer.

250 Also, given that sexual arousal and orgasm: Exton, M. S., Bindert, A., et al. (1999). "Cardiovascular and Endocrine Alterations after Masturbation-induced Orgasm in Women," *Psychosomatic Medicine* 61:280–89.

250 In a recent study conducted in the Meston Lab: Hamilton, L. D., Rellini, A. H., and Meston, C. M. (2008). "Cortisol, Sexual Arousal, and Affect in Response to Sexual Stimuli," *Journal of Sexual Medicine* 5:2111–18.

250 In another study conducted in the Meston Lab: Frohlich, P. F., and Meston, C. M. (2002). "Sexual Functioning and Self-Reported Depressive Symptoms Among College Women," *Journal of Sex Research* 39:321–25.

251 At times masturbation may provide benefits: Gallup, G. G., Burch, R. L., and Platek, S. M. (2002). "Does Semen Have Antidepressant Properties?" *Archives of Sexual Behavior* 31:289–93.

252 In fact, some of the hormones: Benziger, D. P., and Edelson, J. (1983). "Absorption from the Vagina," *Drug Metabolism Reviews* 14:137–68.

252 Both of these hormones have been shown: Abdullah, Y. H., and Hamadah, K. (1975). "Effect of ADP on PGE1 Formation in the Blood Platelets from Patients with Depression, Mania and Schizophrenia," *British Journal of Psychiatry* 127:591–95.

252 . . . and estrogen has been shown: Coope, J. (1996). "Hormonal and Non-Hormonal Interventions for Menopausal Symptoms," *Maturitas* 23:159–68.

252 Among younger women: Roy-Byrne, P. P., Rubinow, D. R., Gold, P. W., and Post, R. M. (1984). "Possible Antidepressant Effects of Oral Contraceptives: Case Report," *Journal of Clinical Psychiatry* 45:350–52.

253 As we saw earlier, low testosterone levels: Wester, R. C., Noonan, P. K., and Maibach, H.I. (1980). "Variations in Percutaneous Absorption of Testosterone in the Rhesus Monkey Due to Anatomic Site of Application and Frequency of Application, *Archives of Dermatological Research* 267:229–35.

253 Using duplex ultrasonography: Becher, E. F., Bechara, A., and Casabe, A. (2001). "Clitoral Hemodynamic Changes After a Topical Application of Al-prostadil," *Journal of Sex and Marital Therapy* 27:405–10.

253 And in a later study: Padma-Nathan, H., Brown, C., Fendl, J., Salem, S., Yeager, J., and Harning, R. (2003). "Efficacy and Safety of Topical Alprostadil Cream for the Treatment of Female Sexual Arousal Disorder (FSAD): A Double-blind, Multicenter, Randomized, and Placebo Controlled Clinical Trial," *Journal of Sex and Marital Therapy* 29:329–44.

257 Women's ideal durations of foreplay: Miller, S. A., and Byers, E. S. (2004). "Actual and Desired Duration of Foreplay and Intercourse: Discordance and Misperceptions Within Heterosexual Couples," *Journal of Sex Research* 41:301–9.

257 The average is somewhat higher: Laumann, E. O., Gagnon, J. H., et al. (1994). *The Social Organization of Sexuality: Sexual Practices in the United States* (Chicago: University of Chicago Press), 368–74.

257 One study that questioned men and women repeatedly: Palmore, E. B. (1982). "Predictors of the Longevity Differences: A 25-Year Follow-up," *Gerontologist* 22:513–18.

258 A recent study of nearly 2,500 elderly Taiwanese: Chen, H., Tseng, C., et al. (2007). "A Prospective Cohort Study on the Effect of Sexual Activity, Libido and Widowhood on Mortality Among the Elderly People: 14-Year Follow-up of 2453 Elderly Taiwanese," *International Journal of Epidemiology* 35:1136–42.

258 One study showed that nuns: Meurer, J., McDermott, R. J., and Malloy, M. J. (1990). "An Exploratory Study of the Health Practices of American Catholic Nuns," *Health Values* 14:9–17.

258 But once a woman goes through menopause: U.S. Department of Health and Human Services (1988). *Vital Statistics of the United States 1986. Volume 11—Mortality. Part A.* (Hyattsville, Md.: Centers for Disease Control, National Center for Health Statistics).

258 Even younger women who have had both of their ovaries removed: Stampler, M. J., Colditz, G. A., and Willett, W. C. (1990). "Menopause and Heart Disease: A Review," *Annals of the New York Academy of Science* 592:193–203.

258 In contrast, there is an abundance of research: Stampler, M. J., and Colditz, G. A. (2004). "Estrogen Replacement Therapy and Coronary Heart Disease: A Quantitative Assessment of the Epidemiologic Evidence," *International Journal of Epidemiology* 33:445–53.

259 But men and women in poor relationships: Kiecolt-Glaser, J. K., Glaser, R., et al. (1998). "Marital Stress: Immunologic, Neuroendocrine, and Autonomic Correlates," *Annals of the New York Academy of Science* 840:656–63.

259 To examine whether how often a person has sex: Charnetski, C. J., and Brennan, F. X. (2004). "Sexual Frequency and Salivary Immunoglobulin A (IgA)," *Psychological Reports* 94:839–44.

260 . . . but one study found that too much opioid peptide: Van Epps, D. E., and Saland, L. (1984). "Beta-endorphin and Metenkephalin Stimulate Human Peripheral Blood Mononuclear Cell Chemotaxin," *Journal of Immunology* 132:3046–53.

260 One study found that postmenopausal women: Leiblum, S., Bachman, E., et al. (1983). "Vaginal Atrophy in the Post Menopausal Woman: The Importance of Sexual Activity and Hormones," *Journal of the American Medical Association* 249:2195–98.

ACKNOWLEDGMENTS

Cindy M. Meston

My parents did not have great expectations for me. My mother wanted me to marry the manager of Safeway so that she could get a 10 percent discount at the meat counter, and my father wanted me to marry someone who could fix my carburetor. They were from a time and place that valued hard work and self-sacrifice, but not education. For giving me the confidence to forge my own path in life, I will forever be grateful to the late Maradine Portt and to my lifelong cheerleader, Claudia McNeil. For laughing at my every stupid story, believing in my every new plan, and standing by me through every heartache since we first became friends in Miss Funk's grade 2 class, I am indebted to Sherry Rempel (p.s., I'm sorry for all the times I tormented you as a child—especially when I dressed you up as a Christmas tree and plugged you in at my parent's dinner party).

There are several people who have had an enormous impact on my academic career. Thanks to Boris Gorzalka, my graduate supervisor, whose amazing teaching skills lured me from the world of sewing machines to the field of psychology. Thanks to Julia Heiman, my postdoctoral supervisor, for your continued sage mentorship and support, to Irwin Goldstein for your unbridled enthusiasm for my research, and to Sandra Leiblum, Ray Rosen, and Lorraine Dennerstein for saying all the right things. I am hugely grateful to the psychology department at the University of Texas at Austin for the support I have received over the past eleven years. Special thanks to Randy Diehl, the dean of liberal arts; Jamie Pennebaker, the chair of the psychology department; and Caryn Carlson, the clinical area head: Your continuous support and guidance have made all the difference. For the energy, enthusiasm, creativity, and intellectual stimulation that they have brought to my lab over the past decade, I thank my former and current graduate students: Penny Frohlich, Alessandra Rellini, Katie McCall, Annie Bradford, Brooke Seal, Lisa Dawn Hamilton, Christopher Harte, Tierney Arhold, Yasisca Pujols, Kyle Stephenson, and Cory Ann Pallatto.

Special thanks to Times Books and Henry Holt and Company for bringing the voices of the women in this book to you, and to Robin Dennis, our editor, whose brilliant insight and magic pencil have been invaluable.

Friendships have always been the most important thing in life to me and I have many dear friends to be thankful for. Special appreciation to those who played a role in my writing this book: Sam Gosling, Jane Spencer, Dale Severyn, Laureen Miki, Lisa Timar, Linda Edworthy, and Lucia O'Sullivan. Super-duper thanks to writer extraordinaire Mary Roach for your encouragement and for all the times you made me laugh so hard my stomach hurt. Particular thanks to my coauthor, David Buss, whose collaboration and friendship have made this book, and the studies on which it is based, especially rewarding projects. For keeping me warm, helping me sleep, and distracting me from worry, I am hugely indebted to my cats Rudy and Mimi, and to my Maltipoo Charlie. Finally, Tom, for so many reasons and in so many ways I could not have written this book without you. Thank you—you are my anchor.

David M. Buss

Through more than two decades of conducting scientific research on the complexities of women's sexual psychology, I have been greatly blessed by the many brilliant women scientists who have collaborated with me on empirical studies: April Bleske-Rechek, Lisa Chiodo, Jaime Confer, Lisa Dedden, Judith Easton, Maryanne Fisher, Diana Santos Fleischman, Cari Goetz, Mary Gomes, Arlette Greer, Heidi Greiling, Mariko Hasegawa, Martie Haselton, Dolly Higgins, Sarah Hill, Sabine Hoier, Karen Lauterbach, Marguerite Lavallee, Cathrine Moestue, Carin Perilloux, Elizabeth Pillsworth, Jennifer Semmelroth, Emily Stone, Viviana Weekes-Shackelford, Margarete Vollrath. Indeed, working with these coauthors made me realize that the limitations of my male brain absolutely necessitated collaborating with women in the scientific exploration of female sexual psychology.

I also express thanks to my many male research collaborators, who, although perhaps suffering from similar limitations due to possessing a Y chromosome, nonetheless made outstanding contributions: Alois Angleitner, Mike Barnes, Kevin Bennett, Mike Botwin, Bram Buunk, Jae Choe, Sean Conlan, Ken Craik, Todd DeKay, Josh Duntley, Bruce Ellis, Harald Euler, Steve Gangestad, Aaron Goetz, Joonghwan Jeon, Peter Jonason, Doug Kenrick, Lee Kirkpatrick, Barry Kuhle, Randy Larsen, Greg LeBlanc, David Lewis, Norm Li, Neil Malamuth, Will McKibben, Richard Michalski, Victor Oubaid, Jay Peters, Kern Reeve, David Schmitt, Todd Shackelford, Bill Tooke, Paul Vasey, Martin Voracek, and Drew Westen.

Many other friends and colleagues contributed in various ways, through discussions or through their published work, to deepening my understanding of women's sexual minds: Richard Alexander, Rosalind Arden, Robin Baker, Jerry Barkow, Laura Betzig, Nancy Burley, Anne Campbell, Liz Cashdan, Leda Cosmides, Helena Cronin, Martin Daly, Laura Dane, Richard Dawkins, Mike Domjan, Kristina Durane, Bruce Ellis, A. J. Figueredo, Helen Fisher, Mark Flinn, Robin Fox, Robert Frank, David Frederick, Shirley Glass, Karl Grammer, Bill Hamilton, Heide Island, Doug Jones, Zigy Kaluzny, Bobbi Low, Janet Mann, Linda Mealey, Geoffrey Miller, Paul Mullen, Randy Nesse, Geoffrey Parker, John Patton, Steve Pinker, David Rakison, Catherine Salmon, Dev Singh, Barb Smuts, Beverly Spicer, Don Symons, Del Thiessen, Andy Thompson, Nancy Thornhill, Randy Thornhill, Lionel Tiger, Robert Trivers, Paul Turke, Bill von Hipple, Gregory White, George

Williams, D. S. Wilson, E. O. Wilson, Margo Wilson, and Richard Wrangham.

Don Symons must be singled out for his seminal work on human sexuality, and for offering intelligent insights through dozens of discussions over the course of many years. I offer special thanks to our agent, Katinka Matson of Brockman, Inc., who saw the potential in this book. Every author should be blessed by the incomparable editor, Robin Dennis, who helped in a zillion ways, large and small, to improve the quality of this book. Special thanks go to my spectacular friend and coauthor, Cindy Meston, without whom this book could not have been written. Finally, I'd like to thank those who endured my long hours of work and who offered love, support, encouragement, and insight throughout the writing process—most of all, Cindy R., and my daughter, Tara.

INDEX

ABOUT THE AUTHORS

CINDY M. MESTON is one of the world's leading researchers on women's sexuality and a professor of clinical psychology at the University of Texas at Austin, where she directs the Sexual Psychophysiology Laboratory, a cutting-edge lab on women's sexual experience. DAVID M. BUSS, one of the founders of the field of evolutionary psychology, is a professor at the University of Texas at Austin and is the author of several books, including *The Evolution of Desire* and *The Dangerous Passion*. Their jointly authored article "Why Humans Have Sex" garnered international attention when it was published in the *Archives of Sexual Behavior*.